Jade Christine Angelica, MDiv

We Are Not Alone
A Guidebook for Helping Professionals and Parents Supporting Adolescent Victims of Sexual Abuse

Pre-publication
REVIEWS,
COMMENTARIES,
EVALUATIONS . . .

"**I**n *We Are Not Alone*, Jade Christine Angelica provides a valuable resource to teens who have been sexually abused and their parents. With compassion and eloquent prose, she walks people through the criminal justice system—from disclosure to final outcome. I believe that her book will be a lifeline to families of teens who have disclosed sexual abuse."

Kathleen Kendall-Tackett, PhD
Research Associate,
Family Research Laboratory,
University of New Hampshire,
Durham

"***W****e Are Not Alone* is a must read for all who work or live with kids who have been abused. It explores abuse through the eyes of the victims, sharing their fears, hopes, and wishes. It inspires us to work harder to meet kids' needs, answer their questions, calm their fears, and protect them from their abusers and a system that is often not designed to respond to them in a language they understand.

We Are Not Alone highlights the fact that to those of us who work with abused kids, it is our job; but to the kids, it is their life. We must never forget that. *We Are Not Alone* helps us realize that we are also not alone, and that is a great thing. We must all work together to end abuse, and this wonderful book offers tremendous insights into kids and how best to achieve that goal."

Kevin L. Ryle, JD
Assistant District Attorney,
Middlesex, Massachusetts

More pre-publication
REVIEWS, COMMENTARIES, EVALUATIONS . . .

"I have the utmost gratitude and praise for Jade Christine Angelica's *We Are Not Alone* guidebook and companion workbooks. They are long-awaited comprehensive and compelling resources for victims and families involved in the child protection and criminal justice systems and the many professionals who work to assist and support them. As a professional working in victim services for almost twenty years, I know how complex and intimidating the system is for victims of all ages and their families. It is particularly daunting for children and adolescents, since the criminal justice system was not designed to meet their unique physical, emotional, and developmental needs. The guidebook points out the harsh realities of the system, but also clearly and sensitively highlights the strides that the child protection and criminal justice systems have made over the past two decades and the efforts to prevent those systems from re-victimizing those they seek to protect. True, the systems are complicated to navigate, but the author is extremely successful in demystifying the system and informing the reader of the positive ways in which the system can and does respond. She strongly encourages victims and their families to participate in the system in an effort to heal from their victimization, seek justice, and hold offenders accountable for their heinous and harmful crimes.

The guidebook is useful not only for victims and their families, but also for professionals working with teen victims and participating as members of multidisciplinary teams. With high staff turnover in many of the agencies involved, this is an exceedingly vital training tool as well. And, of course, the workbooks provide the means by which to engage adolescents in their own care—supporting them in the aftermath of their victimization, helping them engage in quiet introspection, guiding their interactions and conversations with helping professionals and family members, and assisting them to gain the courage necessary to participate in the criminal justice system. Ultimately, these publications will enable them to achieve the goals of vindication, justice, and healing."

Janet E. Fine, MS
Director,
Victim Witness Assistance Program
and Children's Advocacy Center,
Suffolk County District Attorney's Office,
Boston

HMTP

The Haworth Maltreatment and Trauma Press®
An Imprint of The Haworth Press, Inc.
New York • London • Oxford

We Are Not Alone

A Guidebook for Helping Professionals and Parents Supporting Adolescent Victims of Sexual Abuse

We Are Not Alone
A Guidebook for Helping Professionals and Parents Supporting Adolescent Victims of Sexual Abuse

Jade Christine Angelica, MDiv

HMTP

The Haworth Maltreatment and Trauma Press®
An Imprint of The Haworth Press, Inc.
New York • London • Oxford

Published by

The Haworth Maltreatment and Trauma Press®, an imprint of The Haworth Press, Inc., 10 Alice Street, Binghamton, NY 13904-1580

Material excerpted from John E. B. Myers, *The Future of Children,* Volume 4, pages 87-88 is reprinted with the permission of the David and Lucile Packard Foundation.

Material excerpted from an article by Alison Bass, February 25, 1992, pages A1, A4, is reprinted with the permission of *The Boston Globe.*

PUBLISHER'S NOTE
All of the characters in the *We Are Not Alone* workbooks are fictitious. Any resemblance to actual persons, living or dead, or events in their lives, is entirely coincidental.

Cover design by Jennifer M. Gaska.

Library of Congress Cataloging-in-Publication Data

Angelica, Jade C. (Jade Christine), 1952-
    We are not alone: a guidebook for helping professionals and parents supporting adolescent victims of sexual abuse / Jade Christine Angelica.
        p. cm.
    Includes bibliographical references and index.
    ISBN 0-7890-0924-2 (hard : alk. paper)—ISBN 0-7890-0925-0 (soft : alk paper)
    1. Sexually abused teenagers. 2. Child sexual abuse. I. Title.

HV6570 .A54 2001
362.76'8—dc21

2001016623

For all the abused children
who lie awake at night, feeling helpless,
hopeless, and forsaken,
longing for merciful sleep.

You are not alone.

ABOUT THE AUTHOR

Jade Christine Angelica, MDiv, Director of The Child Abuse Ministry, has been working on behalf of victims of child sexual abuse since 1987. A graduate of Harvard Divinity School, Ms. Angelica leads workshops and training sessions for religious leaders and communities, develops programs and conferences, preaches, lectures, and writes on the topic of child sexual abuse. From 1989 to 1993, Ms. Angelica researched and developed special projects for the Child Abuse Unit of the Middlesex County District Attorney's Office in Cambridge, Massachusetts. In order to provide a sorely needed court-oriented resource for adolescent victims of child sexual abuse, Ms. Angelica wrote the first edition of *We Are Not Alone: A Teenage Girl's Personal Account of Incest Through Prosecution and Treatment,* which was printed in 1992 with a grant from the Massachusetts Bar Association.

Also during her time at the Child Abuse Unit, Ms. Angelica realized the importance of involving faith communities and religious leaders in the multidisciplinary efforts of prevention and healing of child sexual abuse. She is also the author of *A Moral Emergency: Breaking the Cycle of Child Sexual Abuse,* a handbook for religious leaders.

CONTENTS

Chapter 6. A Teenage Boy's Personal Account of Child Sexual Abuse from Disclosure Through Prosecution and Treatment   105

Foreword

One of the hallmarks of adolescence is the compelling, sometimes desperate, need to belong. For too many teens, this desire is thwarted by a seemingly impenetrable barrier that sets them apart from their peers: the experience of sexual abuse. In her choice of title, Jade Angelica captures an essential component of any effort to reach troubled adolescents. The helping professionals need to help these adolescents understand that they are not alone.

Despite the outpouring of attention and concern that has focused on child sexual abuse over the last two decades, by far the lion's share has been directed toward the youngest victims. Across the country, state legislatures have enacted laws allowing certain departures from traditional jurisprudence to enable young sexual abuse victims to tell their stories in a somewhat less intimidating environment. Many of these innovations are not available to teens. The vast majority of research on children's capabilities as witnesses—the accuracy of their memories, their credibility with jurors, their vulnerability to suggestion, the emotional effects of testifying—has focused on the youngest children. Far less is understood about the experience of teenaged sexual abuse victims as they traverse the criminal justice system and the consequences of that experience on their mental health.

In *We Are Not Alone,* Ms. Angelica helps readers place the adolescent victim's experience in context by providing background on the prevalence of child sexual abuse; adolescent reactions to sexual abuse, disclosure, and the aftermath; and fundamental components of the criminal justice system. The workbooks for victims, one for boys and one for girls, are expressly designed to resonate with adolescent readers, to acknowledge and respect their feelings—about themselves, about the perpetrators, about their role in the court process.

With great skill and sensitivity, Ms. Angelica models in these workbooks the empathy and compassion that she promotes among the helping professionals who work with teen victims and their parents. The result is a valuable reference that will benefit the many thousands of adolescents who disclose sexual abuse, persevere through the grueling justice system, and emerge as survivors, understanding—perhaps for the first time—that they are not alone.

Debra Whitcomb, MA
Director, Grant Programs and Development
American Prosecutors Research Institute
Alexandria, Virginia

Preface

In 1990, I was commissioned by The Child Abuse Project of the Middlesex County, Massachusetts, District Attorney's Office to write the original manuscripts of *We Are Not Alone (A Teenage Girl's Personal Account of Incest from Disclosure Through Prosecution and Treatment; A Teenage Boy's Personal Account of Child Sexual Abuse from Disclosure Through Prosecution and Treatment)*. The purpose of the project was to provide a court-oriented resource for adolescent victims of child sexual abuse involved in the prosecution process. Although there were many "going to court" books, pamphlets, and videos available at that time for young children, few existing resources were geared specifically toward adolescent victims and the issues they face during the investigation and prosecution of child sexual abuse cases. A few more, but not significantly more, resources have been produced for adolescent victims during the past decade.

The revised edition of the *We Are Not Alone* workbooks include generic, yet detailed descriptions of the policies and procedures of the social service and criminal justice systems, legal information, and a glossary of terms that provide practical guidance so that adolescent victims of child sexual abuse can better understand what is happening. The workbooks also include descriptions of a wide range of psychological and physiological reactions adolescent victims typically experience during disclosure, investigation, prosecution, and treatment.

The workbooks were written as first person accounts with the intention of helping victims realize that this abuse happens to other children and teens. The first person genre provides victims with a peer who is going through a similar process. Although no two victims will experience the same process or the exact feelings or physical responses, peer reactions are critically useful and comforting to adolescents. Feedback from teens and professionals who have used the workbook for girls published in 1992 by Justice for Children, Inc., indicates that the adolescent victims both crave and absorb the psychological, physiological, and personal information shared by Jane, the victim character in the workbook.

Because the workbooks are written at about the ninth grade reading level, the information is accessible for adolescents as well as adult readers. These resources will, therefore, easily communicate basic legal and psychological knowledge, and will enable victims and adults to formulate and ask clarifying questions of the social service and legal professionals. Studying the workbooks will help adult readers converse with adolescent victims about the court processes and the victims' fears in a supportive way. If given to parents, guardians, and/or caregivers early in the investigation process, these resources will inform them about possible situations and outcomes, and help them to prepare themselves and their children for whatever might happen.

Involvement in a social service or law enforcement child abuse investigation and/or a criminal justice process is a distressing experience. Few Americans actually know much about these processes in advance of being thrust into them. This fact makes the reality of having to learn about and deal with these processes at a highly stressful time invariably more difficult. Even the most confident adults can be so confused and frightened by a courtroom experience that they do not know what to ask or what to do. It is, therefore, essential that courageous adolescents who disclose sexual abuse be able to trust social service, legal, and clinical professionals to hear them, to help them, to support them, and to expertly guide them through the confusing fog and treacherous terrain of the criminal court system.

The title of this resource, *We Are Not Alone,* is intended to send a dual message to adolescent readers. It lets victims know that sexual abuse happens to other kids too, and that trained, professional adults are available who know what to do and who will help them through this grueling process. Toward our shared goal of preparing adults to support and protect adolescent victims as they find their way through the criminal court system, Robert A. Geffner, PhD, president of the Family Violence and Sexual Assault Institute; clinical research professor of psychology at the California School of Professional Psychology; and Senior Editor of The Haworth Maltreatment and Trauma Press, had the vision of creating a guidebook to accompany the workbooks. Reading the workbooks for boys and girls and using the guidebook with the victims and their families will aid multidisciplinary helping professionals to better understand both systems and victims. These resources will inform legal professionals about the psychological issues abused adolescents face and how they may be affected by legal intervention. They will also educate social service caseworkers, community mental health professionals, and therapists about the legal system, and give these professionals a blueprint of what could happen when the legal system and sexually abused adolescents intersect, thus preparing them for proactive counseling.

The *We Are Not Alone* guidebook and workbooks are intended for and will be helpful to three distinct groups: adolescent victims, parents, guardians, or caregivers of victims, and multidisciplinary professionals who work with victims.

The most important and primary population for which the workbooks will be helpful is adolescent victims, and there are many. Although exact statistics regarding the number of child sexual abuse cases referred to prosecutors' offices nationwide every year is impossible to acquire, in 1996 child protective service agencies determined that in forty-eight states, 120,000 children were identified as victims of substantiated sexual abuse (U.S. Department of Health and Human Services, 1998). Actual statistics from Middlesex County, Massachusetts, indicate that adolescent victims (age thirteen to eighteen) constituted 41 percent of the 774 cases of child sexual abuse reported to their office in 1997 (Pini, 1998). It is also reasonable to consider some eleven- and twelve-year-olds as readers, therefore projecting that at least 50 percent of all child sexual abuse victims involved in the prosecution process could benefit from this resource.

Parents, guardians, and/or caregivers of adolescent victims as potential readers and beneficiaries of this resource equals, and perhaps exceeds, the number of potential victim readers. It is recommended that adults be given their own workbooks so that the victims can feel a sense of privacy and control over their copies. Both audiences—victims and adults—may find that they want to read the workbook slowly and make notes about questions or feelings. Therefore, a personal copy for each is advisable. The parents in the workbooks act and react in exemplary ways, thus giving parents, guardians, and/or caregivers of actual victims ideas and role models for interacting with their own children in a situation that is new, distressing, and frightening.

The primary readers for the guidebook also include multidisciplinary professionals working with victims of child sexual abuse—prosecutors, victim witness advocates, law enforcement officers, social workers, therapists, religious professionals, and school guidance counselors. Research indicates that any means of enhancing the knowledge and understanding of the plight of children in the court system will heighten the awareness of professionals who come in contact with abused children of their responsibility for child protection (Pence and Wilson, 1994). This is imperative because "there are many opportunities for the law enforcement, child protection, mental health, medical, and legal professions to deepen society's understanding of and improve its response to child sexual abuse" (Larson et al., 1994, p. 24). *We Are Not Alone* provides another opportunity for heightening awareness.

Attorney, law professor, and child advocate John E. B. Myers has been repeatedly amazed throughout his legal career by the gaps in understanding of the legal system many people have, including law students (Myers, 1997). The guidebook and workbooks, when used specifically as a training tool for new social service caseworkers and mental health workers, have the potential to fill in some gaps about the legal system for these helping professionals. The resources can also be a particularly useful training tool for prosecutors, victim witness advocates, law enforcement officers, and other legal professionals, reminding them of the human, vulnerable, child elements associated with sexual abuse cases involving adolescent victims.

Myers (1997) insists that parents of abused children *must* understand the legal system. Toward this goal, parents, guardians, and caregivers of adolescent victims may choose to read the more comprehensive guidebook in addition to the workbooks. This could be especially beneficial if a particular victim is not involved in a therapeutic relationship. The key points, guiding questions, and glossary in Section IV of the guidebook may be of specific interest and help to adults as they support their children through the court process.

Adolescent victims and supportive adults, like the majority of Americans, have probably had little personal contact with the criminal justice system. Therefore, it is important for them to understand that once child sexual abuse has been disclosed, state laws dictate that the social service, law enforcement, and/or criminal justice systems become involved in their lives. And "once the court involvement begins, all the individuals affected face an elaborate system of laws, rules, and procedures, which is certainly confusing and often intimidating" (Feller et al., 1992, p. vii). So, it makes sense to learn something about the laws and the processes that will inevitably take place. Using the *We Are Not Alone* guidebook and workbook may lessen the confusion and intimidation by helping adolescent victims and the supportive adults in their lives know what is happening, what questions to ask, and how to make appropriate and healing decisions.

I invite all who read the *We Are Not Alone* guidebook and workbooks to consider that the court system is one very important method for protecting children—although not the only way, and not the most desired way. However, many professionals in both the legal and therapeutic fields believe that the leverage of the criminal justice system provides children with possibly the most effective protection from abuse that our society has to offer (Whitcomb, 1992). Therefore, understanding the system, and the ways victims react to the system, is crucial for any professional involved in child protection, as well as parents, guardians, and/or caregivers of abused children. As we accompany a victim of child sexual abuse through the legal process, we must always remain aware and respectful of the sacrifice this child has made—and is making—in order to protect himself or herself and others. Awareness and understanding can evolve into compassionate and effective support.

While working at the Middlesex District Attorney's Office and conducting the research for this book, I had the privilege to observe, meet, and interview numerous child and adolescent victims and their families, as well as multidisciplinary professionals. As a result, I deeply comprehend and feel the distress that child sexual abuse and the investigation and prosecution of these crimes creates for victims and those who want to protect them. I, therefore, chose to write a resource in a style that I hope will be accessible, supportive, and compassionate to the varied groups of people I intend to reach: adolescent victims, parents, guardians, and caregivers, and multidisciplinary helping professionals. You are already the experts on this subject, or soon will be by virtue of your own personal experiences. I can only hope I have been a worthy scribe.

Jade Christine Angelica
Scarborough, Maine

Acknowledgments

With gratitude, I acknowledge the following people for their generous contributions to the creation of *We Are Not Alone:*

Robert A. Geffner and Suzanne White, I thank you for your guiding vision and for providing me with the opportunity to develop your ideas into a helpful and healing resource for adolescent victims of child sexual abuse;

Jane Walsh, I thank you for your thorough, patient lessons about the criminal justice system;

Janet Fine, Deborah Fogarty, Susan Goldfarb, Janis Lynch, Kellie Pini, and Lea Savely, I thank you for your enduring and enthusiastic support;

Renee Brant, Lynn Rooney, Kevin Ryle, Trish Sullivan, Debra Whitcomb, the staff of Middlesex and Suffolk County District Attorneys' Offices, and numerous other professionals in the field of child sexual abuse, I thank you for sharing your time, knowledge, and resources;

John E. B. Myers, I thank you for your gracious response to a call for help from a complete stranger. You exemplify the generosity and commitment of child advocates all across the nation;

All of the teen victims of child sexual abuse and their parents who I interviewed and observed, I admire you and thank you for your perseverence, your bravery, and your willingness to share yourselves with others who face a similar challenge;

The Haworth Press production staff, I thank you for your care and attention in bringing this project to life. Your understanding of the importance of providing support to victims of child sexual abuse and your respect for this work is evident in the finished product.

Without your contributions, this resource would not exist.

PART I:
SEXUALLY ABUSED
ADOLESCENTS AND THE CRIMINAL
JUSTICE SYSTEM

Adolescents and the criminal justice system—an odd couple, indeed. Each is a mystery to the other, and yet every day across our nation, this unlikely alliance meets in the search for justice, and lives will never be the same.

Once an adolescent victim of child sexual abuse discloses his or her abuse, that adolescent is catapulted into a foreign and frightening world of established and elaborate policies, laws, protocols, and procedures. For awhile—perhaps a week, perhaps a year or more—the typical adolescent life consisting of school, sports, friends, TV, music videos, telephones, and social activities fades into the background, and a life filled with forensic investigations, police officers, social workers, prosecutors, courtrooms, testimony, cross-examinations, judges, and juries takes its place.

In this foreign world, an adolescent victim may feel alone and lost in the deep woods without a map or a compass, without protection, and without nourishment. For the criminal justice system, on the other hand, an adolescent victim represents business as usual. Thousands of criminal cases, involving thousands of victims, come before thousands of courts every year. A lost adolescent, whose life has just been turned inside out, is merely one more victim in the daily life of the court.

Chapter 1

Identifying Pertinent Aspects of the Adjudication Process

REASONS FOR INVOLVING THE CRIMINAL JUSTICE SYSTEM

In spite of difficulties commonly experienced by victims who seek justice through the courts, involving the criminal justice system in the lives of children and adolescents who have been robbed of their innocence and their childhood by sexual abuse is appropriate and necessary. If all of our social and individual efforts at preventing child sexual abuse have failed, legal intervention to protect children and hold abusers accountable is critical.

Over the past twenty years we have learned that child sexual abuse is a serious problem, with serious ramifications for individuals and society, affecting hundreds of thousands of children every year (Whitcomb, 1992). Because of the grave and far-reaching effects of child sexual abuse, a need exists to take sexual abuse allegations seriously by involving the criminal justice system, "not only to exact retribution on behalf of society, but also to validate the victim's position and to shift the blame where it belongs: with the perpetrator" (Whitcomb, 1992, p. 10). On its own, the criminal justice system cannot be expected to provide the solution to the tragedy of child sexual abuse. However, state and federal legislatures intent on protecting children and social service agencies dedicated to the welfare of children join the criminal justice system in sending a critical and urgent message to society about the importance of protecting children and securing justice on their behalf (Pence and Wilson, 1994). It is up to everyone to respond.

Protecting children from sexual abuse requires more action than jailing the perpetrator. Child sexual abuse causes physical, psychological, spiritual, and social harm, and prosecuting these crimes is

consequential for victims, perpetrators, and society. Through prosecution, the innocence of the child victim can be established, placing
the responsibility for the crime solely where it belongs—with the
abuser. Successful prosecution usually results in a jail sentence,
which keeps the abuser away from children for a time, and/or court
mandated treatment for the abuser, which may reduce recidivism. An
abuser who is found guilty will be labeled with a criminal record, and
in many states will be included on the sex offender registry. This may
result in neighbors being alerted when any convicted sex offender
moves into their neighborhood, increasing parents' opportunities to
protect their children from a known threat. Prosecuting child sexual
abuse "validates the victims' and society's sense of fairness that an
older person has no right to violate or exploit the relative weakness of
children," (Peters, Dinsmore, and Toth, 1989, p. 654) and to inform
and educate society about child sexual abuse. Raising the social consciousness and informing people about child sexual abuse is another
important aspect of child protection. Although child molesters do not
expect to be caught, public prosecutions and subsequent jail sentences may deter other abusers from acting on their desires and sexually violating more children (Peters, Dinsmore, and Toth, 1989).

Another critically important reason to prosecute child sexual abuse
is the sheer magnitude of this crime. In 1996, child protective agencies from forty-eight states determined that "one million children
were identified as victims of substantiated or indicated abuse or neglect in 1996" (U.S. Department of Health and Human Services,
1998, p. xi). About 12 percent, (119,397) of these substantiated victims were sexually abused. These are startling statistics, but even
more startling, according to David Finkelhor, is that it is "widely
known that reported crimes represent only the tip of the iceberg. The
Bureau of Justice Statistics estimates that only 37 percent of all
crimes, and 48 percent of violent crimes, are reported to police"
(Whitcomb citing Finkelhor, 1992, p. 2). Statistics reported by the
National Crime Victim Survey using data from 1995 and 1996 esti-
mate that sexual assault of adolescent victims is reported in only 36
percent of the cases (Finkelhor and Ormrod, 1999).

ADOLESCENT REPORTING

The discrepancy between actual cases of sexual abuse and reported
and substantiated cases may be even greater among adolescent vic-

tims than among younger children. Professionals believe this wider discrepancy may be due to the way society views risks to young children and risks to adolescents. As children mature, the general public perceives the risks of abuse to diminish. Due to their growing physical stature and maturing cognitive ability to reason, adolescents are often seen as having more options to fight, run away or protect themselves in other ways from sexual abuse. If, in fact, a sexual encounter did occur between an adolescent and an adult, society could perceive that a sexually developing adolescent asked for it, initiated it (Gil, 1996), or consented to it since he or she did not choose to fight or run away or find other forms of protection.

Because of these social preconceptions, the adolescent victims themselves may be confused about what happened to them in a sexual encounter with an adult. Adolescents are able to recognize that they possess sexual feelings and thoughts, but because of their emotional immaturity and cognitive limitations, they may not be able to distinguish "between purposeful sexual activity and sexual activity in which they have been coerced, seduced or manipulated" (Deaton and Hertica, 1993, p. 7).

In spite of the speculation that the number of sexual abuse reports made by adolescent victims is the tip of the iceberg of actual incidents, a review of the statistics will reveal that preteens and teenagers comprise the largest percentage of reported sexual abuse victims. In 1997, The Child Abuse Division of the Middlesex County, Massachusetts, District Attorney's Office received 774 substantiated reports of child sexual abuse. Forty-one percent of these victims were between the ages of thirteen and eighteen (Pini, 1998). According to the DHHS review of 1996 statistics, 36 percent of the substantiated sexual abuse victims were twelve years old or older (USDHHS, 1998, pp. 2-9). However, we cannot let statistics confuse the reality of child sexual abuse. These statistics represent the age at which a report was made; they do not necessarily represent the age at which the abuse happened. Victims of chronic child sexual abuse often report years after the abuse began; and some victims do not report a single incident of sexual abuse until years after it occurred. The "higher incidence of reporting among older children is not evidence of higher vulnerability in older ages" (Finkelhor, 1994, p. 48). Finkelhor and Baron (1986) conducted a review of available studies and found that both boys and girls are most vulnerable to abuse between the ages of seven and thirteen. It is believed that a child may not report acute or chronic abuse, which began or happened much earlier, until he or she reaches adolescence, has developed some independence, and has found the courage and support to disclose the abuse (Finkelhor, 1994).

CASES ACCEPTED FOR PROSECUTION

A disclosure of child sexual abuse is the catalyst for the criminal justice process, but a disclosure does not necessarily, or even usually, result in a trial (Cross, Whitcomb, and De Vos, 1995). A number of steps happen during the investigation phase to determine if the abuse allegation can be substantiated. If an allegation is substantiated and referred to a prosecutor's office, numerous aspects of the case are considered before a determination is made regarding prosecution.

The criminal investigation and prosecution of child sexual abuse are complex processes, and more intricate and complicated than imaginable. Contrary to what our society has come to believe from our common cultural experiences with *Court TV* and legal dramas, no standard, clear-cut, or easy criteria exist for determining whether a child sexual abuse case—or any criminal case—will be accepted for prosecution. Facts are weighed and discretionary judgments are made at "each decision point from intake to final disposition . . . [and] there is an intricate configuration of contextual and legal factors that contribute to each decision" (Gray, 1993, pp. 19, 23).

The decision whether to prosecute a child sexual abuse case is burdened by legal, social, moral, and psychological implications which a team of professionals must carefully consider. Whatever the decision, it will have a major impact on the victim and his or her family. If the case is not accepted for prosecution the victim may feel that the investigators and prosecutors did not believe him or her; and in fact, the decision not to prosecute may affect how much, or if, the family actually does believe the child (Cross, De Vos, and Whitcomb, 1994).

Since criminal prosecution and conviction cannot and should not be our sole determinant for validating victims of child sexual abuse, it is useful for parents and helping professionals to understand the criteria prosecutors use for choosing to file or not file charges, or offering and/or accepting plea bargains. It is imperative for professionals, parents, and victims to understand that it is unethical for prosecutors to file charges that cannot be proven. Armed with an understanding of the guidelines and limitations of the criminal justice system, parents and professionals will be better equipped to provide victims with appropriate support and advocacy whatever the outcome of the case.

In their 1994 study of four urban jurisdictions, Cross, De Vos, and Whitcomb indicate that only 61 percent of the substantiated child sexual abuse cases referred to prosecutors were accepted for prosecution. Various and numerous personal and legal issues comprise the reasons that cases are not accepted for prosecution (Cross, De Vos, and Whitcomb, 1994; Whitcomb, 1992). After disclosing, some victims recant and refuse to testify. In most child sexual abuse cases, the victim is the only witness, and his or her testimony is the only evidence. Under these circumstances, if a victim refuses to testify, the case cannot move forward. This point is of particular importance in regard to adolescent victims. Developmentally, adolescents are seeking independence and control over their lives. Sexual abuse, by definition, has already stolen the victims' control over their bodies, and the result is often a feeling of powerlessness. The criminal justice system can compound this experience unintentionally through its "snowball nature" of protective interventions (Whitcomb, 1992, p. 22). These efforts to protect can cause victims to feel as if they have lost control over the process and, once again, their lives. This is a reasonable reaction, because the prosecution process is not controlled by the victim. The victim is not filing charges; the victim is not taking the abuser to court; the victim is not putting the abuser in jail. These steps are being taken—and controlled—by the prosecuting attorney and the court on behalf of the people of the state. The victim is a witness for the prosecution. However, some abused adolescents have overwhelming feelings of fearfulness and a belief that they are helpless against danger and random victimization. It is especially important to help these victims maintain the perception that they have some control over what happens to them during the adjudication process (Chaffin et al., 1996), for them to know that they have choices, and to trust that their input and feelings will be taken seriously.

Cases are also declined because they involve victims who are considered unreliable witnesses. This situation most commonly occurs with preschool-aged victims simply because they are limited by their immature language and ability to reason. Cases involving older children are, therefore, more likely to be accepted. A large increase in case acceptance was identified with victims at age seven with another increase noted with victims at age eleven (Cross, De Vos, and Whitcomb, 1994). Older children and adolescents are considered to be better and more effective witnesses because they are more capable of providing accurate, consistent information. However, adolescent victims can be considered unreliable when they are too psychologically wounded or severely disturbed (probably as a result of the sexual abuse) to present themselves and their account of the abuse in a way which jurors would consider credible. This, the most tragic reason for prosecutors declining a case, is a "sad irony." "When victims [are] more vulnerable or damaged, and the alleged crime therefore arguably more heinous, cases [are] less likely to be prosecuted" (Cross, De Vos, and Whitcomb, 1994, p. 675).

Cases are declined also because testifying and otherwise participating in the investigation and prosecution processes are judged not to be in the best psychological interest of the victim. The experience of relating details about the abuse and perhaps reliving horrendous episodes while facing the abuser in court and being cross-examined by an adversarial defense attorney may be more harmful than helpful to a young, vulnerable victim. Throughout the prosecution, victim witness advocates, interviewers, and mental health professionals remain alert for signs that a victim may be in distress as a result of the process. Parents, therapists, and other supporters can help a victim consider and determine what is best for him or her.

Another personally and socially tragic reason that child sexual abuse cases are not prosecuted is because the parents of the victim will not allow the victim to testify. This happens most often in intrafamilial cases in which the abuser is the mother's partner and she is emotionally and financially dependent on him. According to Cross, De Vos, and Whitcomb (1994), only 41 percent of the cases alleging sexual abuse by a biological parent are accepted for prosecution.

Cases are also not accepted for prosecution due to legal reasons, such as lack of evidence, testimony or evidence being tainted during the investigation, and the type, severity, and frequency of abuse. In 53 percent of the cases referred to prosecutors the only evidence available is the victim's testimony (Cross, De Vos, and Whitcomb, 1994). This, in itself, is considered the least strong evidence, and is not likely to be enough to convict a defendant. "In Western society, there is a long tradition of disbelieving women who claim they were raped or sexually assaulted. This tradition of disbelief extends equally if not more so to children" (Myers, 1997, p. 126). Declining to prosecute a case because the only available evidence is the victim's testimony is another social tragedy.

Every day, prosecutors confront the uphill struggle of proving the secret crime of child sexual abuse in court (Myers, 1997). Cross, De Vos, and Whitcomb (1994) report that corroborating physical evidence is available in only 9 percent of the child sexual abuse cases referred for prosecution, and that eyewitness testimony is available in only 15 percent of the cases. The evidence most likely to lead to prosecution in a child sexual abuse case is the perpetrator's confession, and surprisingly, this evidence is available in 32 percent of the cases; over 90 percent of the cases involving perpetrator confession are prosecuted.

Prosecutors have a moral and a legal responsibility to bring charges against an accused abuser only when the evidence of guilt is strong. If, in the prosecutor's trained opinion, not enough evidence exists to win the conviction in court, it would be a disservice to the victim and society to bring charges and initiate the trial court process. In many cases, prosecutors believe that the child was a victim of sexual abuse, but cannot accept the case for prosecution because they know the abuse cannot be proved in court. It is "not uncommon for prosecutors to tell parents, 'I'm sorry, I can't file charges. I believe your child was molested, but there isn't enough evidence to prove it in court'" (Myers, 1997, p. 89). Again, a social tragedy compounds the personal tragedy.

Testimony can be considered tainted when a victim is improperly questioned by parents, a counselor, a mandated reporter, or even an investigator who uses leading questions. It is understandable that parents or other adults want to show concern and support to a child who discloses sexual abuse to them, and asking questions about what happened is one way to be compassionate and supportive. However, doing so improperly, even with good intentions, may preclude the possibility of filing legal charges in the future. Defense attorneys seek out any and all means of freeing the defendant from the charges; and the defenses that the child was coached by a parent, that these preposterous ideas were planted by a zealous therapist, or that an investigator is conducting a witch-hunt, all have a track record of successful acquittal (Myers, 1997). In some instances, testimony becomes tainted because parents perceive that the investigators are not doing enough or being assertive enough. They lose faith in the process and begin their own investigation (Lanning, 1996). A prosecutor faced with testimony gathered through improper interview techniques is unlikely to bring that case to trial, and, therefore, cases with tainted witness evidence are usually lost forever. It is therefore imperative for all mandated reporters, all parents of abused children, and all concerned citizens to understand that they can most effectively further justice for a victim of child sexual abuse by involving trained professionals immediately, and then allowing the process to work. Child interview specialists and other professionals working with child witnesses in the court system are trained to ask open-ended questions intended to illicit enough detail about the abuse to support the case for prosecution. It will be difficult for the defense attorney to refute testimony given at a properly conducted, properly documented interview. Maintaining faith in a process which is outside of our control is difficult, at best. But for the good of the child and the good of the case, parents may need to seek out professional support and guidance for themselves and their entire family to achieve the justice their child and society deserve.

One would think that the type of child sexual abuse most often prosecuted would be sexual intercourse. In their 1994 study, Cross, De Vos, and Whitcomb found that this was not the case. They discovered that 77 percent of the cases prosecuted involved oral genital contact. In comparison, only 58 percent of the cases involving penetration, and 57 percent of the cases involving digital-vaginal penetration were prosecuted. The researchers speculated that cases of oral genital contact were more likely to be prosecuted due to the general lack of physical evidence available in child sexual abuse cases. Jurors do not expect physical evidence to be presented in cases of oral genital contact; however, if a child was vaginally or anally raped by an adult, the lack of physical evidence could create an opening for reasonable doubt.

Although many reasons prevent prosecutors from bringing child sexual abuse cases to court, in their 1995 study of the criminal justice outcomes of the prosecution of child sexual abuse, Cross, Whitcomb, and De Vos (1995) indicate that these cases are more likely to go to trial than other felony cases. In their study, 9 percent of child sexual abuse cases were referred for trial in comparison to 3 percent of felony cases overall. Based on anecdotal data gathered from their discussions with prosecutors, judges, police officers, and investigators, the researchers hypothesize that some of the reasons child sexual abuse cases go to trial more often than other felonies are:

1. Defendants may think they have a better chance of being acquitted because child sexual abuse cases usually lack physical evidence.
2. Many defendants in child sexual abuse cases are gainfully employed and can afford the cost of a trial.
3. Because of the stigma attached to child sexual abuse, these defendants may have more to lose than other felony defendants, and they want to persist in regaining their reputation.
4. Child sexual abuse carries a severe prison sentence, and the vast majority (94 percent) of cases taken to trial end in conviction (85 percent by guilty plea; 9 percent by guilty verdict). (Cross, Whitcomb, and De Vos, 1995)

Although the percentage of child sexual abuse cases going to trial far exceeds the percentage of other felony cases, 9 percent is still a small number. Therefore, in addition to focusing a great deal of deserved attention on the children involved in the cases that go to trial, we also need to attend to the needs of the victims involved in the 91 percent of the cases that do not go to trial. Whether or not they end up in the witness stand of Superior Court, 100 percent of the victims intersect in some way with the investigative processes of the social service and criminal justice systems. Research shows that victims are questioned far more often in forensic interviews than they are in the courtroom, and it is important to keep in mind that *all* victims need support, encouragement, understanding, and guidance *throughout* the criminal justice process—regardless of the eventual disposition.

The majority of the work of the criminal justice system happens before a case appears in court. Preparation for trial is a complicated and lengthy process, with the preferred goal of case disposition before it reaches the courtroom. The victim's testimony during the interview stage can influence whether justice prevails, (Saywitz and Goodman, 1996), and if the prosecutor prepares a strong case with strong, irrefutable victim testimony, the defendant may plead guilty and a trial can be avoided.

TYPICAL EVIDENCE

In child sexual abuse cases the evidence gathered by the prosecutor typically consists of

- the testimony of the child victim;
- the testimony of lay witnesses regarding their observations of abuse or opportunity for abuse to occur, and/or any hearsay testimony the witnesses received from the victim if this is allowed by law;
- the testimony of expert witnesses, including physicians who testify to physical evidence or explain the lack of physical evidence;
- mental health professionals who testify about sexual abuse and its effects on psychological behaviors of children; and
- other corroborating evidence about the defendant such as prior offenses. (Bulkley et al., 1996)

Child sexual abuse charges are serious and complex, and proof of these crimes may boil down to a child's word against an adult's. Therefore, "the accuracy of children's testimony and the best way to obtain children's statements become matters of substantial societal concern" (Saywitz and Goodman, 1996, p. 298). Because the testimony of older children and adolescents is sometimes considered more credible, the investigation of cases involving this population of victims usually focuses on the adolescent's "statement and efforts to corroborate it" (Bulkley, 1996, p. 281). Support for victims during the investigation may be the determining factor in gathering credible evidence and achieving a pretrial guilty plea and/or a guilty verdict at trial. It is, therefore, important to understand more about the criminal justice system and adolescent victims within the system in order to know what kind of support the victims need and how to provide it.

INHERENT BARRIERS FOR CHILD VICTIMS

Documented evidence of child sexual abuse has been evident throughout recorded human history (Rush, 1980; de Mause, 1988; Angelica, 1993). However, public outcry against these crimes began bombarding our social consciousness and our social service and legal systems in the 1980s. In 1983, psychiatrist Roland Summit wrote: "[this recent] explosion of interest creates new hazards for the child victim of sexual abuse since it increases the likelihood of discovery but fails to protect the victim against the secondary assaults of an inconsistent intervention system" (Summit, 1983, p. 178). Although Summit brought these "new hazards" to our attention over seventeen years ago, victims of child sexual abuse who disclose their abuse are still "thrust into an adult system that traditionally does not differentiate between adults and children" (Whitcomb, 1992, p. 15). In his 1982 testimony before the President's Task Force on Victims of Crime, attorney D. Lloyd said:

> Child victims of crime are specially handicapped. First the criminal justice system distrusts them and puts special barriers in the path of prosecuting their claims to justice. Second, the criminal justice system seems indifferent to the legitimate special needs that arise from their participation. (Whitcomb, 1992, p. 15)

Every state has a child abuse reporting law which requires certain people and professionals to report suspected child abuse to the authorities, (O'Brien and Flannery, 1991) and "all states provide criminal penalties for sexual abuse of a child under the age of sixteen or seventeen without regard to force or coercion because a child is deemed incapable of consenting" (Bulkley et al., 1996, p. 280). These laws are designed and intended to protect children; however, it is with these laws—at the threshold of the criminal justice system—that the barriers imposed by society onto child victims actually begin.

Victims of child sexual abuse hesitate to report the abuse because they know that our society does not routinely take children seriously, particularly when adults contradict them. They fear that they may be disbelieved, blamed, ignored, terrorized, abandoned, or punished by further abuse. Victims who disclose sexual abuse may be accused, outright, of lying or fantasizing or trying to stir up trouble. Adolescents, especially, do not report because they are humiliated or angry that the abuse happened and ashamed that they did not protect themselves. Many victims are threatened into silence. Fearing for their lives or the lives of loved ones, they do not know where to turn, who to trust, or what to say. Most adolescent victims understand the seriousness of child sexual abuse and know that telling may, in some way, disrupt their homes. This disruption may include the threat of the child being removed from the home and sent into the foster care system. Victims of child sexual abuse are more likely to be subjected to this fate than victims of other types of abuse, (Pence and Wilson, 1994) and an abuser may use the threat of foster care to keep the child quiet. Even brutally abused children resist the protective intervention of being removed from their homes. Adolescents have more complex emotional and intellectual abilities and they may choose not to report because they feel sorry for the abuser, or deeply love the abuser, and do not want to cause trouble for him or her. The possibility of saying or doing something that will result in the abuser going to jail, especially if he or she is a friend or family member or respected person in the community, is a weighty burden for a child to bear (Whitcomb, 1992). Abused adolescents, especially, are acutely aware of the outcomes which could result from their efforts to seek protection. Both extremes—being disbelieved or the abuser being convicted and sentenced to prison—present deterrents to reporting the abuse. Particularly in cases of intrafamilial sexual abuse, victims are afraid to endanger the family or cause anger if negative consequences from a prison sentence are expected, such as income loss or divorce (Saywitz and Goodman, 1996).

The need to repeat the account of the abuse is another barrier occurring early in the justice-seeking process which makes involvement with the criminal justice system especially difficult for child and adolescent victims. In a typical child sexual abuse case, a witness may be interviewed several times by social workers, police, prosecutors, and the defense attorney. Formal questioning occurs at preliminary hearings, grand jury appearances, and the trial (Whitcomb, 1992). It is often difficult to imagine how a child victim of sexual abuse finds the strength, the courage, and the resiliency to cope with the abuse he or she has endured, and even more difficult to imagine how a victim manages the distress experienced when revealing private, abusive sexual experiences to a legion of strangers.

Perhaps the most oppressive barrier in our criminal justice system for a child victim of sexual abuse is the defendant's presumption of innocence. In criminal cases the state must prove beyond a reasonable doubt in a court of law that the defendant is guilty. This high standard of proof is based on the social judgment that it is worse for an innocent person to be found guilty and held accountable for a crime he or she did not commit, than for a guilty person to go free (Saywitz and Goodman, 1996).

Victims, their families, and all the professionals who work with them need to understand that the intent of our child abuse reporting and protection laws is to protect children, but that the implementation of these laws through the criminal justice system protects the rights and well-being of the accused. If a case is accepted for investigation and/or prosecution, the parties to the investigation and litigation are the defendant and the people of the state, represented by the prosecutor. The victim is not actually a party to the criminal case, and therefore has fewer rights than the defendant. This imbalance of rights is difficult to rationalize to victims and their families. But our legal system is designed to protect against the miscarriage of justice, and toward this goal, the Sixth Amendment to the United States Constitution provides a number of protections for any defendant accused of a crime. The defendant has a right to a jury trial which is open to the public, a right to be protected from unreasonable searches, a right to present witnesses on his or her behalf, and a right to confront witnesses against him or her in court (Bulkley et al., 1996). These protections, particularly the right to a public trial and the right of confrontation, are often experienced as barriers to justice by victims of child sexual abuse.

The right to a public trial granted to the defendant by the Sixth Amendment is reinforced by the First Amendment which gives the right to open trials to the general public. Child sexual abuse cases that reach the courtroom are often considered newsworthy, and the general public, including reporters, television cameras, and any other interested parties may choose to attend. Victims have no control over who may or may not witness their testimony. The growing awareness of sexuality and issues of sexual identity experienced by adolescents make these victims particularly sensitive to the public aspects of a trial. Developmentally, adolescents seeking independence tend to have a need for privacy and secrecy (Whitcomb, 1992). The last place a fifteen-year-old boy or a sixteen-year-old girl wants to be is in an open courtroom revealing humiliating details of sexual abuse by his Boy Scout leader, or her father, before a group of reporters and strangers. Although most state laws require that the name of the victim be withheld from the press, the risk of public exposure of the sexual abuse at a trial may deter adolescents from testifying.

The right of confrontation is the cornerstone of our criminal justice system which "guarantees persons accused of crime the right to face-to-face confrontation with the witnesses against them, including children" (Myers, 1994, p. 88). Actually facing the defendant in court is usually the most frightening part of the prosecution process for victims of child sexual abuse. Victims feel exposed and vulnerable, often fearing that the abuser will retaliate and cause physical harm to themselves or loved ones. The right of confrontation gives the defense attorney the opportunity to cross-examine any witnesses presented by the prosecution, and in an attempt to discredit their testimony or blame them for the abuse, adolescent victims, specifically, are often harshly treated during this process. Knowing that cross-examination could be adversarial, many victims experience a great deal of anxiety in anticipation. Children worry about their public speaking abilities, about losing control on the stand and crying or yelling, about not being believed by the judge and jury, and about being punished for making a mistake in their testimony and being sent to jail (Saywitz and Goodman, 1996). Child and adolescent victims, with their limited understanding of the legal process, often misunderstand the burden of proof and feel that they must prove that they are innocent.

COURTROOM MODIFICATIONS

John E. B. Myers, author and legal advocate for abused children, describes child witnesses as "particularly vulnerable."

> Imagine the emotions that grip young children required to speak publicly in the forbidding and foreign environment of a courtroom. The courtroom itself, however, is seldom the greatest impediment to testimony. Many children are required to describe on the witness stand the unspeakable acts of an adult sitting a few feet away. In many cases the child testifies against a loved one, even a parent. Finally, once the child tells what happened, defense counsel may cross-examine with an eye toward destroying the child's credibility. (Myers, 1994, pp. 87-88)

Imagining these challenges makes the impressive courage of every victim of child sexual abuse who comes forward and overcomes the barriers of the criminal justice system humbling to witness. But knowing that children face these barriers leads to the logical question: *Must* it be this way? Can the courtroom be adapted in ways that meet the needs and emotional and cognitive developmental abilities of child and adolescent witnesses? Josephine Bulkley and colleagues (1996) indicate that many states have responded to the needs of child victims by providing options for accommodations in some situations.

Myers (1994) elaborates that although the constitutional right to a public trial is important, it is not absolute. In appropriate cases, the judge may close the courtroom to the public and the press. Nor is the right to confrontation absolute. The 1990 Supreme Court decision in *Maryland v. Craig* "ruled that, in selected cases, children may be spared the ordeal of face-to-face confrontation" (p. 89). However, before offering this modification, the judge must determine that such an "encounter would cause the child serious emotional distress that interferes with the ability to communicate" (p. 89). Some states allow video testimony for child witnesses; however, some state supreme courts have completely struck down laws allowing video testimony. The 1986 Supreme Court decision in *Delaware v. Van Arsdall* gives judges the authority to protect child witnesses from intimidation and harassment during cross-examination.

Some other courtroom modifications for children have included the use of child-sized furniture and microphones, allowing child witnesses to face the jury while testifying rather than face the defendant, and having support people available to the victim during testimony.

Massachusetts prosecutor Kevin Ryle (1999) hesitates to use any courtroom modifications for child witnesses because such efforts to make testifying easier on child witnesses, even those allowed by Supreme Court decisions, have been prohibited by the Massachusetts Appeals Court. Therefore, Ryle believes that any conviction currently achieved under modified circumstances will ultimately be overturned on appeal. The convictions of the Amiraults, defendants in the Fells Acre Day School case, prosecuted by Ryle's office in the mid-1980s, have been reversed and reinstated several times, at great expense to the Commonwealth, and at great emotional distress to the victims and their families. The Amiraults' defense objected to the court-approved modification which allowed the children to face the jury during their testimony. When asked to identify their abusers, the children turned around, looked at the defendants, and identified them by pointing. These convictions were appealed based on the Sixth Amendment right of confrontation.

Research shows that prosecutors tend to avoid use of courtroom reforms designed to reduce stress for child witnesses, instead choosing accommodations which will enhance the jury's ability to hear and understand the facts of the case. This may seem a cruel choice on the part of the prosecutor; however, it may ultimately be the most helpful choice for the victim. Painful testimony that results in an irrefutable conviction may be more healing for a victim of child sexual abuse in the long term than testifying under less stressful, but inherently uncomfortable circumstances, thus losing the conviction (Gray, 1993).

During the 1980s much attention was focused on courtroom modifications for child victims. In the early 1990s researchers began to notice and acknowledge that the innovative accommodations designed to make testifying in child sexual abuse cases easier for the victims were not actually the panacea so many child advocates had hoped to create. Instead, researchers concluded that emphasis would be more wisely placed on improving the investigation and interviewing phases of child sexual abuse cases, enhancing the cooperation of various agencies, courts, and professionals involved in these cases, and providing more and appropriate preparation and support to child victims and their families (Whitcomb, 1992).

PREPARING THE VICTIMS

Because of their peculiarity, *cases* involving crimes against children need specialized attention. Often these cases have no witnesses except young, wounded victims (Gray, 1993) who are ashamed and bewildered about the abuse, naive about the legal system, and confused about the common legal terms used in court (Saywitz and Goodman, 1996). The young, wounded *victims* represented in these cases need specialized attention as well.

According to Massachusetts Attorney General Thomas F. Reilly (1990), even the most confident adults are intimidated by the proceedings of the criminal justice system. Therefore, it must be acknowledged that child victims—even older children and adolescents— "may not communicate at their optimal level of functioning" in forensic interviews or in court (Saywitz and Goodman, 1996, p. 304). A review of the treatment literature on child sexual abuse will quickly reveal that the investigation and prosecution of child sexual abuse cases can be stressful for the victims. Recognizing and addressing this inevitable stress is critical. Throughout the concentrated effort to prove the child sexual abuse allegations and win the conviction, legal and social service professionals need to maintain focus on the child victim and his or her needs for healing (Myers, 1994). John J. Wilson, in his Foreword to the 1994 Justice Department Research Report, *The Child Victim As a Witness,* poignantly reminded us: "In our zeal to bring the perpetrator to justice, we must not overlook the impact on the victim—we must not re-victimize the child" (p. iii).

As with any industry, the criminal justice system, with its unique routines, procedures, and vernacular is mysterious to outsiders. My own contact with the criminal justice system was the result of an educational inquiry. As part of my research for this resource, I attended all court-related aspects of child sexual abuse proceedings. I discovered that even peripheral involvement with the criminal justice process caused anxiety. I felt nervous in court, and I was merely an observer. The environment, itself, was stressful and confusing. I heard words that sounded familiar—arraigned, subpoena, and indictment— words I had heard thousands of times on television programs or news reports. Familiar words. I had a vague sense of what they meant, but if I were asked to define them, I could not.

Studies show that by age ten, most children have a basic understanding of the investigative and judicial processes, recognize basic legal vocabulary, and understand the fact-finding mission of the interviews and the trial (Saywitz and Goodman, 1996). However, this basic grasp of the justice system must not be overestimated. As with most Americans, children's understanding of the legal system and the vocabulary is naive. On the other hand, the distress caused to child victims by the prosecution process must also not be overestimated. Humans are resilient creatures, and professionals indicate that testifying against the person who sexually abused them may, in fact, be empowering for some children (Bulkley et al., 1996). Whitcomb et al. (1994, p. 2) observed that any stress caused to child victims of sexual abuse "by their involvement with the legal system appeared to be mitigated by the passage of time, as well as other interventions and life experiences."

Child advocates believe that adequate, sensitive preparation is a critical intervention which can influence the quality of a child victim's subjective experience of the prosecution process as well as the quality of his or her testimony (Spencer and Flin as cited in Saywitz and Goodman, 1996). Since the child victim's testimony in court is usually essential for conviction, it is more advisable to seek ways to improve this testimony, and the psychological strength of the victim, rather than to attempt to keep child witnesses off the stand or to request modifications in standard courtroom procedures. The first step to improving a child's testimony and strength is to acknowledge the communicative, cognitive, and emotional challenges child and adolescent victims face (Saywitz and Goodman, 1996), and to reduce as much stress and pressure as possible.

In a criminal court proceeding, stress and pressure are inherent obstacles, but not insurmountable ones. Most prosecutors begin tackling these obstacles by familiarizing a child victim with the process through available, age-appropriate written materials, a review of vocabulary, a review of the facts of the case, a visit to the victim witness waiting room in the courthouse, a tour of the actual courtroom where the case will be heard—including the opportunity to sit in the witness stand and answer questions—and perhaps even by introducing the child to the bailiff, court reporter, and other courtroom personnel. Some professionals recommend including clinical methods for anxiety reduction—such as deep breathing, guided imagery, self-monitoring and positive affirmations: I CAN DO IT!—to the trial preparation process of child witnesses (Saywitz and Goodman, 1996). The quest for justice for children can be more adequately advanced by providing information, attention, and emotional support for the victim; and, *this* support violates none of the constitutional rights of the defendant (Myers, 1994).

It is important to focus on the quality of the victim's testimony even if the case does not culminate in a jury trial. At many steps in the criminal justice process, a victim is expected to relate his or her eyewitness account of the crime, and given the reality of many child sexual abuse cases—that "the case may boil down to a child's word against an adult's—the accuracy of children's testimony and the best way to obtain children's statements become matters of substantial societal concern" (Saywitz and Goodman, 1996, p. 298). The quality of testimony during forensic interviews, a grand jury hearing, depositions, or other preliminary hearings may determine whether the case will be carried over for trial or whether the defendant will plead guilty. In fact, researchers Cross, Whitcomb, and De Vos (1995) concluded that improving the quality of forensic investigations and victim testimony may have greater influence on the prosecution outcome than courtroom innovations or rulings affecting the admissibility of evidence.

One basic and critical method of preparing victims and their families for the investigation and prosecution process is to share available resources with them. There are age-appropriate booklets, videos, and even court "schools" in some jurisdictions, all of which are designed to educate children and adults who are unfamiliar with the justice system about common practices, experiences and outcomes. Although there are numerous resources for preschool and elementary-aged child victims of sexual abuse, age-appropriate resources for adolescents are scarce. The research of Cross, Whitcomb, and De Vos (1995) as well as national reports (USDHHS, 1998) and statistics compiled by individual prosecutor's offices (Pini, 1998) indicate that adolescents represent the largest percentage of victims of child sexual abuse in the court system. In stark contrast to their numbers, however, few studies have been done regarding the specific abilities and needs of adolescents as they relate to the criminal justice system. Saywitz and Goodman (1996, p. 313) "hesitate to provide many guidelines concerning the interviewing of adolescents because research on [their] testimony in regard to sexual abuse allegations is lacking."

The contrast between the demand for information and materials supporting adolescents and the existence or availability of materials may reflect a lack of understanding about this category of victims. It is important to underscore the vulnerability of *all* victims of child sexual abuse, even adolescents and teenagers. As children mature and grow physically, sometimes larger than the adults around them, individuals and society may tend to overlook their vulnerability. According to Eliana Gil (1996), when working with adolescent victims, it helps to be familiar with basic theories of childhood development and to be mindful that victimization makes children—even big children—feel more vulnerable.

An aspect of preparation that cannot be overlooked is the importance of preparing nonoffending parents for the investigative and prosecution procedures their child will endure. Research indicates that support from parents is a critical factor in how well a child copes with the criminal justice experience and succeeds in the subsequent recovery process. In a case in which a victim has been abused by a father or other adult (e.g., a mother's boyfriend, etc.), support for the adolescent victim from his or her mother is key, and it is imperative to devote time and energy *specifically* preparing the nonoffending mothers of victims, and to acknowledge and help the mothers address and manage their own conflicting emotions and needs (Whitcomb, 1993; Deblinger and Heflin, 1996).

It is common for nonoffending parents to experience substantial apprehension and heightened stress and anxiety after their child discloses sexual abuse; and these reactions may significantly impair their ability to provide comfort and support to their child (Deblinger and Heflin, 1996). Professionals (including law enforcement officers, prosecutors, medical personnel, therapists, counselors, caseworkers, victim witness advocates, and clergy) at every step in the adjudication and recovery phases are urged to pay close attention to the reactions and needs of the nonoffending parents of victims, in particular their mothers. A 1992 study by D. K. Runyan clearly determined that guidance, support, and assistance from these professionals was directly related to the parents' ability to provide emotional sustenance for their sexually abused child (Whitcomb, 1993).

The workings of the justice system are mysterious to all—children and adults alike. Therefore, if helping professionals pay close attention to the parents' reactions and needs, and help them to unravel the mystery by providing information, resources, emotional support, and encouragement, the parents will be more prepared and better able to give their child comfort and support in a concentrated, consistent, caring, and empowering way.

IN SUMMARY

Over the past twenty years, state legislatures, social services agencies, and the criminal justice system have taken on the crime of child sexual abuse with zeal and determination. The rising number of reports and prosecutions of child sexual abuse reflect our society's commitment to protecting children from harm. The intent of the criminal justice system, however, is to punish the perpetrator of a crime, and we must constantly remind ourselves not to lose sight of the victim's need for healing in the pursuit of punishment.

The ultimate goal of the criminal justice system is to achieve justice. Yet even when justice for the children prevails, it is important to keep other realities about child sexual abuse cases in clear sight: the child victim may be faced with a lifelong healing process, the abuser may face a long prison sentence, and the family or families of both may be blown apart. However, the just conviction of a child molester indeed sends a social message of irrefutable truth: Child sexual abuse is wrong. It is an extraordinary betrayal of trust and causes extraordinary harm to the victim. Child sexual abuse will not be tolerated.

Chapter 2

Understanding and Reaching Out to Victims

Teenage and preteen victims of child sexual abuse pose challenges to the criminal justice system which can be exacerbated by our social attitudes about adolescence. Helping professionals often begin working with this population of victims with the firmly rooted assumption that they are *difficult,* and that adolescence is a developmental stage inherently fraught with rebellion, disorder, struggle, peril, tumult, anger, and pain. Adolescents are *expected* to be demanding and defiant (Gil, 1996).

Every teenager experiences and manages the journey into and through adolescence uniquely, and it is not helpful to project defiance, rebellion, and anger onto every teen victim. It is considered normal development for children entering adolescence to seek independence and a sense of control over their own choices, lives, and destinies. Sexual abuse in childhood robs teen victims of personal control. Since the court system can cause victims to feel that they are yet again being robbed of control over what happens to them, adolescent victims may act out during the adjudication process in ways which highlight their developmental setbacks, or which assert their need for independence and personal control. It will benefit victims and aid the investigation and prosecution processes if helping professionals keep in mind that the developmental process of sexually abused adolescents most likely has been compromised or disrupted by the abuse (Gil, 1996).

Children and adolescents react uniquely to the experience of sexual abuse. Although research indicates that there are "typical" or "common" reactions to child sexual abuse, it is important to be wary of labeling, generalizing, or projecting reactions onto any individual victim. Sexual abuse in childhood does not necessarily result in immediate or delayed symptoms that are always consistent or predictable. One victim may exhibit symptoms of depression, diminished self-esteem, and passivity, while another is anxious, self-medicating, and sexually promiscuous, and yet another is grandiose, manipulative, and righteous. Although most victims do experience some type of trauma reaction as a result of sexual abuse, these reactions will range from minor to intense to life altering (Friedrich, 1995).

Adolescents—like all human beings—are vulnerable and resilient. The transition for teen victims of child sexual abuse from vulnerability to resilience can be aided by interactions with trustworthy adults or hindered by adults who are not trustworthy. The presence of another person who provides an adolescent victim with consistent empathy, care, and continuity of attention is one of the most important ways to counteract the negative effects and vulnerability caused by child sexual abuse (Gil, 1996).

ADOLESCENT REACTIONS
TO CHILD SEXUAL ABUSE

The reactions of victims of child sexual abuse will differ according to numerous variables including age at the time the abuse happened or began, type of abuse, duration of the abusive interactions, relationship to the perpetrator, and family reaction and support. As noted in Chapter 1, research indicates that parental support after the disclosure of child sexual abuse is of significant importance to a victim's reactions and recovery. If nonoffending parents believe the victim and provide support during and after the disclosure, the victim is likely to experience fewer and less intense psychological and physical symptoms. If a victim's disclosure is met with disbelief, criticism, rejection, or punishment by his or her parents, increased symptomology is likely (Briere and Elliot, 1994).

To interact most effectively with an adolescent who discloses sexual abuse, it is important to determine if the abuse was recent, if it occurred earlier in life, or if it began earlier and was/is on-going. According to Eliana Gil (1996), a victim's reactions to sexual abuse and the type of symptoms exhibited will vary depending upon the stage of development at which both abuse and disclosure occur. In cases of chronic sexual abuse, victims may display an impaired ability to protect themselves due to "what they perceive as 'learned helplessness' or the futility of trying to stop long-standing abusive patterns" (Gil, 1996, p. 24). Adolescent victims of chronic sexual abuse tend to be more vulnerable than their nonabused peers or peers who were sexually abused only during adolescence. Many victims of chronic abuse have diminished ability to exercise personal control, identify and weigh options, or make use of available resources because the ongoing abuse has damaged their self-esteem and sense of entitlement. Adolescent victims who have had a respectful and loving relationship with their parents throughout their lives are more likely to be motivated for therapy after acute abuse and resilient enough to endure the adjudication process with fewer setbacks (Gil, 1996).

William Friedrich quotes a 1985 study by Finkelhor and Browne which suggests that child sexual abuse is "deleterious because of four traumatic factors: betrayal, stigmatization, powerlessness, and traumatic sexualization. Each . . . has a potential impact on both overt behavior and internal psychological processes, including cognitions" (Freidrich, 1995, p. 5). Behavioral reactions include: withdrawal, noncompliance, aggression, and inappropriate sexual behavior. Psychological difficulties and cognitive distortions include: anxiety, dysphoria, anger, shame, and beliefs which lead to distrust of others, feelings of self-blame, and sexual dissatisfaction. Victims of child sexual abuse also experience physiological symptoms including headaches, stomach aches, and startle reactions (Deblinger and Heflin, 1996).

Deblinger and Heflin (1996) indicate that the majority of victims of child sexual abuse experience at least partial symptoms of posttraumatic stress disorder (PTSD). According to the American Psychiatric Association's *Diagnostic and Statistical Manual of Mental Disorders* (Fourth Edition), the symptoms of PTSD are:

1. Reexperiencing the traumatic event through intrusive memories, dreams, and flashbacks.
2. Avoiding memories and reminders of the trauma. Experiencing reduced interest in activities, detachment from others, limited affect range, and a sense of a foreshortened future.
3. Experiencing increased anxiety or arousal, sleep disturbances, irritability, difficulty concentrating, hypervigilance, or heightened startle response.

Many studies have been done to identify reactions to child sexual abuse, and the list of the most common reactions displayed by adolescent victims is alarmingly long and complex. Adolescent reactions include: alienation from school and peers, anger, anxiety, denial, depression, dissociation, drug and alcohol abuse or addiction, eating disorders, fear, feeling defective, guilt and shame regarding the abuse, hyperarousal, inability to trust, insomnia, low self-esteem, lying and manipulating to gain power and control over others, negative self-perception, panic attacks, school problems, self-mutilation, sexual promiscuity, suicide ideation or attempts, and vulnerability to stress (Briere and Elliott, 1994; Deblinger and Heflin, 1996; Elliott and Briere, 1992; Friedrich, 1995; Gil, 1996, cites Bagley, 1995; Lee, 1995). Often adolescent victims try to communicate about the abuse they have endured through acting-out behavior instead of words. Unfortunately, observers and recipients of these behaviors, viewing them through the stereotypical lens of "difficult adolescent," could mistakenly interpret these cries for help as abuse of others, carelessness, or rebellion.

REACTIONS AND THE PROSECUTION PROCESS

Typical adolescent rections to child sexual abuse that may specifically interfere with the legal process or impact the outcome of the investigation and prosecution of these cases include: denial, fear, inability to trust, and vulnerability to stress.

According to Lyn Sanford, one of the typical feelings victims experience following the disclosure of child sexual abuse is fear. "Child sexual abuse represents a total disruption to the normal developmental process, forcing children to experience intense fear long before they have the ego strength to do so successfully. Without effective intervention, free-floating fears can continue into adulthood" (Sanford, 1987, p. 3). After disclosing sexual abuse, victims may feel panic about how the exposed secret will affect them, their families, and the perpetrator. Distorted cognitions might cause victims to fantasize that the perpetrator will kill them or members of their family, or that the truth of the abuse will actually destroy a nonoffending parent. It is not uncommon for these distorted fears to lead victims into denying the abuse and recanting their disclosure. It is important for helping professionals and supportive adults who are interacting with adolescent victims of child sexual abuse to have awareness about the complexities of retractions. Some reasons for retractions are fear of retribution by the perpetrator, fear of disruption to the family, coaching or threats by parents, confusion about what actually happened (this is particularly significant for adolescents who may have sexual feelings or otherwise be sexually active), and dissatisfaction with a foster care placement (Besharov, 1994).

Child sexual abuse threatens and disrupts a victim's sense of security, and so it is not surprising that abuse produces individuals who experience chronic fear and anxiety (Briere and Elliott, 1994). When working with adolescent victims, awareness of this fear is essential for attaining and maintaining their participation and cooperation throughout the investigation and prosecution. Victims may feel anxious and fearful in the presence of people who express kindness toward them and who offer to help them. They may be particularly frightened of judgment or evaluation, and especially anxious when interacting with anyone who is perceived to be in a position of authority (Briere and Elliott, 1994).

For victims of child sexual abuse, fear can be a double bind. Although they may feel excessive fear *after* disclosing the sexual abuse, fear was often the impetus for the disclosure in the first place. Adolescents are often afraid for the well-being of other potential victims, for their own safety, or for their own health. As victims of child sexual abuse begin to mature, they will likely realize the risks of sexual activity due to information that bombards them via the media, peer pressure, and guidance and counseling they receive in school. A health risk that may torment teen victims of child sexual abuse into disclosing is the threat of HIV and other sexually transmitted diseases (STDs). The reality of AIDS and the increasing awareness of this deadly virus can burden victims of child sexual abuse with life and death worries. Sometimes the only way for children or adolescents to feel peace of mind and obtain treatment or protection for themselves is to disclose the abuse.

Toward the goal of providing appropriate treatment and/or peace of mind to victims of sexual assault or sexual abuse who may have been exposed to HIV, state and federal laws have been enacted to address the issue of mandatory HIV testing for convicted defendants. (See The Federal Crime Control Act of 1990, Section 1804; Federal Statute 42 U.S.C., Section 3756; Pennsylvania Statute 35 P.S. 521.11a—

added by Act of September 29, 1994, P.L. 516, No. 75, 2; Omnibus Crime Control and Safe Streets Act of 1968, Public Law 351-42 U.S.C., 3756). Unfortunately, fears about child sexual abuse and health consequences such as STDs, AIDS, and/or pregnancy do not and will not end with convictions, testing and counseling of victims, or laws requiring mandatory testing of perpetrators. Child sexual abuse could have far-reaching and serious implications. "Feelings of guilt [for the sexual abuse], sexual acting out, and self-destructive behaviors may contribute to former victims [of childhood rape] becoming infected with HIV [or other STDs] in later life." (Grubman-Black, 1990, p. 45). In *The Boston Globe* (February 25, 1992), Alison Bass indicates that sexually abused children

> often develop serious self-esteem and developmental problems that interfere with their ability to make decisions or consider the consequences of their actions. . . . Female victims are less likely to use contraception even when they have access to contraception and family planning . . . and male victims are less likely to use condoms to protect themselves from the threat of AIDS. (p. 4)

Researchers conclude that child sexual abuse is one explanation for the large percentage of adolescents who do not respond to pregnancy-prevention programs or AIDS-prevention information.

Younger children are usually perceived and expected to be more vulnerable to abuse and the stress of the adjudication process than are adolescent victims; therefore, it is often assumed that younger children need more support and protection than do adolescents. This assumption is not always accurate, and operating as if it were could adversely affect the victims and ultimately the outcome of cases. When interacting with and assessing the vulnerability of adolescent victims, it is important to remember that "prolonged and intrusive sexual abuse imposed on the physically immature body and the developmentally immature psyche of a child frequently creates an adolescent who cannot find adequate solutions to the dilemmas of identity development. . . . As a result, the adolescent[s] are extremely vulnerable to stress" (Gil, 1996, p. 16). Since adolescent victims of chronic sexual abuse have endured the stress of the abuse for longer periods and through more developmental stages than have the younger victims, it follows that adolescents even need more support, not less, than the young children.

The level of stress hardiness of a victim can influence the choice to prosecute and the ultimate outcome of the adjudication process. Many cases do not go forward because it is determined that the process will be detrimental to the well-being of the victim. In these cases, particularly, it is likely to help the victim's sense of safety and self-esteem in the long term if the perpetrator were convicted and incarcerated; however, the emotional status of the victim must be guarded in the short term.

GENDER DIFFERENCES

In our society it is generally assumed that victims of sexual assault are female and sexual aggressors or abusers are male. This assumption exists because girls and women are expected to be gentle and are rewarded for passive behavior; boys and men are expected to be self-reliant, stoic, and aggressive, and they are rewarded for manifesting these behaviors. The majority of child molesters are male—but not *all* molesters are male, and not all victims are female. In 1996, findings of child maltreatment indicated that 23 percent of reported and/or substantiated victims of child sexual abuse are male (U.S. Department of Health and Human Services, 1998). The *actual* number of male victims could be considerably higher. Because of social pressures and differences in sex role expectations, boys are likely to hide their abuse, and even more likely to be overlooked as victims by society. Typically, boys are viewed as stronger and more resilient than girls, and this view leads to the assumption that child sexual abuse is less harmful or damaging for male victims. Clinical evidence indicates that this view is inaccurate. Child sexual abuse harms boys as much as it does girls. In some cases, the double standard and denial surrounding male sexual victimization may cause child sexual abuse to be even more harmful to boys (Porter, 1986).

Adolescents victims are often blamed for being sexually abused. Girls are blamed for being pretty and flirtatious and wily. Simply because they have reached puberty, adolescent girls are often perceived as "objects of sexual behavior" and, therefore, they are at least "partially responsible" for their abuse (Gray, 1993, p. 108). Regarding an incest case in which the father gave his daughter expensive gifts, a professional was heard to say, "That girl knew what she wanted and how to get it" (Gil, 1996, p. 14). Male victims are *very* often blamed for their sexual abuse. Common responses to a teenage boy's disclosure are that it was/is no big deal, *or* that he is responsible because he should have been able to protect himself and stop the abuse.

If a boy was molested by a female, he may feel foolish for reporting the abuse because society tells boys they are *supposed* to enjoy *all* sexual interactions (Grayson, 1989). Regrettably, some adults—even well-intentioned adults—may consider abuse of a boy by an older woman to be a positive encounter and a fortunate opportunity for the boy to learn about sex (Porter, 1986). Because males are rewarded and females are condemned for having numerous sexual partners and casual sex (Friedrich, 1995) a gender-related double standard concerning sexual mores festers in our society. The reality and the power of this double standard in relationship to child sexual abuse must not be glossed over, passed over, dismissed, or underestimated. Unfortunately, even educated, enlightened adults are not immune. Eliana Gil (1996, p. 14) "overheard an investigator call the adolescent [male] victim 'a lucky bastard' because he had sexual intercourse with the thirty-five year old mother of one of his friends." In my own experience working with prosecutors of child sexual abuse cases, I observed a male prosecutor exclaim with a grin, "Lucky day," in reference to a teenage boy who had intercourse with his female teacher.

The vulnerability of adolescent male victims, like the vulnerability of adolescents in general, must not be overlooked. Boys themselves deny and cover up the abuse because admitting it is evidence of their failure to be masculine and their inability to protect themselves. In his 1988 article, "Hidden Victims, Hidden Pain," Roland Summit discusses historical and social reasons for denying and avoiding the reality of child sexual abuse. It seems that the degree of hiding—of both victims and pain—exists on a continuum, and that adolescent boys are most likely to be hidden victims.

Boys may make a valiant effort to be tough and unemotional during the adjudication process, believing this is what is expected of them. Helping professionals and parents are encouraged to be attentive to the masked vulnerability and the deeply buried, and heavily guarded pain of adolescent male victims.

Sexual abuse during childhood can affect the sexual behavior and sexual identity of victims throughout their lives; and as developing adolescents begin to experience and express their sexual feelings, the after-effects of abuse may first become manifested. Female victims tend to believe that sexual abuse has made their bodies into damaged goods, and that no one will ever want to touch them or to love them. These girls believe that their bodies—and their whole beings by extension—are unclean, "dirty, disgusting, and bad" (Lee, 1995, p. 52). This belief becomes visible in adolescent promiscuity in which it appears that the girls do not care about what happens to them or their bodies. Teen pregnancy and teen prostitution are the most overt manifestations of the damaged goods syndrome.

Studies suggest that adolescent victims tend to disclose sexual abuse when they are caught behaving inappropriately and are least likely to be believed (Goodwin, 1985, cited in Jackson and Nuttal, 1993). The female victims of child sexual abuse who are pregnant or involved in prostitution do not usually elicit much compassion from juries who can too easily conclude that these rebellious, promiscuous teens got what they wanted or deserved (Gray, 1993). Prosecutors can enhance their chances of winning justice on behalf of adolescent female victims by educating judges and juries about how child sexual abuse impacts sexual behavior. According to Debra Boyer, cultural anthropologist at the University of Washington, "If you have an adolescent whose sexual experiences have all been involuntary and who has never perceived herself as a good girl, it may be impossible for her to say 'No' " (Bass, 1992, p. 4). The impossibility of refusing sex underscores abused girls' learned powerlessness and "translates into an inability to protect themselves from unwanted sexual experiences" (Bass, 1992, p. 4).

The sexual abuse of boys frequently includes physical force, and since the boys are not big enough or strong enough to fight back in ways that accomplish protection, they may also retreat into a feeling of powerlessness. To combat the powerlessness, abused boys often exhibit external sexual aggression, (which can be inappropriate attempts to reassert their masculinity), and sexual preoccupation and excessive masturbation, (which can be symptomatic of lack of control) (Elliott and Briere, 1992; Finkelhor, 1984; Friedrich, 1995; Grayson, 1989). If the combination of sexual abuse and physical aggression continues over a long period of time, male victims are likely to construct an impermeable emotional wall between themselves and others, and to seek power and control in all future relationships (Bass, 1992). They may also come to view "aggression and sexuality as naturally coexisting processes. This combination can . . . result in reduced empathy [for others, particularly others] over whom they have control" (Friedrich, 1995, p. 8).

Surrendering to the powerlessness may cause abused boys to feel worthless, used, and hopeless (Friedrich, 1995), and to recreate experiences of sexual victimization, just as girls do. According to Eli Newberger, a pediatrician at Childrens' Hospital in Boston, "A higher than average number of young men who were sexually abused as children . . . become passive and self-destructive, particularly when it comes to protecting themselves during sexual encounters" (Bass, 1992, p. 4).

Confusion and anxiety about sexual identity is commonly reported by male victims of child sexual abuse, particularly if the perpetrator was also male. Heterosexual boys fear that the sexual abuse will make them homosexual; and homosexual boys fear that they caused or invited the abuse or that the abuse caused their homosexuality. If boys experience erection or ejaculation during the sexual abuse, confusion becomes intensified by guilt. "Not understanding fully how sexual abuse happens, boys assume these responses 'prove' that they desired the experience" (Grayson, 1989, p. 6).

The confusion about sexual identity and gender stereotyping should be kept in mind when working with adolescent victims of sexual abuse. It may be difficult or impossible for them to trust and/or to feel safe or comfortable or close to a person of the same gender as their abuser (Friedrich, 1995). Since the vast majority of abusers are male, particular attention to this issue is needed by male professionals. Adolescent girls may flirt with male helping professionals or cower with fear in their presence; and sexually abused adolescent boys may act out their rage against male professionals (Friedrich, 1995). Victims of male perpetrators may just not be comfortable with male social workers, therapists, victim witness advocates, or prosecutors, and their discomfort may sabotage the adjudication process. A simple shift in the gender of the personnel handling a case may transform it from chaos into cooperation. On the other hand, if a victim is open to another kind of transformation, connecting in a healthy and safe way with a person of the same gender as the abuser could be a corrective and life-changing opportunity.

LEARNING TO TRUST

Sexual abuse that occurs early in a child's life or sexual abuse that continues over a long period of time is likely to derail a victim's normal development of a sense of self and healthy self-esteem (Briere and Elliott, 1994). By the time they reach adolescence, many victims of child sexual abuse do not know themselves. As a result, they have difficulty sharing themselves with others and real friendships do not happen naturally or easily. As they mature, it becomes increasingly difficult for victims to identify their own feelings and thoughts and to be honest about them because they have little experience at doing this. Many victims have been systematically taught not to believe their own thoughts and feelings—not to trust themselves (Lee, 1995).

Victims of child sexual abuse often develop into loners—life is safer that way. They learn to distrust others, particularly those who they perceive to be in positions of power. Victims feel both fear and anger in relation to authority figures, and manifest these feelings in passive behavior by deferring to the person in authority, in passive-aggressive behavior by avoiding direct communication about their feelings, acting out inappropriately, or exhibiting overtly defiant behavior (Briere and Elliott, 1994).

Trust becomes an elusive concept and an even more elusive reality for victims of child sexual abuse. Often the abuse they experienced by a trusted adult provided them with opportunities to feel good, possibly even to feel loved and wanted (Grubman-Black, 1990). This preposterous combination of abuse and good feelings deeply confuses victims who are usually lonely and needy children, seeking love and approval. Sexual abuse, which may bring the victims longed-for attention, tends to increase their gullibility and reduce their capacity for self-protection. Victimization then proliferates in all areas of their lives: victims of child sexual abuse have a "greater likelihood of being victimized or exploited by others" (Briere and Elliott, 1994, p. 59).

Eliana Gil (1996) noticed the positive impact adults can have on adolescents simply by taking the time to ask how they are doing or to briefly converse with them. Teachers showing a special interest, physicians taking the time to really listen, or the parents of friends who consider their company worthwhile, can help to heal victims' wounded souls and psyches. This is an important point because it represents a double-edged sword. Children and adolescents are vulnerable to attention directed toward them by adults. Perpetrators of child sexual abuse know this, and they can lure children into abusive and exploitive relationships by providing the attention the children crave.

When working with children and adolescent victims of child sexual abuse during the adjudication process, it is paramount to ensure that they will be safe in the company of all the adults they meet (Friedrich, 1995). Surely they will be safe from further sexual abuse while in the care of helping professionals, but other forms of safety are also critical. During the investigation and prosecution of child sexual abuse, it is important to protect the victims from experiencing additional feelings of loss of power and further separation from themselves.

According to Gil (1996) adolescents develop trust through the experience of having clearly defined expectations. During the investigation and prosecution of child sexual abuse, paying attention to simple interpersonal interactions and meeting agreed-upon expectations can make a major impact on the victims' feelings of safety. Of utmost importance is clear communication. Keep victims and their families informed about the process and any changes that occur. Keeping promises—even small ones—is critical to helping victims understand that their needs and feelings are important and that adults can be trustworthy. A typical promise that is likely to fall through the cracks is a promise to call. Even if there is nothing new to report, it is essential to keep that promise to call. For many victims, the promise kept is more helpful than the information received. Fulfilling clearly defined expectations can provide victims with the opportunity to have experiences with a trustworthy adult that they may remember and refer to for strength and clarity throughout their lifetimes. Never underestimate the healing power of fulfilled expectations.

IN SUMMARY

Adolescent victims, in particular, may resist support that is offered to them during the criminal justice process. When faced with this resistance, it is necessary to assess a victim's feelings of safety, understanding that as long as adolescents "feel unsafe and distrustful, they will stay on guard" (Gil, 1996, p. 3). At this juncture, every helping professional has the opportunity and the power to provide abused adolescents with corrective, healing experiences in the presence of a trustworthy adult. Victims of child sexual abuse "often simply need someone to believe in them, [respect them], and care for them in order for them to believe in themselves, [respect themselves], and take steps on their own behalf" (Gil, 1996, p. 49).

PART II:
CONNECTING
WITH THE SOCIAL
SERVICE AND CRIMINAL
JUSTICE SYSTEMS

The United States social service and criminal justice systems are foreign territories for most Americans—young and old, victims and their families, thrust abruptly into these systems, become reluctant pioneers. The professional "guides" who are acquainted with the territories are the only hope of survival for these pioneers. Their questions, whether acknowledged and articulated or not, are abundant and diverse, vague and specific.

"What happens next?"

"What's an arraignment?"

"Will my husband be arrested?"

"Where do we go from here?"

"Will everyone know this happened to me?"

"Why can't Mom be with me in court?"

The unarticulated questions are usually the most troublesome ones for the pioneers. Wandering in the unknown, unable to identify a familiar landmark, creates apprehension and anxiety. Legal and social service "guides" typically describe the processes in great detail to adolescent victims and/or their nonoffending parent(s). But the reluctant pioneers are usually experiencing heightened levels of physical and emotional distress, and expecting them to remember or comprehend descriptions and explanations or foreign details and words is unrealistic. The *We Are Not Alone* workbooks will supplement a helping professional's explanation and provide victims and their families with a springboard for formulating and asking questions.

Every case of child sexual abuse is unique, and the process any given adolescent victim of child sexual abuse experiences in the court system, anywhere in the country, *will never be exactly the same* as the process described by the characters in the workbooks. It would be impossible to identify all the potential procedural and policy differences for every jurisdiction in the nation, so that attempt will not be made. However, some areas where differences are inevitable are highlighted in Chapter 3.

Helping professionals, parents, and supporting adults are encouraged to find out precisely what the policies and procedures are in their jurisdiction so that victims can be adequately informed about and prepared for what will likely occur. In her book, *Unequal Justice: The Prosecution of Child Sexual Abuse,* Ellen Gray (1993) provides an overview of social service and criminal justice policies and procedures from eight jurisdictions across the United States as they existed in 1987. Gray's "Eight Jurisdictions: Study in Differences" is both enlightening and discouraging because it points out that there are so many differences. This is why it is so critical for professionals, parents, and victims to become familiar with the policies and procedures in their particular jurisdiction. The criminal court system is an important mechanism for protecting children, and understanding its policies and procedures is a crucial ingredient for any professional involved in child protection, and for any parent whose child is a victim.

Chapter 3

Social Service and Criminal Justice Policies and Procedures

REPORTING PROCEDURES, DIVERSION, AND INVESTIGATION

Every state has laws requiring certain individuals to report suspected child abuse. Our federal government underscores the importance of these laws by making receipt of funds under the Child Abuse Prevention and Treatment Act (CAPTA) contingent upon states having formal child abuse reporting laws. Thirty states have a specific reporting mandate only for professionals who, through their work, are expected to come into regular contact with children. The other twenty states require "any individual" (professionals, relatives, friends, strangers) to report known or suspected abuse to child protection authorities (Pence and Wilson, 1994). Who receives the report, how and when it is investigated, and by whom, and how, when, and where the case is referred for prosecution, all vary according to jurisdiction. Most states have a child abuse hotline, so even a person calling directory assistance to find the number for reporting abuse would not have difficulty connecting with a human services office. A call to the local police could also begin the process. However, figuring out which to call—Child Protective Services or police—may not be obvious. Some states require that Child Protective Services (CPS) receive reports only when the child is abused by a caregiver (i.e., a parent, baby-sitter, teacher, or other person in a custodial role); abuse by all other persons must be reported to the police. According to DePanifilis and Salus (1992) this distinction is statutory in most states. If a child is molested by a parent or other caregiver, this is considered "sexual abuse" and Child Protective Services becomes involved. If a child is molested by a person who is not a caregiver, these acts are considered "sexual assault" and the initial report is made to the police.

What happens after a report is filed also varies. In some jurisdictions, CPS and the police are mandated to inform each other (cross-report) of any report of child sexual abuse they receive. In some jurisdictions police and/or CPS must notify the District Attorney's office (Gray, 1993). In other jurisdictions CPS is not required to notify the District Attorney of cases diverted to counseling. The time limit for cross-reporting also differs. In her research, Ellen Gray (1993) found that the Texas Family Code requires the Department of Human Services to notify the police of serious cases of child sexual abuse within twenty-four hours. In the counties surrounding Jacksonville, Florida, CPS is mandated to notify the state's attorney about child sexual abuse reports verbally within one hour and in writing within three days.

The distinction between "sexual assault" and "sexual abuse" becomes more focused as the investigation of the report begins. A report of sexual assault, usually reported to the police, will go directly into the criminal justice system, whose primary focus is to adjudicate allegations of crime. After receiving a report of child sexual abuse, the primary concern of Child Protective Services is to protect the child and, if possible, to keep the family together (Larson et al., 1994). In some states, the desire to preserve the family leads CPS to divert the case into a mandated treatment program for the defendant, the victim, and other members of their family, or, depending on the jurisdiction, into juvenile court rather than to the criminal justice system. Juvenile courts have the authority to place children in foster care, to order at-home supervision, and to mandate treatment for abusive parents (Myers, 1994). The criminal courts have power to mandate treatment but only after conviction, most commonly as a part of a sentence or a condition of probation. In some jurisdictions diversion is preferred over a trial in support of an underlying philosophy to maintain the family unit unless the defendant is perceived as a threat to society (Gray, 1993). Diversion is one explanation for the number child sexual abuse cases that are not prosecuted.

Investigations of child sexual abuse cases will vary according to type of abuse and policies of a particular jurisdiction. A report may be investigated by Child Protective Services, the police, and/or both, or a multidisciplinary team consisting of social service, mental health, law enforcement, and legal professionals. According to John E. B. Myers (1994), the multidisciplinary approach to investigating child sexual abuse cases is a positive innovation that has been developed and utilized in some jurisdictions since the early 1980s. This approach helps investigators organize and coordinate their efforts in a way that expedites the process and protects the child victim by limiting the number of investigative interviews. Gray's (1993) research results indicated that all eight of the jurisdictions studied had a special unit for handling sex abuse cases. Some units were established in the police department, some in CPS, and some jurisdictions had a special unit which combined law enforcement and social service investigators.

INTERVIEWS, PRETRIAL HEARINGS, AND PLEA BARGAINING

In most cases, the victim is the only or the primary witness to the crime of child sexual abuse, and his or her eyewitness testimony is essential to achieving a conviction. The child's description is gathered through forensic interviews. Victims need to be prepared for and supported during the interviewing phase of the investigation, as it can be stressful. The number of interviews required of a victim as well as the interviewing process will vary according to jurisdiction. Gray's (1993) data indicate that the number of victim interviews ranged from three (this was the maximum number allowed by mandate in the Jacksonville area in Florida) to six to "many" (Gray, 1993, pp. 42-43).

Forensic interviews may be conducted by social service workers and/or police for the purpose of substantiation, and/or by police or prosecutors for purposes of credibility and discovery, or by a multidisciplinary team for any or all of the aforementioned purposes. Over the past decade, many jurisdictions have made an effort to significantly limit the number of victim interviews. The establishment of the multidisciplinary teams supports this effort, and the use of innovative techniques, such as two-way mirrors and videotaping, can reduce the number of investigative interviews required. Through the use of a one-way mirror, the multidisciplinary team can view the original interview without overwhelming or intimidating the victim. Through the use of videotape, members of the investigative team can review it later to gather additional information or impressions without reinterviewing the victim. A videotaped interview can also help in situations in which the credibility of the interviewing techniques or the suggestibility of the child victim are called into question. By viewing the videotape, a judge and jury have a realistic picture of how the interview was conducted (Larson et al., 1994).

Victims may or may not be required to testify at pretrial hearings, which could consist of a preliminary hearing and/or a grand jury hearing. At the preliminary hearing, which takes place before a judge for the purpose of determining if the defendant should be tried, both the defense and the prosecution are represented by legal counsel. The prosecution calls witnesses to testify, who are cross-examined by the defense. A grand jury hearing is held for the purpose of determining if the evidence is sufficient to charge the defendant. However, the grand jury is held in private—neither the defendant nor his or her counsel is present—and only the prosecution presents evidence (Feller et al., 1992). Which hearings are required depends upon the mechanism for bringing forward criminal charges in the state where the crime was committed. In most states, either a preliminary hearing or a grand jury hearing is required, however, "in a few states, the prosecutor can file charges by simply filing an information or complaint and a supporting affidavit summarizing the evidence" (Bulkley et al., 1996, p. 283). In some states, a grand jury is convened for felonies only, which usually include sexual crimes against children.

After a defendant is indicted, a plea bargain may or may not be an option. There are pros and cons to plea bargains. In exchange for a reduced charge (which usually results in a reduced sentence or probation) the defendant pleads guilty. This relieves the state of the expense of a jury trial and protects the victim from the stress of testifying. Parents of victims may actually pressure prosecutors to negotiate plea bargains to shield their child from the witness stand. In many cases, prosecutors will defer to the wishes of the parents in negotiating pleas (Gray, 1993).

Plea bargains may save the state money and spare the child victim from testifying. However, depending on how they are implemented, plea bargains in child sexual abuse cases may not be in the best interest of society. Gray (1993) points out that plea bargaining is used extensively in child sexual abuse cases, and identifies this process as another reason that the majority of the cases referred for prosecution do not go to trial. She also highlights a significant drawback to plea bargaining. The charge reduction required to secure the defendant's guilty plea "may leave a convicted defendant with a record not easily identified as child molestation" (Gray, p. 3). As with most legal procedures, the use and implementation of plea bargaining differs by jurisdiction.

WITNESS COMPETENCY, COURTROOM INNOVATIONS, AND TRIAL VARIANCES

Our legal system insists that all witnesses who testify in court be competent (Feller et al., 1992). However, this competency, particularly when children are called to testify, is not always presumed. Under federal law and in many states, *all* witnesses, including young children, are assumed to be competent. Nevertheless, in some states, on the motion of the defense attorney, the prosecutor, or the judge, a competency hearing can be scheduled. Approximately one-third of the states still require competency testing for children younger than ten, twelve, or fourteen, depending on the state (Bulkley et al., 1996). In these states, young witnesses *must* be questioned by a judge to determine their competency, which is based on the following elements:

1. The child's mental capacity at the time of the event to observe or receive accurate impressions of the event.
2. The child's memory to retain independent recollection of the observations.
3. The child's ability to communicate his or her memory of the event and understand simple questions about the event.
4. The child's understanding of the difference between truth and falsity, and appreciation of the responsibility to tell the truth. (Bulkley et al., 1996, p. 288)

Courtroom innovations available and used in child sexual abuse cases will vary from court to court, and from jurisdiction to jurisdiction, based on a number of factors:

1. State statutes.
2. The type of litigation (criminal court, juvenile court, family court). Criminal courts are less likely to allow innovations.

3. The stage of the prosecution process. Accommodations for child witnesses are more likely to be allowed during preliminary hearings than during the actual trial.
4. The rulings of the judge. This is a significant factor. Since many of the courtroom accommodations for child victims are available at the discretion of the judge, the use of them may even vary *within* a specific jurisdiction. (Feller et al., 1992)

The actual trial process will also be unique for every child sexual abuse case. Different staffing policies in prosecutors' offices will alter the course of the case, as will the judge assigned to the case. Some prosecutors' offices are now using a procedure called "vertical prosecution" with child sexual abuse cases which allows one prosecutor to follow the case from the beginning to the end (Gray, 1993, p. 47). Before the Child Abuse Unit was established in Dallas County, Texas, "child sexual abuse cases had been randomly assigned to a prosecutor in one of the fourteen different district courts. Prosecutors frequently rotate to different courts in this jurisdiction, so that victims may have had several different prosecutors working on their case by the time it was brought to trial" (Gray, 1993, p. 47). Although it would be preferable for one prosecutor to handle a case involving a child victim so a sense of trust and safety can develop, this cannot always be assured. Helping professionals and parents of young victims need to be prepared for the possibility of a change in staffing at any time, and to be aware of the affect this change may have on the victim. A change in the prosecutorial team may cause an increase in frustration, fear, and confusion.

The judge assigned to any given case can often cause a great deal of variation in the trial process and the sentencing outcome. Some jurisdictions have a lot of judges, so a lot of variation can be anticipated. Gray's (1993) study indicated that Baltimore County, Maryland, had thirteen judges who could be assigned to child sexual abuse cases, Dallas County had fourteen judges, and Jefferson County, Kentucky, had sixteen judges. Part of the variation in the trial process caused by the assigned judge is due to the judge's individual awareness about the issues of child sexual abuse cases and his or her attentiveness and responsiveness to the needs of young victims.

After the trial begins, variations will be discovered at each step. The following are various possibilities.

If a young victim lives in the Jacksonville, Florida area, and he or she is expecting to see a twelve-person jury in the courtroom, that victim will be surprised and confused by the six-person jury that appears. Florida is one of six states permitting a jury of less than twelve to sit for felony and misdemeanor trials (Gray, 1993).

Witness sequestration is a usual trial procedure. The purpose of requiring witnesses to be out of the courtroom when they are not testifying is to prevent them from being influenced to change their testimony based on what they hear from other witnesses. In child sexual abuse cases, this rule might be flexible in some states, allowing a parent or other support person to be in court during the victim's testimony for the purpose of offering support, even though the parent or support person will later be called as a witness.

Hearsay evidence, which is usually not admissible in court, may— under certain circumstances—be admissible in child sexual abuse cases. Hearsay exceptions that play a role in child sexual abuse cases include excited utterances and other special exceptions. Admissibility of hearsay evidence may be interpreted differently by different courts. According to Bulkley et al.

> Statements made by someone under the immediate stress of a startling event are considered reliable because they are made *spontaneously or without time to reflect.* . . . Although traditionally the statement must be made nearly contemporaneously with the event, in child abuse cases, some courts have been liberal in admitting statements made long after the sexually abusive event (e.g., hours, days, week, or even months). Other courts, however, have not admitted a child's statements made more than a few minutes after the experience under this exception. Courts have also admitted excited utterances statements made by children in response to direct questioning. (1996, p. 285)

Not all states allow for a Victim Impact Statement to be formally and publicly presented to the court during the sentencing proceedings. Some judges may invite the victim to present such a statement in writing or in private to the judge. Whether or not the court invites or receives such a statement from a victim of child sexual abuse, it will be helpful for the victim and his or her family to prepare an impact statement. This statement represents a way for victims to express themselves clearly and concisely and to have an overview of the affects that the abuse and prosecution experiences have had on their lives.

Sentencing guidelines regarding convicted sex offenders can also vary by jurisdiction and by judge, although some states do have and implement mandatory sentencing guidelines for felony crimes. In Massachusetts, each crime has a statutory sentence attached to it, along with proposed sentencing guidelines. But, since these guidelines are only proposed, the judge is not obligated to follow them. As long as the judge does not exceed the statutory limits, any sentence may be imposed (Ryle, 1999). Feller et al. (1992, p. 25) indicate that "there has been a trend toward enacting more severe criminal penalties for child abusers." However, sentences for convicted defendants could range from a suspended sentence or probation or mandatory counseling, requiring no jail time, to twenty or more years served in a state prison. Young victims need to be prepared for this variance. Sometimes the fear and vulnerability child and adolescent victims experience in anticipation of the perpetrator being free after the trial is so overwhelming that the victim cannot go forward with prosecution. Supporting the victim by providing information about what could happen during sentencing, what is likely to happen, and how these differ from or are similar to what the victim wants to happen, will be helpful.

IN SUMMARY

As with any process or procedure involving individuals, the criminal prosecution process is vital and volatile. It must be. Each case of child sexual abuse includes individuals and specifics requiring the processes to contract and expand within their limits to meet the needs and the demands of the case.

Coaching victims to expect and anticipate variances rather than allowing them to grasp onto a rigid outline of the process, will help victims to be more resilient during prosecution. Rigid, unmet expectations will serve only to further erode the trust of already skeptical and wounded victims, and this should be avoided if possible. When describing the prosecution process, and/or giving victims or their parents the *We Are Not Alone* workbooks, "expect variations," would be helpful advice.

Chapter 4

Multidisciplinary Teams and Helping Professionals Support Victims

Over the past decade, multidisciplinary teams for the investigation and prosecution of child sexual abuse have advanced in quantity, expertise, and effectiveness. Similarly, the growing awareness about the reality of child sexual abuse in our culture has encouraged helping professionals (including social workers, community mental health providers, psychologists, psychiatrists, school counselors, and pastors) to become more knowledgeable about the short-term and the lasting effects of this abuse on victims and society. Yet the ultimate goal of blending prosecution and healing, along with legal regimes and psychological issues, remains a resistant mix.

In order for the mix to coalesce, prosecutors and police officers working with victims of child sexual abuse need to be informed about child development and abuse-reactive behavior as well as being experts in constitutional law and the procedures and nuances of the criminal justice system. Child and adolescent clinicians, as well as other helping professionals, need to be knowledgeable about criminal legal proceedings as well as developmental theories of behavior and clinical techniques. There is no question that the special needs relative to child sexual abuse cases require a team of hybrid professionals to achieve the most efficient, effective, and healing outcomes.

This difficult challenge of attending to personal/psychological issues, while preserving the integrity of the legal case, is undertaken daily by the dedicated professionals who have chosen to protect and advocate for child victims of sexual abuse. It is difficult to imagine the skill and the strength of spirit which must be available and combined for legal and helping professionals to undertake this challenge. These professionals are required to seek out distressing details about a despicable crime, and the evidence in child sexual abuse cases *is* distressing. During the time I spent working at the Middlesex District Attorney's Office I witnessed a piece of trial evidence that horrifies me to this day. A prosecutor had a pornographic photograph of violent sexual activity taking place between a perpetrator and an adolescent male victim. I glanced at this photograph for only seconds— three or four seconds, maybe—but that image remains burned into my consciousness, and my life will never be the same.

How do the legal professionals involved in these cases manage to do this work? How do they deal with hundreds of vulnerable victims of this terrible crime every year? How can they gather and work with this evidence? Prosecutors have responded to my questions, and their answers highlight how difficult their work is. Prosecutors who are working on child sexual abuse cases *must* become desensitized to the reality of the crimes—out of necessity, for self-preservation. They must approach these cases through objective and detached eyes, focusing on the business of the law, developing a hard shell . . . or else they would go home every night and cry. Because they witness a real and shocking part of life that most of us could never imagine—even in our worst nightmares—they develop a camaraderie among their colleagues which involves transforming horror into absurdity. They also break their cases down into small pieces, analyzing each aspect according to the law, focusing on convicting the perpetrator and protecting the victim and other children from the threat of further abuse (Rooney, 1999; Ryle, 1999).

The addition of the victim witness advocate to the multidisciplinary team has helped both victim and prosecutor. Throughout the investigation and prosecution processes the victim witness advocate can intercept many of the victim's personal and psychological issues and needs, and provide direct information and support. Some victims and their families may want to discuss their cases and their feelings directly with the prosecutor, and this is certainly permissible. However, in most instances, the victim witness advocate is the conduit and/or the lightning rod between the prosecutor's more focused attention on the legal case and a victim's feelings.

The police officer or the social worker investigating the case may be the first person the victim and his or her family meets following the initial disclosure. These professionals may be the ones with whom a victim feels safe and connected, and therefore, they may be the ones receiving the confused and pleading calls for clarity and support throughout the prosecution process. All professionals along the investigative continuum need to be specially trained and prepared to deal with the emotional issues of adolescent victims and their parents.

Counseling support for the victim and his or her parents, and perhaps other family members, throughout the investigation and prosecution of child sexual abuse, will be invaluable—in the long term as well as the short term. Clinicians who are aware of the legal process and how child and adolescent victims are likely to react to the process will provide the most beneficial support.

The *We Are Not Alone* guidebook and workbooks are designed to support legal and helping professionals in developing more effective interactions with adolescent victims of child sexual abuse and their parents. The workbooks are intended to help legal and law enforcement professionals better understand the victim's personal and psychological issues relative to prosecution. Reading the stories presented in the workbooks will highlight some of the human aspects involved and remind these professionals that, although they have been involved in *hundreds* of these cases, each victim is going through the distress of investigation and prosecution for the very first time. The workbooks will also give clinicians and other helping professionals an overview of the legal process and help them prepare the victims for what will likely occur. The guidebook will inform both legal and helping professionals and coach them in using the workbooks with adolescent victims and their parents.

This chapter provides an overview of how multidisciplinary professionals working with adolescent victims of child sexual abuse throughout the prosecution process can, themselves, benefit from reading the workbooks and enhance their professional effectiveness, and how the workbooks can be used to support victims and their families. The information in this chapter was drawn from interviews with social service, law enforcement, legal, and clinical professionals who work daily with child and adolescent victims of sexual abuse in the legal setting.

GETTING STARTED

Any professional along the continuum of the investigation and prosecution of child sexual abuse may have the opportunity to give an adolescent victim a copy of the *We Are Not Alone* workbook. A vic-

tim and his or her parents could be given the workbook by the school
counselor who receives the initial disclosure, by the social worker or
police officer doing the screening investigation, by the victim witness
advocate or prosecutor assigned to the case, or by a clinician working
with the victim on therapeutic issues. Whoever gives the workbook to
the victim needs to do so with explicit guidance attached. Abused adolescents may present with a strong need to be in control of what happens to them, and under the stressful circumstances surrounding a
child sexual abuse investigation and prosecution, adolescent victims
will not have much tolerance for deviations from their expectations.
Therefore, any adolescent reader needs to clearly understand that his
or her experience in the court system *will not* mirror the experiences
described by Jane or Joe, the victim characters in the workbooks; and
that no two experiences in the criminal justice system are ever the
same even though most stages and practices will be in common.

The workbooks are not intended to answer every question a victim
and his or her parents might have, but instead provide a foundation
for understanding the process and to raise more questions. The story
told by an adolescent peer intends to create opportunities for the victim to talk about his or her own experience and to ask questions. For
each chapter in the workbooks, a few guiding questions can be found
at the end, which will help victims focus their thoughts and feelings
in productive ways. The professional who gives the workbook to a
victim will be most helpful if he or she offers to answer any questions
generated by reading it, to discuss the feelings described in it, and to
take the initiative to follow up by contacting the victim rather than
waiting for the victim to call.

One of the things that may prove to be most difficult for an adolescent victim is the reality that *many* professionals will be involved in
his or her case. The faces, temperaments, and responsibilities of the
professionals may change daily depending on the progress of the
case, the standard procedures in any given jurisdiction, and the events
in the lives of the professionals assigned to the case. A victim may be
interviewed once by a police officer or social worker, and never see
that person again. Since victims of child sexual abuse have difficulty
trusting and feeling safe, it is important to prepare the victim early in
the process for this possibility and to seek to provide some stable support. In the volatile criminal justice system where faces and schedules can change on a daily basis, the characters in the workbook could

offer some needed stability by being there—day or night—to answer and generate questions, and to provide support and understanding.

ENHANCING PROFESSIONAL EFFECTIVENESS

The *We Are Not Alone* resources can best enhance professional effectiveness when used as a training tool. New social workers are hired into the child protection system every day. Likewise, new police officers, new prosecutors, and new victim witness advocates are always being hired and assigned (or reassigned) to multidisciplinary teams investigating child sexual abuse cases. It is a heart-wrenching profession, and staffing changes are common. Even seasoned clinicians will be faced with their *first* case of child sexual abuse in the court system. Because the general population has only basic knowledge about the criminal justice system, and very limited knowledge about the realities of child sexual abuse, entry level social service, legal, law enforcement, and clinical professionals cannot be expected to be much more informed than the average citizen about practices and procedures of legal investigations or prosecutions, or how they relate to issues experienced by adolescent victims of child sexual abuse. Therefore, including the workbooks and guidebook in training sessions for these multidisciplinary professionals will introduce them to their challenge in an accessible way that is easy to read, comprehend, and retain.

The professionals I interviewed all agreed that the workbooks are most helpful to their colleagues when given to entry-level professionals in their packet of standard training materials, and that having one or more copies of the guidebook within their offices for shared use is the most effective combination for using the *We Are Not Alone* resources. Prosecutors also recommended that lawyers assigned to child sexual abuse cases read the workbooks periodically to remind them of the personal issues and human aspects of each case and that this is a foreign and frightening experience for the victim.

SUPPORTING VICTIMS AND THEIR FAMILIES

An interview conducted by a social worker from the state Child Protective Services department is often the first link in the chain of the investigation and prosecution of child sexual abuse. At this phase in the process, the workbooks can provide support to adolescent victims and their families/nonoffending parent in various ways. The parental characters in the workbooks rise to the occasion of supporting their children in exemplary ways, but in real life, this is not always the case. Often parents whose children have been sexually victimized are confused, frightened, and reluctant to become involved with the prosecution process, knowing the stress which may result from the protracted and public aspects of a criminal trial. The reluctant parents of actual victims could be inspired by the workbook characters to defend and protect their children in ways they might not have imagined. When their child's case is in the beginning stages of disclosure and discovery, parents may not realize how beneficial and empowering the prosecution process can be for victims. They may not realize the importance and healing properties of believing their child; they may not realize how critical it is for the victims to feel strength coming from their parents, to know that their parents are in charge and advocating for them, as well as believing and protecting them. Having the workbooks early in the process can demystify the process for parents, and perhaps give them the courage to allow their child to move forward with a process that is consequential both to individuals and to Society (Lynch, 1998).

What happens following a disclosure of child sexual abuse can actually cause victims to feel that their lives are being overtaken by an alien system. Most victims do not think beyond the disclosure, and when they find out what happens next, they often get scared and decide that they will not tell anyone else. At this juncture, CPS workers face a challenge. They know the victims have been harmed, and may still be at risk. They do not want to send children back into perilous situations, or allow perpetrators to roam freely on the streets of their town. Therefore, it is important to help the victims move beyond this initial fear. Giving adolescent victims the workbooks, encouraging them to read the books to discover what happened to other teenagers, and reassuring them that teenagers can handle the experience might infuse the victims with courage, and help turn the events in a way that will protect more children and incarcerate more perpetrators.

In all jurisdictions, police officers are involved in child sexual abuse cases at the early stages. According to Detective Trish Sullivan (1998) of the Medford, Massachusetts, Police Department, community officers working in the schools receive a high number of disclosures of child sexual abuse. Children and teenagers develop personal and trusting relationships with these specialized detectives and feel a greater sense of safety when revealing such details to a police officer. Depending upon the case, police officers will also conduct part of the investigation. In Middlesex County, Massachusetts, during the initial intake report, officers routinely explain the entire interviewing process as it occurs to victims and their parents. It is at this point that Sullivan believes the victims and their families can best benefit from receiving a copy of the *We Are Not Alone* workbook. She witnesses the fear and panic victims experience because they do not know what will happen to them now that they have disclosed, and she feels that the workbook has a reassuring and calming tendency. Sullivan believes that in cases of child sexual abuse, the unknown is worse than anything, particularly when victims are depending upon others to help them and protect them. Therefore, a sense of knowing will always be welcomed. Having a resource to give to victims and their parents can also be very reassuring to the detectives handling the investigation. They can offer a resource which can provide support at times when an actual person working on the case cannot be reached. Nights and weekends are times when many dark and lonely hours can make the mind run wild with worry. Sullivan highlighted the importance of the glossary in the back of the workbooks, citing much confusion by the public about legal terms.

The Medford Police Department also receives a substantial number of phone inquiries from school guidance counselors about child sexual abuse. Many police departments have a budget line item for resources, and having workbooks and guidebooks on hand to give to guidance counselors who are searching for ways to support victims of child sexual abuse is an enormous public service.

After an allegation of child sexual abuse has been investigated and substantiated, the torch is passed to the legal professionals within the prosecutor's office. Depending upon the jurisdiction, these professionals include a child interview specialist, a victim witness advocate, and a prosecuting attorney. (See the glossary to identify the term used to refer to the prosecuting attorney in your state.) Legal professionals who have reviewed the *We Are Not Alone* workbooks believe they will be useful and helpful to adolescent victims and their families. They do, however, offer a caution regarding the timing of the distribution of the workbook. Child interview specialist Lea Savely (1998) warns *legal professionals* not to give the workbook to a victim during the disclosure and investigation phase or before the allegations have been supported by either Child Protective Services or the police. The criminal justice system must always be mindful of the possibility that a defense attorney could accuse the prosecutor's office of coaching the victim if any resources are given to the victim by the legal professionals prior to the prosecution's investigation. Savely (1998) suggests that the workbook be given to victims *by legal professionals* immediately after the prosecution's initial interview. However, from her perspective as a child interview specialist, it is more ideal for the victims and their families to receive the workbook as early in the process as possible; however, it would be easier on the case if the workbook was given in the earliest stages by a clinician, school counselor, CPS social worker, or police officer.

Legal professionals know how critical parental support is for the outcome of the case, and Savely believes that the workbook will help parents feel safer about what could happen. She suggests that parents read the workbook (and the guidebook if they are so inclined) so they can effectively participate in preparing and supporting their child. Although the social worker or police officer conducting the initial investigation routinely will explain the process, the workbook has it all written down as a reminder. Legal professionals meeting the victim for the first time will explain the process again in order to establish direct contact; and, in these cases, repetition is a good and necessary thing. Adolescent victims, especially, need as much information as they can get.

Former Chief of Victim Witness Services of Norfolk County, Dedham, Massachusetts, Deborah Fogarty (1997), believes it is important for a legal professional to give the workbook to adolescent victims and their families when he or she has time to prepare the victims to read the resource and to go over some of the major differences in processes. Fogarty also believes that it is critical to mention the individual differences that can be expected of any given victim or any given family members regarding reactions and feelings.

According to Fogarty (1997), the best way to use the workbooks is in an ongoing dialogue that includes the victim, his or her parents, the treating clinician, and the victim witness advocate who is assigned to the case. However, this process could be problematic for the legal case in certain jurisdictions where the prosecution is required to disclose knowledge of counseling to the defense who can then request that the victim's counseling records be brought into court. If an ongoing dialogue between legal professionals and clinicians is allowed by law, does not jeopardize the case, or put the victim in a vulnerable position, combining legal and clinical expertise could be a highly effective way of using the *We Are Not Alone* resources with adolescent victims and their families.

If a victim and/or his or her parents and family are involved in a therapeutic relationship during the prosecution process, the resources can provide substantial support when used in this context. Child and adolescent psychiatrist, Renee Brant (1998), suggests that any clinician who has not previously guided a teen victim and his or her family through the prosecution process might not know what to expect, and will especially benefit from reading and using *We Are Not Alone*. Many of Brant's clients and their parents routinely ask her for supporting written material so they can gain a better understanding of their situation. Parents, particularly, are often looking for materials that are experiential—not merely informative or descriptive—to help them make the agonizing decision about whether or not it is the best for their child to go forward with prosecution.

Brant (1998) believes that the workbooks will be helpful to teen victims as a jumping-off point for therapeutic discussions, even if their cases do not go to trial. The fictional characters in the workbooks offer the opportunity for victims to displace their feelings onto Jane or Joe, perhaps making it easier for teens to talk about their abuse experiences or their perceptions of the investigation and prosecution processes. In Brant's experience, this type of displacement can facilitate the therapeutic process for a teen victim by generating healing discussions without the victim having to directly reveal his or her feelings.

Brant (1998) feels that effectively using the workbooks in a therapeutic setting with teen victims of child sexual abuse will make it less likely that the victims will be retraumatized by the court system. She sees the possibility of a paradigm shift in therapy with this traumatized population. Most therapy with child sexual abuse victims is geared toward helping them understand and integrate the trauma of the abuse experience. They are encouraged to talk about what happened in the past. Using the workbooks to support victims who are going through a stressful time in the present as a result of the prosecution process, can provide a corrective experience and help them to learn that they are not just reactive creatures. The workbooks can prepare victims for the prosecution process, helping enormously with what Brant (1998) refers to as "damage control." Prosecution puts victims face to face with an extreme situation that is a direct result of the sexual abuse. However, through the characters in the workbooks, victims can see and comprehend that they are not helpless in the present. Clinicians who artfully use the workbooks to anticipate what might come up for victims, will be better able to prepare the victims and support them during this stressful time. Victims may actually develop a sense of mastery and power through the therapeutic process by identifying what might happen and feeling prepared and in control.

IN SUMMARY

The primary purpose of the *We Are Not Alone* resources is to guide and support teen victims of child sexual abuse who are involved in the investigation and prosecution processes by providing them with a map and a peer who knows the territory. In addition, the resources will provide parents of victims, and the full spectrum of helping professionals working to support this population of victims, with general information about the systems and prepare them for potential victim reactions. Professionals are especially encouraged to use the workbooks as a training tool to educate themselves about the legal processes and the psychological issues, and to discover creative uses for the resources.

PART III:
ADOLESCENT VICTIMS
SHARING THEIR EXPERIENCES

INTRODUCTION

Renee Brant

I am honored to introduce you to *We Are Not Alone,* a sensitive rendering of two teenagers' experiences in the criminal justice system. You will soon meet Jane, a sixteen-year-old girl who was sexually abused by her father, and Joe, a sixteen-year-old boy who was sexually abused by his neighbor and boys' club leader. In the wake of their disclosures, Joe and Jane meet many professionals. Each professional has a role to play in the complicated drama that unfolds as Joe and Jane tell school administrators and protective service personnel what happened, begin therapy, and wind their ways through the criminal justice process.

Joe's and Jane's sagas are based on the accounts of many teenagers who generously shared their experiences with the author, Jade Angelica. A "child-friendly" and healing spirit permeates *We Are Not Alone,* and I commend Ms. Angelica for her remarkable capacity to empathize with and learn from the teenagers she interviewed. She translated their experiences into a most readable narrative. In addition, *We Are Not Alone* provides examples from actual encounters with dedicated professionals who labor daily on the "front lines" of-

---

Renee Brant, MD, is the founder of the Sexual Abuse Treatment Team, Children's Hospital, Boston, and is in private practice in child and adolescent psychiatry in Newton, Massachusetts.

fering protection, comfort, therapy, support, and legal representation to victimized children and their families.

We Are Not Alone is based on the policies and procedures that are practiced in Middlesex County, Massachusetts, a part of the Greater Boston area. These policies and procedures evolved over a number of years as a result of legislative changes, legal innovations, and the dedication of prosecutors. In 1983, following the passage of a new Child Abuse Reporting Law, contact between children and teenagers and the criminal justice system in Massachusetts increased significantly. This law required the Department of Social Services to report certain cases of severe child abuse and child sexual assault to the district attorney's office. As a result, a tremendous influx of cases involving child and teenage victims poured into the criminal justice system. The unique needs of young victims challenged professionals working within the system. These professionals rose to this challenge by developing specialized, interdisciplinary child abuse protection teams and units such as the Middlesex County Child Abuse Division within the Family Protection Unit of the District Attorney's Office.

The people and systems interacting with sexually abused children have a significant impact on these young victims. Professionals involved in child abuse investigation, protection, and prosecution can, unfortunately, become a part of the problem if they are insensitive to the needs of child and teen victims and their families. In Joe's and Jane's cases, however, the child-friendly and knowledgeable helping professionals they met played a significant role in their healing and recovery. Nothing can undo the trauma of child sexual abuse. However, victimized children and adolescents can have a contrasting and profoundly healing experience in relationships with adults when the adults are attentive to the victims' needs, protective of their vulnerabilities, empathetic to their feelings, and validating of their experiences. Thus, in the best of circumstances, professionals can offer child and adolescent victims a trustworthy, respectful relationship which can help them overcome the isolation, shame, and stigma of sexual abuse.

We Are Not Alone serves multiple purposes for adolescent victims. It is a resource for teenagers who are facing the unknowns of the criminal justice system. It provides a guide that introduces teenagers to the key players and procedures of the legal process, and a map for them to follow as they travel through the justice system. The central message of *We Are Not Alone* is its title. Teenagers reading this book will experience connections on various levels. They will learn about the network of professionals who are available to help and support them, and they will have a means of identifying with other teenagers who have traveled this difficult road. Through Joe's and Jane's experiences, teenagers who have been sexually abused will find a path to realizing and understanding their own feelings and perceptions. They will find a comfort in knowing that "we are not alone."

WELCOME TO TEEN READERS

Dear Reader,

We Are Not Alone was written specifically for teenagers who have been sexually abused and are involved in the prosecution process. However, adults—including parents, relatives, therapists and social workers, doctors, lawyers, judges and other legal professionals, ministers, priests and rabbis, teachers and school administrators—will also find this resource book informative and helpful in their efforts to support and guide teenage victims of child sexual abuse. If you would like supportive adults in your life to have more information about what you are experiencing in the court system, please ask them to read this book.

We Are Not Alone describes the step-by-step process that Jane, a teenager who was sexually abused by her father, and Joe, a teenager who was sexually abused by his neighbor, experienced in the Massachusetts Superior Court System. On pages 102 and 147, "How It Happened for Me: A Diagram," illustrates a "typical" superior court process. This diagram should be used only as a guideline, because the actual court process will vary from case to case. The legal process and the support systems will also vary from place to place. Each state and county develops and implements its procedures based on particular needs and available resources. Therefore, it is recommended that you use *We Are Not Alone* as a springboard for helping you understand how the systems operate in your county or state.

Some of the words and phrases used in the legal system may be unfamiliar to you. Therefore, a **glossary** is included. Definitions of the words and phrases found in **bold type** within the text are listed alphabetically in the glossary.

As well as describing the legal process, *We Are Not Alone* highlights some of the feelings and reactions experienced by teenagers who are involved in legal proceedings. However, not all teenagers will experience things in the exact way that Joe and Jane do. Again, their feelings and reactions represent the "typical." Actual feelings and reactions will vary according to each individual. Also included is a section of **guiding questions.** Thinking about and answering these questions may help you identify and better understand your own feelings and reactions.

Jane's and Joe's personal accounts of child sexual abuse, from disclosure through prosecution and treatment, can be read like a novel, from beginning to end. Or, you may prefer to read only the parts that are of particular interest to you. Each chapter title describes the information covered in that chapter so you can easily locate topics of specific interest. Joe and Jane express some intense emotions. Therefore, the account of their experiences may be difficult and upsetting to read at times. If it becomes too distressing, put the book down for awhile. You can always come back to it later. But, even if it is hard, do try to keep reading at your own pace. Having detailed information about the legal system will make the difficult process seem less overwhelming and less frightening.

In many ways, Joe's and Jane's accounts present an idealistic scenario of what happens after a child or a teenager discloses details of sexual abuse. Some child and teen victims who have been sexually abused do find support from their families as Jane and Joe do. However, not all victims are so fortunate. The legal system is designed to provide some support—so young victims do not feel all alone—but it is important for victims to also seek the additional support of relatives, friends, other caring adults, and a qualified therapist.

We Are Not Alone is the result of observations of and interviews with professionals in the legal, victim witness, and mental health fields, as well as conversations with and observations of teen victims of sexual abuse and their families. Although Joe's and Jane's account are fiction, the spirits of actual victims and helping professionals are alive in this narrative.

The purpose for creating *We Are Not Alone* was to help people learn about child sexual abuse and the legal system. I had no idea that being in the presence of children and teenagers who had been sexually abused, and their families, would teach me invaluable and life-changing lessons. It has been an honor for me to be with you all.

Chapter 5

A Teenage Girl's Personal Account of Incest from Disclosure Through Prosecution and Treatment

IDENTIFICATION OF CHARACTERS

Mr. Burger: The district attorney on *Perry Mason,* the television show.

Dr. Catherine Clayton (Cathy): Jane's therapist.

Dan: Jane's high school friend.

Ms. Feldman: Jane's high school guidance counselor.

Joy: Jane's high school friend.

Andrea Kane: The victim witness advocate from the district attorney's office who worked with Jane and her family throughout the prosecution process.

Lisa Lance-White: The child interview specialist from the district attorney's office who met with Jane and conducted the investigative interviews.

Mr. McCarthy: The defense attorney for Jane's father.

Patricia O'Neill (Patty): The DSS (Department of Social Services) social worker who investigated Jane's disclosure of sexual abuse.

Detective Anthony Rapucci: The local police officer who was part of the team that investigated the allegations against Jane's father.

Nina Santiago: The assistant district attorney who was in charge of prosecuting the case against Jane's father.

Tree-Girl: Jane's cat, who likes to climb trees!

Mrs. Winston: The school nurse at Jane's high school. The first person Jane told about the sexual abuse.

SECTION 1. I'M JANE

My name is Jane. I'm sixteen years old and a junior in high school. From the time I was a little girl about five years old, I guess, my father was sexually abusing me. And until I saw a video at school in ninth grade, I didn't even know it was "abuse." I always felt pretty weird about it, you know, scared, ashamed, and sick to my stomach a lot, but Dad told me it was OK. It was "good," he said, because I was "special," and he loved me "so much." Even though it hurt me sometimes, I thought he was loving me, not abusing me.

And then I saw this video about sexual abuse in my health science class at school. I knew for sure, right then, that what my dad was doing was wrong. I felt really confused, dirty, and scared. Oh, I felt stupid, too. Stupid and mad at myself because I didn't know what was happening.

I didn't know what to do, but I just kept getting more and more upset inside. I was nervous all the time. I cried a lot and had headaches every single day. I was really tired because I was so nervous I couldn't sleep at night. I didn't want to talk to any of my friends or go to school anymore. But I did. I did everything as usual. I kept pretending, like always, that everything in my life was just fine. It was the worst feeling.

I was truly confused. I didn't want to tell Dad to stop because I didn't want to hurt his feelings, and I didn't know if he would stop anyway. I didn't want to tell him that I knew he was abusing me, and I especially didn't want him to think that I didn't love him anymore. Besides, what we did felt really good sometimes. I liked getting the attention from my dad. I was afraid to tell Mom because I didn't think she'd believe me, or if she did, I was afraid she would blame me. I was afraid that nobody would believe me, and everyone would blame me. I was so scared all the time, that finally I prayed to God to help me, just because I didn't know who else to ask.

SECTION 2. THE FIRST TIME I TOLD

One day at school, about three weeks after I first saw the video, I was really tired and feeling very sick. So after lunch period, I went to the school nurse's office and asked Mrs. Winston, the nurse, if I could rest for awhile. I guess I looked pretty bad, because she wanted to send me home. Since my mom works downtown and didn't have the car, Mrs. Winston asked me for my dad's telephone number at work so he could come and pick me up.

I don't know what happened to me, but I couldn't move, and I couldn't talk either. I sat like I was frozen, just staring at the floor. And I remember hot, stinging tears. They started pouring out of my eyes, but I still didn't make a sound. I covered my face with my hands, and cried for what seemed like forever.

Mrs. Winston sat next to me, patiently handing me tissue after tissue. When I finally started to stop crying, Mrs. Winston quietly asked, "Jane, can you tell me what's wrong?"

And I just said it. In between quivering sobs and hiccups, I whispered, "Mrs. Winston, my dad has sex with me . . . like in the video we saw." For a very long minute after I said it, the whole room was so quiet and still, I thought for sure the world had ended. But it didn't. I was still there. Mrs. Winston was still there.

Mrs. Winston got me a glass of water. As I sipped it, she told me that she believed me and wanted to help me. She told me what happened with my dad wasn't my fault, and that I was a really "brave young woman" for telling her.

I don't know if I can describe how I felt then, because I felt all mixed up for sure, but I'll try. I felt relief because I didn't have to carry the heavy burden of the "special secret" all alone anymore. I felt grateful to Mrs. Winston for believing me, and for being so nice to me. I felt guilty because I didn't want my dad to get in trouble or my mom to be upset. I felt so very scared that my dad and mom would be really mad at me for making trouble for them, and that they wouldn't want to be my parents anymore. And I felt so ashamed. I felt dirty and used, and I wanted to hide so no one would see me, so no one would know.

I was surprised to learn that my high school had standard procedures for handling the **disclosure** of sexual abuse. Mrs. Winston said it was her responsibility to call **DSS** (The Department of Social Services), to report what I had told her. She said she would also like to have my guidance counselor, Ms. Feldman, come to be with me.

Ms. Feldman came right away, but I couldn't talk to her. I couldn't even look at her. I stared at the floor wishing I could disappear, wishing I was at home watching TV and eating cookies. It was too hard, too horrible, too embarrassing to talk about.

Then Mrs. Winston called DSS to file an official report because of the **mandated reporting law.** As the school nurse, Mrs. Winston is considered a **mandated reporter.** That means she has a legal responsibility to report incidents or disclosures or suspicions of abuse of children to DSS. So when you tell someone who is a mandated reporter, like a teacher, or a doctor, or a counselor, they will help you. That's the law.

SECTION 3. MAKING A REPORT

While Mrs. Winston was filing the report with a **social worker** over the telephone, my guidance counselor explained some things to me about what would happen next. Even though I could not look at her, and could not really even listen to her, she explained anyway. Ms. Feldman told me that she wanted me to have all the information. She said, "Once the report is received and evaluated, a social worker will be assigned to your case. Then DSS will have ten days to investigate." Although they legally had ten days to investigate, Ms. Feldman said that a social worker might be in touch with me sooner.

"These next several days might be particularly stressful for you, Jane," Ms. Feldman said, "and you may have a hard time being at home." Then she gave me this telephone number for a twenty-four-hour **crisis line,** "just in case" I needed to talk to someone. Ms. Feldman said she was trying to prepare me for what was going to happen and how I might feel about it.

She was so encouraging and so nice, and I appreciated her efforts even though I couldn't tell her so at the time. But unfortunately, nothing could have helped me feel better on that day. I was too upset and too confused to be consoled. I needed to think.

Because of my particular circumstances, Mrs. Winston and Ms. Feldman thought it would be best if my parents didn't know about my disclosure until my social worker was involved. So I stayed in the nurse's office for the rest of the day, feeling numb and very stupid, and then I went home.

I went right to my room and turned on the radio—loud! I was so confused and frightened that I just sat and stared out the window through the trees, into the sky. I felt as nervous as Tree-Girl, our cat, who was keeping me company by pacing around my room. I actually jumped out of my chair when I heard the front door close, and Mom yelled, "I'm home." While Mom made dinner, I paced with Tree-Girl, twisting my fingers until they were purple and numb beyond hurting. I didn't know what to do. I felt like I was being torn in two. Part of me felt so relieved that I had told, and part of me wished I had never said a word.

Dad came home, and we all ate dinner. I didn't say much. Everything seemed just the same as usual, except inside me. I was different inside. I knew inside that it was over, and I was so thankful. But I was really, really scared about what would happen next. And I was sad. I looked at Dad across the table, and realized how much I loved him, and how much he loved me. My dad had such a way of making me feel special.

After dinner I watched TV because it was the only thing that I could do.

SECTION 4. THE INVESTIGATION BEGINS

The hardest part of the whole **investigation** and **prosecution** process was having to wait and at the same time not knowing what was going to happen to me, to Dad, and to our family. I cried every time I thought that Dad might not be sitting at the dinner table with us anymore. But I didn't even want to think about that.

Fortunately, at the beginning, I didn't have to wait for very long before things began to happen. It was only three days later, although it seemed like an eternity, when Ms. Feldman called me into the Guidance Office. She told me my DSS social worker, Patricia O'Neill, would like to meet with me the next day at school. Ms. Feldman said it would be best if my mom could be here, too. So she called Mom at work and asked her to come to my school for an important meeting.

At 9:00 a.m. the next morning, I met Patricia O'Neill in the counseling center at school. I was totally nervous from not knowing what to expect. Ms. O'Neill was very nice, and she tried to calm me down. She said I could call her "Patty."

Patty began our meeting by asking me if I knew why she was there to see me. I knew all right, but it was hard to answer her. She repeated the question, "Jane, do you know why I'm here this morning?"

"Because of my dad," I whispered. "Because I told Mrs. Winston that my dad has sex with me."

"Yes, Jane. That is why I'm here."

And then Patty explained her role as my DSS social worker and the procedures that would happen next. When she finished talking it was almost 10:00. She said she was going to meet with my mom, and invited me to be in the room if I wanted. I decided to wait in Ms. Feldman's office until after they told Mom.

Patty told me I was very brave, which took me completely by surprise because I felt so scared. But I guess in order to be brave, you have to be scared first.

As Patty got up to leave the room, I looked at her, and I said, "I need to ask you a very important question."

She sat right back down, looked at me, and said, "OK, shoot."

I looked right into her eyes when I asked, "Why did Dad do this to me?"

Patty was real quiet for a minute, and then she said, "I know this isn't a very good answer, Jane, but it's the only true answer I know right now." She took a very deep breath, kind of like a sigh, and continued, "The truth is, I do not know why your father did this. But I do know you did the right thing by telling us. So now we can protect you, and help your mom and your dad. Your dad really needs help so he doesn't hurt you or any other kids ever again."

I just nodded in response.

Then Patty shook my hand. That made me feel very grown-up and important. She gave me her business card with her office telephone number and address. She said that I could call her anytime if I had questions, or if I wanted to talk to her. Then Patty went to meet with my mom.

I looked at her card for a long time, just thinking about things, I guess. Finally, I put the card in my backpack, and nervously waited for Ms. Feldman to come for me.

SECTION 5. I'M SORRY, MOM

About twenty minutes later, the longest twenty minutes of my life, I think, Ms. Feldman came to get me so I could talk to Patty and Mom. I went into the room, and I could see right away that Mom had been crying. I sat down next to her, and she took my hand. I said, "I'm really sorry, Mom." She hugged me and said, "Oh no, Janie, I'm sorry." She started to cry again.

I guess Mom was pretty shocked and upset because she didn't say much else. It was a good thing that Patty and Ms. Feldman were calm and knew what to do.

Patty said something had to be done to keep me safe from my father. She told Mom that either I had to stay with someone else—she suggested a foster family—or Dad had to leave our house. Mom asked Patty what would be best for me. Patty said it would be best if Dad left so I could stay in my own home with my mom. I was happy to hear that because I didn't want to be alone or with strangers. I was too upset to adjust to that. Mom said that Dad could stay with his brother, my Uncle John. Everyone agreed that would be best. I was so relieved. But sad, too. Like I worried before, I wouldn't see Dad at dinner anymore, and he wouldn't be there to make me feel special. Then I started to cry.

Mom agreed to call Dad at work before she left my school. She asked for Ms. Feldman or Patty to stay with her while she made the call.

Then Patty told us that it might be helpful for me to talk with a **counselor** who works with kids my age. She said, "It's a good idea for kids who have been sexually abused to be able to talk with someone about what happened. And, Jane, you also might need to talk with someone about what's happening now and how you feel about it all."

Patty suggested that Mom might be interested in going with me to the counselor for awhile. Mom took the paper with the referral on it and quietly said, "Thank you." I wondered what would become of that name and telephone number. Mom didn't really believe too much in counselors.

Then Patty started to talk about a meeting she wanted to have, which she called a **team interview.** She wanted Mom's permission to schedule it as soon as possible, which to Patty meant within the next day or two. She explained, "This interview is part of the DSS investigation, and it's done in the team format so Jane won't have to be interviewed too many times by too many different people. Not all places use a team interview because they think other ways are better, but we always use the team interview here because we think it is easier on the kids to only have to say what happened one time during this part of the investigation."

I remember just staring at Patty when she said "easier." Like anything could make this easier.

Patty continued, "For the team interview, we gather all the people who need to know what happened. That's me as the investigative social worker for DSS, the **assistant district attorney,** the **victim witness advocate,** the **child interview specialist,** a police officer, and a **therapist** from a local mental health clinic."

I almost had a heart attack when I realized I would have to say what my dad did in front of all those people, but Patty calmed me down right away.

She said, "You actually only have to tell one person at the **interview,** and that will be the child interview specialist. The others will observe the interview from behind a two-way mirror. They will be able to see and hear you, Jane, but you won't be able to see or hear them."

Well, that sounded a bit better, but I didn't like the idea of telling anyone else. I didn't want more people to know. It was embarrassing enough already, and the more people who knew, the more embarrassed I felt. I mean, really. What was going to happen if the kids at school found out? They would think I was easy, and some slut, you know. I was afraid none of the guys would ever ask me out. Oh, this was so terrible. I felt so dirty. I wanted to disappear.

But Patty said if we were going to stop this abuse from happening to me, we needed to do the team interview. It was nice that she said "WE." I didn't feel so alone.

I was nervous and upset about this, of course, but Mom said, "Yes" right away. She said, "Yes, we need to protect Jane. Please schedule the interview as soon as possible. Jane and I will be there."

Believe it or not, I wanted to go to my classes that day. I needed a distraction. I wanted to feel "regular" for a few hours, or even for a few minutes. Even if I was just pretending again, that was OK.

Mom said it was fine for me to go to class. She said she would call Dad and ask him to pick up his things before I got home from school.

I say felt "nervous," but that's only because I don't know of a word that describes how completely upset I was. I don't know what Mom said to Dad, but when I got home he wasn't there. Mom told me that Dad said I had misunderstood his gestures, that he was merely being really affectionate. Dad wondered where I got such a "silly notion" that he was abusing me. I got that numb feeling again and stared at the floor. I didn't feel, think, or say anything. I just knew I needed my mom to believe me.

SECTION 6. THE INTERVIEW

About 5:30 p.m. that same afternoon, Patty O'Neill called from DSS to let us know about the team interview. It was scheduled for 3:00 p.m. the next day at the district attorney's office. They have a special Child Unit set up there to handle all the child abuse cases in the county.

Mom and I arrived at the office at about five minutes past 3:00. We were late because I kept changing my clothes. I knew it didn't make much sense to care about what I was wearing, but I was just so nervous. Patty met us at the door, and tried to make us feel comfortable. Seeing her familiar face made me feel safe somehow.

The team was already meeting in a big conference room which had a very long table and lots of chairs. Then this woman, Lisa, came out into the reception area where Mom and I were waiting. Lisa was my interviewer. When she shook my hand I did manage to look at her face. I was surprised to see that she looked very friendly. She said, "Hi, Jane." And she smiled at me.

I said, "Hello," and looked quickly down at the floor.

After a few minutes, Lisa and I went into a small, very neat room. In the room were two chairs, a small table, sort of like a coffee table, this huge mirror that covered one whole wall, and a box of tissues. It was weird. You know, sort of uncomfortable to see myself in the mirror. I felt a little self-conscious. Lisa explained that the people from the team were on the other side of the mirror, and they could see and hear us. She said she thought it might be easier for me to talk with only her in the room.

Before the interview started, Lisa explained why certain people needed to observe. She said, "Patty O'Neill will be observing as a part of her investigation for DSS. In her report, Patty needs to indicate whether or not she **supports the allegations** of the sexual abuse.

Nina Santiago, the assistant district attorney assigned to your case, will be making **prosecution** decisions, and the victim witness advocate, Andrea Kane, will be making assessments about your emotional readiness to be a witness in court."

I wasn't sure what all of that meant, but I was sure this interview was very important. As hard as it was for me to talk about the sexual abuse, I knew I had to tell the truth. I didn't want Dad to hurt me anymore.

Then Lisa started asking questions. It helped me sometimes to close my eyes as I answered.

"Can you talk a little louder, Jane? You're whispering."

"Yes," I replied, opening my eyes. "I can talk louder."

I sat up straighter in my chair and opened my eyes. I needed to focus in order to do this.

Then Lisa asked me to tell exactly what Dad did. I didn't say it all, I could never say it all. But I made myself say some of it. Saying the words, "penis" and "vagina," talking about my dad and me, made me feel so ashamed and guilty. I'm quite sure I mumbled a lot. I'm very sure I stared at the floor a lot. I noticed some scratches on my shoes and a piece of navy blue thread on the floor. Lisa's shoes were black suede. And then I started to cry. I covered my eyes with my hands, and Lisa handed me the box of tissues. She told me it was definitely OK to cry, and so I did.

Lisa was very understanding about me being so upset. Like Patty and Mrs. Winston did, Lisa told me I was very brave. I looked at her, I remember, feeling confused, because I didn't feel especially brave at that moment. But buried somewhere beneath the confusion and the upset, I did feel proud of myself for being strong enough to do something that was so scary.

After the interview and after the tears, Lisa explained what would happen next. She said that if Mom and I wanted to talk with my team today, we could wait in the reception area while the team reviewed my interview. We could meet with them today or later, separately or together. There was "no pressure," she said. It was totally my choice. Mom and I talked it over, and we decided to stay and meet my team.

SECTION 7. AFTER THE INTERVIEW

I wandered around the reception area for about twenty minutes while Mom tried to be calm and read a magazine. I felt best about meeting the team with Mom in the room, so when Lisa came to get me, Mom and I went into the big conference room together. It was hard to be with all these people because I felt ashamed that they knew such private things about me. It was a struggle for me to even look at them.

All the people on the team explained their job responsibilities to me, and what would happen next. It was hard for me to understand everything they said. Mostly, it was hard for me to even listen because I was so distracted by my own upset and embarrassment. But everyone was nice to me, and it was clear they were used to working with kids and knew what they were doing. I really got the feeling that they were all on my side.

Patty spoke first. "Based on your interview, Jane, there is enough evidence to support the allegations of child sexual abuse in my report for DSS." Then the Assistant District Attorney, Nina Santiago, talked about the prosecution process. She explained, "With your testimony, Jane, there appears to be enough evidence to proceed with the criminal prosecution of your father. The Commonwealth of Massachusetts will file the charges against him in **superior court**. You will not actually be responsible for taking your dad to court. But in order for the case to go forward, you need to be willing to be a **witness**. Your initial testimony will be videotaped so you won't have to testify live, in person, in front of all the people of the **grand jury**."

"What's a grand jury?" I asked.

Nina replied, "It's a jury of citizens who consider evidence brought before the superior court and decide if there is cause to believe a crime has been committed."

I told her that I had never heard of a "grand jury."

And so, Nina explained more about it. She said that not all states have grand juries, and in those states, the **probable cause hearing** takes place before a judge. She also said that sometimes the states that do have grand juries don't use them for child abuse cases. "It is one of those legal procedures which really varies from state to state, " she said. "And since we do have the grand jury here, we must present the evidence for your case to them. The videotaping of your **testimony** will hopefully make that part of the process easier for you, Jane. But if the case goes to trial, you need to be able and willing to **testify** in court."

This information and my emotions were somewhat overwhelming. Although my team was very nice, they were also very serious about wanting my dad to take responsibility for what he did. I asked what would happen to Dad if the case went forward.

My victim witness advocate, Andrea Kane, replied. She said, "There are a variety of possible **dispositions** of a criminal case, Jane, and if your dad is found **guilty,** Nina and I will talk with you and your mom about what you want to happen before we make a recommendation to the court."

While Andrea was talking, I couldn't keep my eyes off the police officer, Detective Rapucci. I wasn't planning to say anything to him but I just blurted out the question, "Are you going to arrest my father?" I was very upset about the possibility of Dad being in jail! I don't know if I felt ashamed, sad, scared, or guilty about that possibility, but I knew I WAS UPSET!

Detective Rapucci assured me he would not be arresting my dad at this time. He said, "I might ask your dad some questions, but I will discuss every detail of the investigation with the assistant district attorney to decide whether an arrest should be made."

Andrea continued the conversation. "There will be lots of time to talk about what might happen to your dad, and your feelings about what could happen will certainly be considered."

The next person to speak was the therapist from the mental health clinic. She said, "It's clear that this experience is upsetting for Jane, and under these circumstances, upset is a perfectly normal reaction."

I was relieved to be considered "normal." But then I started to cry because she went on to say that it might be helpful for me to talk with a counselor. Everybody, including my mom, nodded.

I was confused. And angry. A second ago I was "normal," and now I felt like there was something really wrong with me because they wanted me to go to a counselor. I wondered if maybe these people thought I was crazy. I asked, angry about it, and they all said they didn't think I was crazy. Patty reminded me how important it would be for me to talk about my feelings and fears with someone I trusted.

Mom mentioned that we had an appointment in a few days with the therapist Patty O'Neill had recommended. That surprised me. Mom said that she made the appointment the same day Patty gave her the number. Patty said, "It's good to know that there will be an additional support person in Jane's life during this difficult time."

Mom asked if she and I could have a few minutes alone together to talk things over, so everyone left the room. Mom said that she knew a public trial would for sure be a hard experience for our family, and especially hard for me. "But," she said, "protecting you is my primary concern, Janie. And, it's important to keep your father away from other kids." She also said, "We need to make sure your dad gets help."

I just nodded.

When the team returned, Mom told them that we would cooperate with the district attorney's office in preparing the case against Dad for trial. They were all very businesslike as, one by one, they thanked us.

Before we left the office, Andrea scheduled an appointment for me to come back in a few weeks to videotape the interview of my testimony for the grand jury. Then she gave me her business card, and told me I could call her if I had any questions about the legal process, or didn't understand something that happened, or even if I just wanted to talk to somebody. I put her card in my backpack along with Patty's. Having their telephone numbers with me all the time helped me to feel protected.

Then, as we were leaving the office, Andrea said, "I'll be in touch with you very soon, Jane. Just remember, it's my job to answer any and all of your questions, explain the court process, provide support to you and your mom, and to keep you notified of the case status. I had hoped to explain the court process to you this afternoon, but that seems like it might be too much for one day. So, we'll do that another time, OK?"

That was fine with me. My mind was spinning.

Then Andrea reassured me that she would be there for me. And I believed her.

SECTION 8. COUNSELING

I went to school the next couple days, and being there was a relief. I wanted to forget about Dad and what was happening to me and my family. Pretending everything was OK had become a way of life for me, and although pretending was harder now, I was still pretty good at it.

I had not told any of my friends or teachers or anyone what was going on, and that was becoming a problem for me. Not telling was making me feel isolated and alone. I wanted some of my friends to know because I really wanted people to understand me. You know, I wanted them to feel sad with me, and I wanted them to feel angry with me, too. Really, I just didn't want to feel alone with all of this.

But I didn't know who to tell. I didn't know who to trust because sometimes kids can be so mean to each other, even kids who you think are your friends. Last year this one girl had an abortion and some other girls left signs on her locker and in the girl's room calling her a baby killer. That was so mean. I'm sure she did what she thought was the best thing for her to do. But when I imagined what they might say about me, I actually thought I would throw up. Oh, and thinking that the boys would find out. Oh no! I couldn't even think about that! I felt so ashamed.

Mom and I went together to see the counselor Patty O'Neill recommended. Her name was Dr. Catherine Clayton, but she said I could call her "Cathy." I liked that. During our first session, I couldn't talk much about anything. I cried a lot, but that seemed OK with Mom and Cathy. We all decided I could come by myself to the next session which we scheduled for two days later.

When Mom and I were leaving, Cathy gave me her business card with her telephone number on it. She told me I could call her any time, day or night, if I wanted to talk to her . . . or if I wanted her to talk to me. I kind of smiled as I put her card into my backpack along with Patty's and Andrea's. I felt like I had a whole team of people in there helping me to get through this.

During my next appointment with Cathy I was calmer, for some unknown reason, and I felt more prepared. I had a list of things I wanted to talk about. I had my questions written on a piece of paper that was folded about thirty times and stuffed into the inside pocket of my jacket.

First on my list was what to do about feeling so isolated. I still had not told anyone. Although I didn't want to feel so alone, I also didn't want anyone else to know.

Second on the list was the feeling of being ruined for life, worrying that no boys would ever go out with me because they would think I was dirty and all used up already. I felt like maybe I was bad in some way because a lot of time the sex and the physical closeness felt good to me.

I was really afraid about what the sexual abuse had done to my body. I wondered if I wouldn't be able to have children, or if maybe I had AIDS or some other disease. I was so sure people could tell I'd been having sex just by looking at me. I wanted to hide, or be invisible, maybe.

I also wanted to talk about my dad, my mom, and my family. When I got to that number on my list of questions, tears started to seep out of my eyes. I tried to blink them back inside me, but I couldn't. I missed my dad. And I was very confused because Dad kept calling me to tell me how much he loved me. I asked Cathy, "Does he really love me? Why did he do this? Why did he ruin our family? Why did he hurt me? And Mom? He hurt Mom, too. And why did he lie and say I misunderstood?" This was just too hard. I kept wishing it had never happened.

Then I managed to tell Cathy that I had been feeling so terrible when I was alone at night that I actually thought I might rather be dead than to feel this way. I was having horrible nightmares.

I also wasn't sure if I did the right thing by telling, or if I was doing the right thing by planning to testify. I felt guilty and confused. My dad might go to jail, and maybe it was really my fault like he said. Maybe I did want him to do it. I felt like screaming! Cathy said it was fine to go ahead and scream, but I was too embarrassed.

Cathy listened while I went down my list of questions and concerns, which I read pretty fast, stumbling over my words sometimes. When I finished, I looked up at her and she smiled at me. Then she leaned forward a little bit, closer to me but not too close. She said, "Jane, I can see that you may be feeling really scared and nervous and sad and confused about all of this. And before I say anything else, I want to tell you that it is completely normal to be feeling all of those things."

Normal, again. What a relief. I sighed, and relaxed a little.

Cathy continued. "This is a great list, Jane. I can see that you worked hard putting it together, and I know it took a lot of strength to put your thoughts and feelings onto paper and bring them here." Then she said that dealing with sexual abuse issues was tough, and that it was "a real act of courage" for me to tell Mrs. Winston about my dad.

Cathy also said she was glad I trusted her enough to bring my list to her. She said we would talk about whatever I wanted to whenever I wanted to, whether it was on the list or not. "We can talk about the details of the abuse when you feel ready to do that, Jane. But it's also important for us to talk about your reactions to what is happening in your life right now, as well as your feelings about your family, your friends and your school experiences." It felt good not to be pressured to talk about what Dad did to me.

Unfortunately, Cathy didn't think we'd be able to answer all of my questions in that hour on that day. I was disappointed about that because I wanted answers. "But," she said, "you can tell me where you want to begin, and we will begin."

And so we did. It was really hard to talk about my feelings, but I made myself. Somewhere deep down inside, I knew it was important to get my feelings out of me and into the world. Cathy helped me to talk by asking me direct questions, by listening to my answers, and by being really gentle with me. The hour with Cathy was painful, but it passed quickly. We decided I would come to see her on Mondays and Thursdays for the next month. That way, Cathy said, I wouldn't feel so alone.

Since talking about wanting to die rather than deal with all of this wasn't what I chose from my list to talk about that day, Cathy said she wanted to take some extra time before I left to talk about those feelings. She said, "I suggest that you keep the telephone number of the twenty-four-hour crisis line Ms. Feldman gave you handy at all times. And I encourage you to use it, to talk to someone there, especially another teenager, if you want or need to talk with someone about what happened. Everything you say will be kept private."

Cathy then asked me to promise that the next time I felt so bad, I would call her, no matter what time. She encouraged me to put the crisis line telephone number and her telephone number on a piece of paper right next to my bed, so they would be there for me at night when I felt so scared and alone.

SECTION 9. PROSECUTION BEGINS

The next week my victim witness advocate, Andrea Kane, called from the district attorney's office. She said that she wanted to follow up on our meeting and to answer any questions I might have. She also wanted to explain the investigation, interview, and court processes to me.

But before doing any of that, Andrea asked, "How are you feeling, Jane? How is your therapy going?"

I didn't say much.

So then Andrea said, "I understand that this is really hard and painful for you. But remember, the case will only be brought to court if your therapist, your mom, and you think it is advisable for you."

It seemed to me that everyone wanted to make sure I would be OK, and that the court process wouldn't be harmful to me or interfere with my healing process.

Andrea and I confirmed a date for the grand jury interview which involved videotaping my testimony. Then she offered me some options for how to go about discussing some details about the prosecution process. She said, "We can talk on the phone, or meet earlier on the day of the interview, or, you can come into my office for a separate meeting." I decided on the separate meeting, so we scheduled a meeting for the next day after school.

When we got together the next afternoon, Andrea explained that the grand jury consists of a group of citizens who are registered voters in our county. They are called for jury duty for a three-month period, and are assigned to review the evidence for superior court cases. Their job is to hear evidence on serious cases and to determine if the case should go forward into the court system.

Assistant District Attorney Nina Santiago would present the case against my dad to the grand jury, and then they would watch the videotape of my testimony. Dad and his lawyer would not be there. After the presentation of the evidence, the grand jury votes on whether or not they think there is sufficient evidence to prosecute. If they think YES, they issue an **indictment.** If they think, NO, the case is closed.

This sounded like a foreign language to me, and it was all pretty confusing. So confusing actually, that I didn't really know what to ask when Andrea wanted to know if I had any questions.

She went on to explain about the **criminal justice system.** She said, "The criminal justice system is designed to protect the rights of the accused. In this case, that's your dad. He is accused of sexually abusing you." Andrea reminded me of the phrase we learned in junior high civics class, "presumed innocent until proven guilty." She said, "The assistant district attorney must convince a trial **jury,** beyond a **reasonable doubt,** that your dad is guilty of sexually abusing you."

Andrea also said, "The criminal court system is really designed for adults and it is sometimes especially hard for kids. Things can be said, and things can happen that kids don't understand. But I'm always here to help you. Please, just ask me. Anything. Feel free to ask me anything."

Finally I did manage to ask a few questions, just to see if I could make some sense of all that Andrea was saying. Then I realized it would be helpful to write some things down in case I forgot, or so I could think about this and ask more questions later.

Before we ended the conversation, Andrea reminded me again that it was OK for me to call her if I wanted to talk or if I had any questions. I didn't know how to respond to her. I'm not the type to ask a lot of questions, or to call people when I need to talk for fear that I will be bothering them. But it seemed that everyone I met—Patty, Cathy, Andrea—kept inviting me, encouraging me, to call, whenever, and to ask whatever. I began to think that maybe I wouldn't be such a bother after all.

Andrea reminded me again of the grand jury interview scheduled in a few weeks with Lisa. She also reminded me that it would only happen if I felt ready. She assured me I could decide if and when the time was right for the interview. Andrea and Nina, the **ADA,** would be there observing the interview from behind the two-way mirror.

Andrea also said she would call my mom sometime during the next few days to tell her what would happen next and to answer her questions.

"Good-bye, Jane." Andrea said as she walked me to the door of the office. "Take care. And call me. I'm here for you." I felt my eyes swell with tears.

"Good-bye, Andrea. And thanks," I said.

I stood outside the building for a long time, just staring at the puffy, pure white clouds floating through the sky. I felt furious that this was happening to me. Why? Why did I have to deal with this?

SECTION 10. PRETRIAL TESTIMONY

Mom and I went together to the district attorney's office on the day of my interview for the grand jury. It had been a hard and painful time for us both. Dad kept calling. He was trying to convince us not to become involved in the legal process. He kept saying how much he loved us, and insisted we could "work things out as a family." But when Dad realized that all the insisting in the world wasn't going to change anything, he tried to convince Mom that the abuse wasn't abuse. And that whatever it was, it was MY fault, not his.

Mom was upset by everything, and she found a therapist to talk to. She was considering a divorce. Dad said that was my fault, too. I wondered if maybe he was right. Cathy told me over and over that the sexual abuse wasn't my fault, and in some ways I could believe that. But I felt that the problems happening in my family were because of me. If only I hadn't told. I was confused but grateful that I had Cathy to help me. She was convinced that I was not to blame for the abuse or for my parents' problems.

Lisa, Andrea, and Nina Santiago were all going to be a part of the interviewing process. Before beginning the taping, they spent some time talking to me, trying to calm me down, I think. Although I felt scared, I also felt like a very important person at a business meeting with other important people. I tried to act especially grown-up, really because I didn't want anyone to know how scared I was.

Andrea asked me how I was feeling.

I said, "Fine."

She asked how my therapy was going and how I liked Cathy.

"Fine. Fine."

Andrea wanted to make sure I would be OK if I gave my testimony that day, and she said that she was happy to hear I would be seeing Cathy later in the afternoon. It was Cathy's idea for me to have an appointment with her after the interview. That way I would feel "supported," she said.

The interview room was the same room I was in before when I talked to Lisa. Everything was just the same, except the navy blue thread had been vacuumed up from the floor. I sat in a chair facing the mirror and the camera hiding behind it. Lisa spoke to the mirror and asked for the camera to be turned on. Andrea and Nina were on the other side of the mirror, so I guess one of them did that.

Lisa spoke to the camera. "Good afternoon. Today is November 16. My name is Lisa Lance-White from the district attorney's office. I'm here today meeting with Jane." Then Lisa spoke to me. "Jane, do you understand that it is important for you to tell the truth when you answer the questions I'm going to ask you today?"

I answered "Yes," but my voice was so soft because there was this huge lump in my throat, that Lisa had to ask me to speak louder. I said it again, "YES."

Then she said, "Do you promise to tell the truth today, Jane?"

I replied, "Yes, I do." I shivered a bit, shut my eyes tight, and took a deep breath. I was really doing this!

Lisa began asking me some simple questions like my full name, my birthday, where I went to school, what grade I was in, my address, and who lives with me. While I was answering those questions, Lisa had to remind me to speak up. I was very nervous, and even laughed a couple times during those first questions. I couldn't believe I laughed, because it definitely wasn't a funny experience, but I was just so nervous. I actually clenched the arms of my chair the whole time, maybe so I wouldn't get up and run away.

And then came the hard questions. Lisa asked, "Jane, did something happen with your father? What happened? When did it begin? How often did it happen? Where did it happen? When did it stop. . . .''

As I answered these questions for Lisa, I remember reaching up to my face, and brushing the tears from my cheeks. My face was so hot. It seemed like I was in the interview room answering these questions forever, and I was really surprised to find out that the whole thing only took about fifteen minutes.

At the end of the interview Lisa thanked me, and she walked with me into the reception area to get my mom. Then we met for a short time in the big conference room. Nina, Andrea, and Lisa said that my testimony was "excellent." But all I cared about, really, was that it was over. I felt so relieved. I just knew I did the right thing.

Andrea said she would call me in a couple of days to discuss the next step. You know what I liked most about Andrea? She always called me when she said she was going to. That made me feel like I could really count on her to be there for me.

When we left the office, Mom took me to McDonald's and bought me a vanilla milk shake. My favorite. Believe me, I really needed that milk shake.

Then I went to see Cathy.

SECTION 11. COUNSELING SUPPORT

Have I mentioned how tired I was? During those weeks after I first told Mrs. Winston about my dad, I was just so tired all the time. I felt sick a lot, too. And confused. Yes, for sure. I felt tired and sick and confused that afternoon when I went to see Cathy.

You know, I love my dad, and I felt so guilty about what I said about him. And now it was on videotape. A grand jury of the superior court was going to hear what my dad did to me. I was too embarrassed to even think about it. But I was also sad because I didn't really want my dad to get in any trouble. When I saw Cathy I told her I was afraid. I was thinking maybe I shouldn't be involved in this prosecution thing.

Cathy said that she understood my confusion. That afternoon she helped me to understand it, too, and to accept being confused. I just wanted everything in my life to be fine and smooth and simple, and everyone in my family to be happy. I felt like such a troublemaker.

Cathy told me that it was OK to love my dad and to still want him to be responsible for his actions. After all, Dad abused me. "Your father has some problems, Jane, and he needs help," Cathy said. "However," she continued, "what he did to you is a crime. Legally and morally, it is a crime." She explained that the child abuse laws were made to protect me, and that I had a right to be protected. Cathy and everyone at the district attorney's office had a way of making me feel like I was somebody important. Since they believed so strongly that I had "rights," I came to believe it, too.

Patty O'Neill told me, and Lisa told me, and Andrea told me that if testifying felt too hard for me, I could stop the prosecution process at any time. After all, I was the primary witness. Without my cooperation there was really no case. Cathy reminded me again that feeling reluctant about the court process is normal. Then she said, "Know that you do have a choice about testifying, Jane."

I left Cathy's office feeling less tired, but I was definitely lost in thoughts about what she told me. I was "important." I had "rights." I could "choose." I felt better because I felt like I had some control over my life.

SECTION 12. WAITING

The next few weeks seemed endless because I didn't know what was happening. And mostly it didn't seem that anything was happening. But I guess even though I couldn't see it, the justice system was, in fact, operating.

Some of the time I was kind of in a panic, and I think I called either Andrea or Nina or both of them at least once a day to see how my case was going. I needed to know. Nina was in court a lot, so sometimes she didn't call me back right away and I would panic even more, worrying that she forgot me. But Andrea always called me, and even though she sometimes didn't have much new information, just talking to her helped me to calm down.

Then finally, one day after school, Andrea called. *The Commonwealth vs. My Dad* would be heard by the grand jury the following Tuesday. "And then a couple weeks after that," she said, "we'll know if an indictment will be issued."

I felt a surge of excitement rush through my body, like an electric current up and down my back and legs and arms. But when I hung up the phone I felt stunned. I sat in the living room for a long time waiting for Mom to come home from work. As the sun went down I watched the house get dark and the shadows appear. I never even turned on the lights. Really, I wasn't even sure if I could move. Tree-Girl waited with me. We sat on the couch, watching the shadows. The only sounds I noticed were the ticking of the clock and Tree-Girl's purring. Waiting . . . waiting . . . it seemed like forever.

SECTION 13. AT SCHOOL

I wanted to go to school—to be distracted mostly—but I also didn't want to go. A few days after the meeting at school with Mom and Patty O'Neill and Ms. Feldman, Mom met with the principal to explain my "situation." The principal then talked with all of my teachers, and without being specific, explained that I was experiencing a family crisis. She told my teachers that I might be late or absent, or sometimes I might have difficulty concentrating, or maybe I would need some extra help with my work or some extra attention. I was embarrassed about this "special" treatment because I didn't want the other kids to notice it and tease me. But down deep, I really appreciated everyone's help and concern. And this truly was a family crisis.

Cathy and Mom helped me decide which of my friends to tell and how to tell them. Cathy also helped to prepare me for their possible reactions. It's hard for some kids to understand about taking your own father to court. I could totally relate, because it was hard for me to understand, too.

Mom helped a lot. She talked to my friends' moms so they could understand what was happening. It felt so weird to me when this secret thing wasn't a secret anymore. My mom, my friends and their moms, and some people at school knew. I felt ashamed. But I really needed the support, so it was good that they knew and could help me.

I sometimes felt like the whole world knew my secret that wasn't a secret anymore. I felt like everyone was looking at me. I wished no one could see me. I prayed that I would just disappear one day and it would be all over.

Even though I went to school most days, I didn't say much in classes because I didn't want to draw attention to myself. I didn't know what to say to people, even my friends. Should I talk about what was constantly nagging at my thoughts—Dad and the trial? Or, should I talk about boys and sports and music and classes, and pretend that everything was cool—like I did before? It was hard, I didn't know what to do, how to be, where to start.

It helped a lot when my friends would come up to me and start conversations. Like at lunch one day, Joy came over and said, "Hey, Janie. So what do you think about that substitute teacher in history class? What a bore!" Joy broke the ice and just acted natural to me. I felt drawn into the conversation. I remember smiling that day. I didn't feel so isolated or weird.

I was pretty nervous a lot, and jumpy. One day at school the hall was kind of empty and I was getting a notebook from my locker. This guy, Dan, who I kind of liked, called to me from down the hall. "Hi, Jane!" He startled me, for sure, and I dropped all my books on my foot. I felt so scared and stupid for dropping everything, I started to cry. Dan said he was "so sorry" for scaring me, and he helped me pick up all my stuff. I don't remember exactly what he said next, but somehow he got me laughing. Crying and laughing, sometimes they happen together.

That afternoon, Dan and I went out for some fries and a Coke. I had fun. We didn't talk about my real life, my dad, I mean. We talked about school and books and movies. I laughed. It felt so good.

As things about the abuse and the trial became public, more people found out. And not all the kids were as nice to me as Joy and Dan. Some were totally cruel, and I hated them. Some days I thought I'd never go back to school. Some days I was going to leave town, change my name, and start a whole new life. Cathy helped me through a lot of tears and hate about those kids. It's times of trouble like this that you find out who your true friends are.

I was beginning to learn about trust. I had been pretty mixed up about that.

SECTION 14. THE INDICTMENT

It had been an uneventful day. I was beginning to feel a little calmer, and didn't even jump when the phone rang at home late that afternoon. It was Nina Santiago calling to tell me that the grand jury had handed down an indictment against my father. She said he would be sent a **summons** to appear in superior court for **arraignment** within the next few days. My hand felt frozen to the phone. My thoughts were whirling.

I knew that Andrea had explained arraignment to me, but I guess I forgot. I stammered as I asked Nina, "What's arraignment?"

She explained. "Arraignment is the public reading in the court of the formal charges against your father. Because of the indictment from the grand jury, your father will receive a summons in the mail which will tell him when to report to court. At the arraignment in court, the charges filed against him will be read to him, and he will **plead** "guilty" or "not guilty." Just so you know, Jane, it is pretty standard for all defendants charged with serious crimes to plead "not guilty" at the time of arraignment. This has nothing to do with whether or not they plead guilty later in the process. Jane? Jane, are you there?"

I was there, but I had drifted off into the frenzy of my whirling thoughts. Was this all really happening?

"Oh, by the way, Jane," Nina continued, "Remember we mentioned that although it's not very common, sometimes indictments handed down by the grand jury might appear in the local newspapers. Your name won't be mentioned in the papers because the law says the media cannot use your name. However, your father's name and address might be in the papers."

"Oh no." I thought. "Now everyone will know." I hid my face in my hands and cried.

SECTION 15. THE ARRAIGNMENT

Life was in slow motion for me, but the day finally came. Mom and I didn't go to the arraignment. It was a really "quick procedure" Nina said, so she was the only one who needed to be there. She said it was important for my father to understand that the charges were being brought against him by the Commonwealth of Massachusetts, not by me or my mom. That fact would be clearer to him if we weren't there for the arraignment. But I might as well have been there. I couldn't think of anything else all day. I imagined the scene over and over in my mind. I was grateful that Dad wouldn't have to be handcuffed. Some of the defendants being arraigned are handcuffed, you know.

Nina finally called late in the day. I stayed home from school, waiting to hear from her. Believe me, it was a very long day. "As expected," Nina said, "Your dad pled 'not guilty.' There was a **bail hearing,** and **bail** was set so he won't have to be in jail." I was glad. Nina said that court dates had been set for **pretrial conferences** and **motions hearings**. But I didn't have to go to them. "The actual trial date," she said, "could be scheduled anytime from three months to one year from now."

I screeched. I know I screeched, "A year!" I was totally shocked.

Nina said, "Jane, it might even be longer. Sometimes there are **continuances** in court that we can't control. Realistically, though, the trial could happen in September or October." This was December. September, October. That seemed like never.

I called Andrea later after I had calmed down. "What's a continuance?" I asked.

And she told me. "A continuance is a change in the date that something is scheduled to happen in court."

Now I had more questions! "Why does that happen? Will it happen to me?"

She answered, "It happens because of lots of different reasons. Sometimes the lawyers need to do more research on the legal issues. Sometimes a witness is not available. Sometimes a previously scheduled trial takes longer than expected, so the judge is busy with that and not ready for us. I don't know if any continuances will happen for your case, Jane, but it's probable, so be prepared." She also said that most likely Mom and I would be notified in advance about any delays or changes. When it was time for the trial we would receive **sub-**

poenas telling us when to appear in court. "By then," Andrea said, "things should be pretty well set and ready to go."

SECTION 16. WAITING AGAIN

I could not believe that it took so long for a trial to be held in superior court. It's about "scheduling" they told me, and lots of cases for the judges to hear. It was hard for me because there was nothing I could do about it but wait. Sometimes I was frantic, but mostly there was just nothing anyone could do about it.

Eventually I settled down into a routine, and a routine felt nice for a change. I still called Andrea a lot, and she called me regularly to check in about how I was doing and to keep me informed about the progress of my case. I saw Cathy every week, and I really started to like her and trust her, too. But sometimes I wasn't sure why I went. I didn't really want to talk about the abuse. Sometimes I just wanted to forget the whole thing.

The house was quieter. Mom seemed to calm down some, too, but there was definitely an empty spot without Dad. He didn't bother us by calling much anymore. Weeks earlier, Nina had filed for a **restraining order** to keep him from seeing me or contacting me. Dad called Mom at her job if he needed to talk to her about something.

Sometimes Mom and I could put our troubles aside. "File them for future reference," Cathy would say. And during those times we had some fun together.

The holidays that year were very strange.

SECTION 17. THE EMPTY COURTROOM

Although Mom and I went on with our regular lives, we both felt like there was this gray storm cloud hovering above us all the time. It followed us. I wondered if Dad had one, too.

In early July, Andrea called to tell me that a trial date had been set for August 18. I shivered, and it was 90 degrees outside! She did remind me, however, that things could come up to cause delays.

During the last week in July and the first week in August, Nina, Andrea, and I met a few times to go over what would happen in court. First they talked to me about the verdict. Andrea said, "We know your dad is guilty, Jane. But during the trial, we need to prove his guilt, beyond a reasonable doubt. Remember? We talked about reasonable doubt."

I nodded.

Andrea was being very serious. She continued talking. "In cases like this, sometimes the **defendant** is found **not guilty**. If that happens, Jane, it doesn't mean that your dad is innocent, or that he didn't abuse you. It means that the district attorney's office did not have sufficient evidence to convince the jury of his guilt beyond a reasonable doubt." Andrea told me this to prepare me for the possibility that my dad might be **acquitted** rather than **convicted.** I knew it was a possibility, but I told Andrea that I didn't want to even think about it.

One afternoon Andrea and Nina took me to an empty courtroom so I wouldn't be going into a totally strange place when the trial started. We went into the courtroom. It looked dark and somber, and it felt cold. In fact, a shiver went up my back as I stood in the doorway and looked around. I knew right away this was a very serious place.

Nina coaxed me into sitting in the **witness stand.** As she and Andrea looked through some papers to decide on the questions I would be asked, I just sat and looked around, slowly. I had to remind myself to breathe. I felt hot tears burning my eyes. I squeezed my eyes shut really tight, hoping the tears would go away, hoping when I opened my eyes I would be away. In Florida maybe, at Disney World, in Hawaii, or maybe Spain. I've always wanted to go to Spain. My hands actually gripped the arms of the chair. I was hoping with all my might.

And then I heard Andrea's voice. "Jane. Jane, what's happening?"

I opened my eyes and was surprised to see her, and Nina and the empty courtroom. It didn't look so scary now because it wasn't the first time I was seeing it. It actually looked familiar. "I'm OK," I said.

So while I was sitting there, supposedly "getting comfortable," Nina spent some time preparing for what might come up in the trial. I knew this was going to be hard.

Then Andrea helped me step down from the stand. I was a little shaky, but I felt very mature and grown-up.

SECTION 18. PRETRIAL DETAILS

A lot of paperwork goes into a trial. I learned that first thing. Before the trial actually happens, the ADA and the **defense attorney**

meet in court with the **judge** and the court workers (the **court officers,** the **judge's clerk,** and the **court reporters**), to submit and decide about the **pretrial motions.** That's when the attorneys request
certain procedures and special conditions. For example, Nina asked
for a microphone to use during my testimony. She knew I talked
softly, especially when we got to the parts that were hard for me to
say. She wanted to make sure the judge, the jury, and everyone could
hear me. The defense attorney didn't want Nina to refer to me as a
victim, but to call me a **complaining witness** instead. Andrea explained that this was because the word victim implied that I was hurt
by my dad, and that's what the ADA had to prove. "It's a technicality," she said. The judge decided to "wait and see" about the microphone, but I wish he hadn't done that. He said I had to be referred to
as a complaining witness. The court process—the whole thing—was
hard for me. Sometimes I didn't understand, and I really wondered
whose side they were on.

SECTION 19. DELAYS AND PREPARATIONS

And there were continuances. I'm glad Nina and Andrea warned
me about them, but even their warnings didn't help my stress about it.
We'd be all ready for the trial to start the next week, and Andrea or
Nina would call to say it had to be rescheduled for later.

It happened a few times, and each time I got mad at Andrea or
Nina, whichever one called to tell me the news. But then I felt bad
about being mad at them. They were really nice to me, and on my
side. I knew that. After all, the judge was the person who was in
charge of the courtroom, and the delays were mostly for administrative reasons. But I could never figure out how those things, whatever
they were, could be more important than people's feelings. I was very
upset about all this waiting and delaying, and so was my mom. I wondered if they cared about us at all. I had waited so long already, and I
didn't know if I could stand waiting one minute longer. Mom called
my upset "apprehension." Fear of future evil! That felt like an accurate description. But in spite of all the distress, I somehow made it
through the waiting.

For months before the trial I spent most of my free time preparing
myself by watching lawyer shows on television. I almost never

missed *Judge Judy* or *Law and Order* or *The Practice*. And some-times I'd stay up late and watch reruns of the original *Perry Mason*. I prayed that Nina was a better prosecutor than poor Mr. Burger!

I was fascinated, yet frightened by this television law. Even though Andrea talked to me a lot about the legal process and the language that would be used in court, I thought I could become some kind of "expert" from my TV research, and then I'd be less afraid. Andrea and Nina had both talked to me about television law, warning me that some of it was "realistic" and some of it was "just drama" geared to entertain TV audiences. But I watched the shows anyway.

Unfortunately those TV shows didn't help me to feel more confi-dent when my real day in court finally came. But they did keep me oc-cupied during the long months of waiting. Watching them helped me feel like I was doing something to prepare myself.

SECTION 20. THE TRIAL BEGINS

The trial was finally scheduled to begin on October 4. "A firm date," Nina said. Mom and I had received subpoenas in the mail re-questing our appearance as witnesses for the prosecution in the case of *The Commonwealth of Massachusetts vs. My Dad*. The documents had a serious, cold look about them, just like the courtroom.

The trial did start on October 4. It lasted for five days from the jury **empaneling** to the reading of the **verdict.** These were by far, the lon-gest, yet the quickest, five days of my entire life. When the trial was in progress, even the minutes crawled by. The days seemed endless. And the sleepless nights were frightfully endless. But when the trial was all over, it seemed to have lasted no longer than the blink of an eye.

SECTION 21. IN COURT

Court was a tense place. It was very organized, and the people who worked there seemed to know exactly what was going on. But in spite of knowing, even they seemed tense.

There were a lot of people in court. There were two lawyers (Nina and Mr. McCarthy, who was the defense attorney for my dad). There were two court officers. They had on uniforms sort of like police officers. There was a court clerk who sat at a desk in front of the judge's bench, and a court reporter who recorded every word of the trial. I was surprised that there were fourteen people on the jury instead of twelve. I kept counting them, thinking I made a mistake. When I asked Andrea, she explained that two jurors were alternates in case someone on the jury got sick or something. There were also a few people in the audience. Most trials are open to the public. I wanted to know who the people were and why they were there. I was upset to see my grandparents and Uncle John sitting behind my dad. They didn't believe me, and at the trial they didn't even look at me. I just knew they hated me, and I was sad and upset and I didn't want them to be there.

I appreciated Andrea more as each minute passed. She stayed with me the whole time. I didn't realize it, but because my mom was also a witness, we couldn't always be together in the courtroom. There's this thing called **sequestered.** It means that one witness is not allowed to hear the testimony of the other witnesses, so as not to be influenced by what someone else says. So I had to spend a lot of time with Andrea in the victim/witness "waiting" room (what a perfect name for that room), wondering what in the world was going on inside the courtroom. There was this huge clock on the wall in the waiting room, and I just stared at it, watching the endless seconds tick by. At first I asked Andrea a lot of questions because I was so nervous. But then I drifted off into my worries. Mom was getting divorced. Dad might go to jail. And I was going to have to say totally embarrassing things in the courtroom.

Mom and I were in court on the third, fourth, and fifth days of the trial. We didn't have to be there for the jury selection or the pretrial motions that happened during the first two days.

First Nina and Mr. McCarthy gave their **opening statements.** That part was sort of like the TV shows. Then Nina called me to the witness stand to testify. I was so nervous my hands were sweaty. My stomach was upset, and I was afraid I would throw up. But I didn't. It was hard to testify, for sure. But I did it. I was OK.

Nina stood across the courtroom and asked me questions. The easy ones were first. My name, address, age, school . . . and then came the hard ones. Nina began to ask me questions about the sexual experiences I had with my dad. "Oh no," I thought, "I can't say this!" Nina kept asking me to speak up, but I could barely speak at all.

Then all of a sudden, the judge jumped up from his chair. His unexpected movement, right in the middle of my testimony, scared me. He abruptly said, "We're in **recess.** Counsel, in my chambers." Surrounded by a cloud of swirling black fabric, the judge disappeared from the courtroom, followed by the lawyers.

I started to cry. I couldn't figure out what was happening. Before I knew it, I was out in the corridor and Andrea was right beside me. I got some water, and Andrea tried to calm me down. A few minutes later, the court officers were installing a microphone on the witness stand for me to use. Nina came out into the corridor and explained that the judge couldn't hear my answers and asked that the microphone be set up. I wished that the judge had approved Nina's pretrial motion for a microphone in the first place, because now I was upset and feeling afraid of him.

Fifteen minutes later court was back in session. The judge spoke to me directly and apologized for the disruption. He asked me to speak clearly into the microphone "so the jury can hear every word." I think he smiled at me. I know I didn't smile. I just nodded.

SECTION 22. CROSS-EXAMINATION

When Nina finished asking me questions, Dad's lawyer, Mr. McCarthy, **cross-examined** me. He was loud and abrupt. At times I felt attacked by him. He tried to confuse me by asking me the same question over in different ways. Later Andrea explained that he was trying to "discredit" my testimony.

Mr. McCarthy's confusing questions made it hard for me to think. I felt those now familiar tears stinging my eyes. My fists were clenched in my lap. I wanted to run out of the courtroom, and not stop running until I got to Spain. But then I would see Andrea—she was like an anchor for me—and I somehow found the strength to sit still and go on.

I answered the questions in the best way I could. But Mr. McCarthy kept saying he didn't understand. So he'd ask the same question again, and again. Finally, the judge interrupted. He rephrased Mr. McCarthy's last question, which had been asked several times, and my answer. He then looked directly at me and asked, "Is this what you're saying, Jane?"

"Yes," I said as I nodded.

The judge turned to Dad's lawyer and said, "Well, then. That's quite enough for this question, Mr. McCarthy. I think that both the jury and I understand the witness's answer. Please move on."

I felt such relief, I can't even say. The judge's interruption helped me calm down, and Mr. McCarthy didn't seem so mean from then on. But still, I was exceedingly glad when it was finally over. I was questioned for almost three hours total.

That afternoon and part of the next day there were other witnesses. My mom, Cathy, and my doctor also testified. After that, my dad testified even though his lawyer didn't want him to, and he didn't have to. Andrea explained that Dad didn't have to testify because of the **Fifth Amendment,** and because the **burden of proof** is on the prosecution. My Uncle John testified for my dad as a **character witness.** I didn't hear any of the testimony because I was sequestered.

At the end of the examination of witnesses, both lawyers gave their **closing arguments** to the court. I was there for that. Hearing Mr. McCarthy speak was very scary. He said that he was completely convinced my dad was not guilty. He said that I was mistaken. "Children misunderstand and misinterpret." He said that I lied. "Children have vivid imaginations, and they sometimes fabricate dramatic tales to get attention." That's what Mr. McCarthy had to say about me.

But then Nina's closing argument restored my faith and confidence. She said I didn't lie, and that I wasn't mistaken.

I felt like I was on a roller coaster. I wondered how the jury felt.

SECTION 23. INSTRUCTIONS TO THE JURY

After the closing arguments, the judge spoke directly to the jury for what seemed like a very long time. I wondered how in the world they could ever remember everything he said.

The judge told the jury to weigh the **credibility** of the witnesses, and to decide whether to believe some, none, or all of what each person said. I thought it must be very hard to be a juror. I mean, I said my dad had sex with me, and he said he didn't. How does the jury decide who's telling the truth and who's telling a lie?

The judge went on to further instruct the jury. He reminded them that my dad was **"presumed innocent."** I shivered when I heard those words. The judge said that the prosecution must prove guilt beyond a "reasonable doubt," but not *all* doubt. I started thinking that must be where the old saying came from, the one about giving someone the "benefit of the doubt."

Then the judge went over the elements of the charges against my dad for the jury to hear, reminding them that Dad was charged with rape of a child. Then the judge read these things called **statutes.** "Whoever has sexual intercourse or unnatural sexual intercourse . . . abuses a child under the age of sixteen." It all sounded so impersonal, I couldn't believe he was still talking about me. The jury was then told that they had two choices for a verdict: not guilty or guilty as charged.

When the judge finished talking to the jury, the court clerk took this wooden box and shook it up. It looked like he was going to draw the winning name for a raffle. I was kind of startled by this familiar, friendly action that seemed so out of place. The clerk drew two names from the box, but instead of winning something, the names identified the alternate jurors. The other twelve jurors left the courtroom and went into the jury room to **deliberate.**

"All rise." The judge swiftly left the courtroom followed by his fluttering black robes. The trial was suddenly over.

I turned to Andrea with hope in my eyes and a question in my voice. "It's over?"

"Not yet, Jane," she replied. "It's not over yet."

SECTION 24. THE VERDICT

Nina suggested that Mom and I go to the cafeteria for lunch. She said we shouldn't go home or leave the courthouse. She wanted us to be close as we waited for the verdict. We went to the cafeteria and ate lunch, and then spent the rest of the afternoon waiting with Andrea in the victim/witness waiting room. I swear, I have every detail of that room memorized!

At 3:30 p.m. Nina appeared in the doorway of the waiting room. The jury had reached a verdict.

And then we were back in the courtroom. I have never in my life been so scared. Andrea stayed right beside me the whole time. This was a totally terrible situation. I was feeling panicky because I wasn't sure what I wanted the verdict to be. If it was "guilty" then maybe my dad would go to jail, or at least he would be in a lot of trouble. He'd have a criminal record. But even worse, if the verdict was "not guilty" probably everyone would think I was a liar. I had this terrible headache. My teeth were clenched so tight. My fists were, too. Andrea kept trying to get me to be more relaxed, but there was absolutely no possibility of relaxed!

The jury filed in. The judge appeared. "All rise." I was becoming accustomed to the routine. "This court is now in session." What followed felt like a dream . . . or a movie. Something unreal, anyway. In fact, if I think about it, I can still play back the entire scene in my mind just as if I were seeing it happen all over again.

The judge spoke. "Men and women of the jury, have you reached a verdict?"

The foreman stood and replied. "We have, your honor." The clerk asked my dad to stand, and he did. So did his lawyer. And then the verdict. **"Guilty as charged."** Guilty as charged . . . guilty as charged. An echo. I'm sure I heard an echo in the cold, hollow courtroom.

Movement and sound happened slowly and distinctly. I couldn't see my father's face, but when the guilty verdict was announced, his whole body slumped forward, looking defeated. My face and hands finally relaxed. Dad sat down and held his head in his hands. Was he crying? I was. My tears were a release of tension mixed with feelings of great loss. Would I ever have a dad again?

The judge spoke. His voice startled me. "The jury is dismissed. The court thanks you for your service. Sentencing will be in two weeks. This court is adjourned." And in that now familiar flurry of swirling black, the judge was gone.

SECTION 25. AFTER THE TRIAL

In slow motion I turned to Andrea. I looked up at her and very softly asked, "It's over now?"

"Well, not quite, Jane," she answered. "The trial is over, but the court process is not. At the sentencing hearing, in two weeks, the judge will hear sentence recommendations from both Nina and Mr. McCarthy. And if you want to say something, there will also be time for you to make a **victim impact statement**. Or, you can write a letter to the judge telling him how you feel about your dad's sentence. In fact, sometimes before the sentencing people write to the judge about the defendant, and you need to be prepared for that. Your father may have character witnesses—like your grandparents and your uncle, or your dad's boss, or his minister—who write on his behalf, suggesting that he receive **probation** and not be sentenced to jail at all, or that he receive a short sentence."

I just nodded in response, and Andrea continued. "Nina will discuss her sentencing recommendations with you directly before she says anything to the judge. I know that you've thought a lot about what kind of sentence you want your dad to receive, Jane. And now is the time for you to decide if you want to make a victim impact statement. You can either say your statement in court the day of the sentencing, or you can write it to the judge. We encourage you to communicate your feelings to the court in some way, so your voice will be heard, but you don't have to. You don't have to say anything. You don't have to write anything. You don't even have to go to the sentencing hearing."

Andrea and I had similar talks before, but hearing it all again left me in a daze. Maybe I was dazed because I thought it was over. I hoped it was over. I wanted it over. Two more weeks seemed like another eternity, but I knew I'd get through it somehow. I mean, really! Look at what I'd been through already!

During the next several days, I spent my time after school alone, going for long walks, mostly. Thinking. It was fall and it felt good to be outside in the bright, crisp sunshine. I walked and walked, trying very hard to get to the bottom of my feelings about Dad. Talking with Cathy helped, but I knew that identifying my own feelings was really a solitary activity. And so I walked some more. Finally, after ten days I sat down very late at night and wrote the victim impact statement I would read in the courtroom.

My statement was short. I thought that was best. I honestly didn't know how much I would be able to say without crying.

SECTION 26. VICTIM IMPACT STATEMENT

Since I'm only sixteen years old, I can't know for sure, but I think that writing this statement, and then saying it out loud in court, may be the hardest thing I will ever do in my whole life.

In spite of everything my dad has done to me, including the actual abuse and that he said I lied about it, and in spite of how bad I feel sometimes, both physically and emotionally, I still love my dad very much. And I know he loves me.

But he hurt me. He scared me and threatened me. He confused me. My own father stole things from me, important things, that I can never, ever recover. My body was violated. My heart is broken, and I think my spirit is too. My family is shattered. We have all suffered so much. Nobody should have to go through this.

Dad did something wrong, something very wrong and bad. He always punishes me when I'm bad. It seems only fair that he should be punished now. I love my dad, and feel very bad about the idea of him being in jail. But I don't want him to hurt me anymore. I want to feel safe. If he's in jail, and can't see me or call me, then, maybe, for the first time in my life, I can feel safe.

I also want my dad to see a doctor or therapist who can help him. So then maybe he won't hurt other people like he hurt Mom and me.

SECTION 27. SENTENCING

The day of the sentencing hearing finally arrived. Mom and Andrea and I were sitting in the courtroom at exactly 2:00 p.m., the time the hearing was scheduled. Except for Nina and the court officers, the room was empty. I was nervous and confused. At five minutes past 2:00, more people started coming, but I didn't know who they were. In and out. People kept coming in and going out of the courtroom.

I whispered to Andrea a question I had asked her several times before. "What kind of sentence will Dad get?"

"Well," she whispered in reply, "there are guidelines regarding appropriate sentencing for every crime, but the decision in each case is really up to the judge."

At ten minutes past 2:00, more people came in. "Who are all these people?" I asked Andrea.

Other activities were scheduled in court that afternoon. They were lawyers and victim witness advocates and witnesses and friends. Some were Dad's friends. I noticed that the lawyers seemed friendly to each other, even if they were on opposite sides. When Mr. McCarthy arrived, Nina shook his hand and spoke to him. I didn't want them to be friendly.

At 2:15, I started going in and out of the courtroom. Getting a drink, going to the bathroom. This waiting made me so nervous. Andrea told me that sometimes the waiting is the worst part. I thought maybe she was right. At 2:20, the court officer started talking on the telephone on his desk and this one lawyer over in the corner was throwing his pen up in the air catching it each time it came down again. Was he nervous, too? Or just passing the time? It seemed to me that nothing at court ever started on time. I don't know why, either, but it made me very nervous. I wondered if whoever was in charge had any idea about how nerve-racking all this waiting was. My heart was pounding so hard, that I worried I might be having a heart attack. But I wasn't.

Finally people slowly began taking their places. They sat down and one by one became quiet. Dad came in and sat on the other side of the courtroom. He didn't even look at me.

"All rise." The judge appeared. "Be seated. This court is now in session." A solemn quiet. The clerk announced the other cases, stated who was present, and who the lawyers were. Now things seemed to happen very quickly, and soon the courtroom was nearly empty.

The clerk announced our case and acknowledged Nina and Mr. McCarthy as the lawyers. Dad went forward and sat next to Mr. McCarthy.

Then Nina stood. I stopped breathing, I think. Nina spoke directly to the judge. Her voice was clear and loud. It echoed in the hollow, quiet space. "Thank you, Your Honor. On behalf of the commonwealth, the district attorney's office recommends a state prison sentence. The sexual abuse of a dependent child is the most heinous of crimes. Jane's father made her childhood into a living nightmare. She was a helpless, defenseless, loving child. A father is supposed to protect and care for his child, not molest her. Jane suffered the ultimate betrayal by her own father, and nothing we do here today can heal her wounds. However, what we can do is hold her father responsible for his crimes. This young girl endured over ten years of abuse. There is physical evidence and psychological damage. Her father was found guilty by a jury of his peers. Although we cannot take away Jane's suffering, we can send a message to other child molesters, through this molester, that our society will not tolerate the mistreatment of our children. Therefore, the commonwealth recommends a state prison sentence, to be followed by a **suspended sentence** from and after the committed sentence, during which time sex offender counseling will be mandatory."

When Nina was finished, it was my turn to speak. I walked up to the witness stand and sat down. I was feeling kind of shaky. I unfolded my paper and looked at Nina and then at the judge. I looked at Dad. I wanted him to look at me, but he was staring at his hands which were fiddling with some papers on the table in front if him. I read my statement, grateful that it was short, because I did start to cry. This whole situation was a terrible nightmare. I still couldn't believe it was happening. I felt so sad, so bad about it all. Why did you do this, Dad?

I finished my statement, folded up my paper, and went back to my place next to Andrea. I was glad the court officer was there to help me step down from the stand.

Then Mr. McCarthy spoke on my dad's behalf. "He is not a one-dimensional person. He is a son, a husband, a father. We cannot deny him his humanity. He has provided for his family responsibly. The judge has received a number of letters from friends and relatives who have known him for more than twenty years. He has a friendly, generous spirit . . . " Mr. McCarthy went on and on saying what a great man my dad was. It was hard for me to believe that Nina and Mr. McCarthy were talking about the same person.

And then the judge talked, for a long time it seemed, before getting to the point. He asked Dad to stand. Then the clerk announced the sentence. "You have been found guilty . . . you are sentenced to a state prison term . . . to be followed by a suspended sentence . . . will include mandatory counseling . . . sentence to begin immediately." The court officers came up to Dad and led him away through the mysterious door in the back of the courtroom.

Time stopped for me. Shocked, stunned. I don't know. A shiver went through my whole body. People were talking to me. I saw their mouths move, but didn't hear their voices. Andrea sort of steered me out of the courtroom and into the victim/witness waiting room. I sat down, and burst into tears.

Well, the trial was finally over. But now the part about putting my life back together was about to begin.

SECTION 28. TOWARD RECOVERY

It hasn't been quite two years since I first told Mrs. Winston about the sexual abuse, but it seems like it all happened centuries ago. Since the trial ended I've felt that I can get on with my life. No, that's not quite right. I feel that I'm finally beginning to live my life.

In some ways I feel lucky. Not lucky that my dad abused me, that wasn't lucky at all. That was frightening and destructive. But, I feel lucky that there are people who care about kids, and that some of those people helped me. In fact, they're still helping me. I see Cathy every week, and probably will keep seeing her for awhile. She's helped me to understand the experience of incest and to work on my feelings about it. Sorting out my feelings can be very, very hard work, and will "take some time," Cathy said. I mostly hate thinking about it and getting upset about it, but then the upset and work seem worthwhile when I finally come to understand more about my experience and to accept it.

I feel sad every time I think about my dad. I probably always will feel sad about him. I'm really angry at him, too. But even though I feel sad and angry about the abuse and what Dad did to our family, I still love him. I can't help it. After all, he's my dad.

He's in jail now. I don't visit him or write to him. I'm still too upset. But Cathy thinks maybe someday I'll want to tell him how hurt and angry I am. I sure hope he learns something while he's in jail. I hope he understands how much he hurt me and that what he did to me was wrong, and that he can never sexually abuse a child ever again. He wants me to forgive him, and I said I would think about it. But I'm not sure I can forgive him. I need to be 100 percent sure he's truly sorry, so sorry that he will never even consider abusing another child.

Given the life I've survived so far, things are going as well as can be expected. I'm doing okay in school. My grades aren't bad, and last spring I even got up the courage to try out for the track team. I made Varsity! I've dated a little, very little, but enough to realize that I have a lot to learn about relationships and sex. "But doesn't everyone!" Cathy said.

Sometimes it's tempting to think about burying my past and my pain with drugs and alcohol, like some kids at school do. But I resist. I know that keeping things buried won't help much in the long run. Sometimes I have nightmares. Sometimes I'm tired and sick with headaches and stomachaches. Sometimes life isn't very fun for me. But now I at least feel like I'm living it, and that I'm in control of my own body and my own life. I really like that feeling. For the first time in my whole life I'm feeling and expressing, and being "me"! I've discovered that "me" is happy and sad and angry and confused and hopeful and discouraged and frightened and courageous and . . .

In a way, I'm sorry I can't end this story by telling you that I "lived happily ever after." But I'm only sixteen years old, so this isn't anywhere near the end. Anyway, that happily ever after stuff is for kids and fairy tales. This is real life, my life. Oh, I'll never forget what my father did, and I'll never forget the pain. But I'm going to keep working at understanding myself and what happened, because I firmly believe that with work and persistence, life will be better. I have lots of hope for the future thanks to Mrs. Winston and Patty O'Neill and Andrea and Nina and Cathy and Mom and . . . well, you know, thanks to everyone who helped me and everyone who cared.

SUPPORT PEOPLE I CAN DEPEND ON

	Name	Telephone #
Therapist/Counselor		
24-Hour Crisis Line		
Victim Witness Advocate		
Child Interview Specialist		
Assistant District Attorney		
Police Officer		
Doctor		
Friend		
Friend		

HOW IT HAPPENED FOR ME: A DIAGRAM

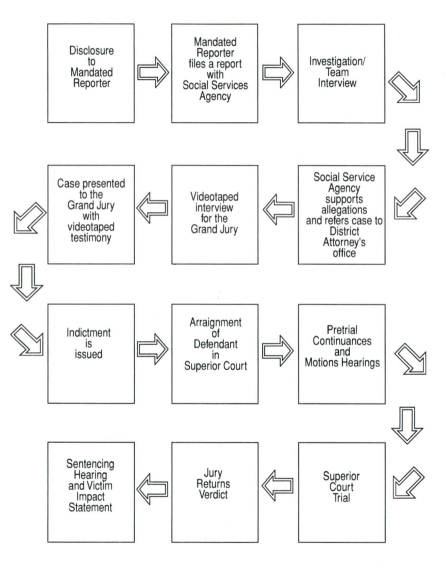

Chapter 6

A Teenage Boy's Personal Account of Child Sexual Abuse from Disclosure Through Prosecution and Treatment

IDENTIFICATION OF CHARACTERS

Bob: Joe's neighbor and youth club leader. He was accused of sexually abusing Joe.

Mr. Burger: The district attorney on *Perry Mason*, the television show.

Dr. Catherine Clayton (Cathy): Joe's therapist.

Dan: Joe's high school friend.

Dave: Joe's friend in his physical education class.

Ms. Feldman: Joe's high school guidance counselor.

Joy: Joe's high school friend.

Andrew Kane (Drew): The victim witness advocate from the district attorney's office who worked with Joe and his family throughout the prosecution process.

Lisa Lance-White: The child interview specialist from the district attorney's office who met with Joe and conducted the investigative interviews.

Mr. McCarthy: The defense attorney for Bob.

Patrick O'Neill (Pat): The DSS (Department of Social Services) social worker who investigated Joe's disclosure of sexual abuse.

Detective Anthony Rapucci: The local police officer who was part of the team that investigated the allegations against Bob.

Nina Santiago: The assistant district attorney who was in charge of prosecuting the case against Bob.

Mr. Stone: Joe's physical education teacher. The first person Joe told about the sexual abuse.

SECTION 1. I'M JOE

I'm Joe. I'm sixteen years old, and a junior in high school. I was sexually abused when I was a kid by someone who I thought was my very best friend.

Bob moved into my neighborhood when I was eight. He bought the house on the corner and right away started fixing up his basement. Lots of guys from the neighborhood would hang around on Saturdays and watch him. Sometimes he'd let us help with small stuff like sawing and pounding nails. He built an awesome "rec room" with a pool table, pinball machine, a big-screen TV for video games, and a bar with a Budweiser sign that lit up. He even had an old-fashioned jukebox and lots of old records. We used to give him a hard time about being an "oldie but a goodie." In the spring, we talked Bob into being a youth leader for our neighborhood club. We figured that way we would get to see him more often.

Bob was about forty and divorced. He used to always say how much he missed his family, and that being around the guys made him feel better. My mom said she thought it was strange that Bob didn't seem to have a woman friend, because Mom thought he was handsome and very nice. But Bob said he worked too much and didn't have time for women. I never knew what Bob worked too much doing, but he wore a suit, carried a black briefcase, and took the bus downtown every weekday.

Sometimes the guys would go over to his house on weeknights, especially after the Jefferson Avenue Neighborhood Club meetings. But mostly we went over on Saturdays. Being with Bob was always fun. We played games and goofed around and talked. Bob was great. He was someone I could really talk to. My dad worked downtown, too, and he was usually pretty tired when he came home. But Bob was never too tired for me. Bob was like a friend, and he was like a dad, too. Bob always had time for all the guys. He took us places, bought us presents, and gave us a place to just "hang out."

The refrigerator and cabinets in Bob's rec room were always over-flowing with candy and snacks. On Saturdays he would make a special trip to the store and buy whatever we wanted to eat. It became a contest: Who could come up with the grossest snack food? Sometimes Bob gave us money. He said we could buy food and cassette tapes and games with the money if we wanted to, and we could bring them over to share.

One Saturday morning, I noticed a dirty magazine on the bar. I checked it out and then showed it to the other guys. When Bob saw what we were up to, he acted a little strange. He said some grown-up friends had been over the night before and the magazine had been left out by accident. He took it away from me. But about a month later, more magazines showed up. From then on, Bob started to get physical with us. Only at his house, though. Never at our neighborhood club meetings. He was like a different guy at the meetings. You know, distant. And then at home he was so friendly and warm.

Bob said he was teaching us about sex so we would be prepared for dating. He said learning about sex was for our own good. It went on for years, and Bob made us promise never to tell anyone about our "private club," and especially never to tell about our "activities."

I liked the attention Bob gave me, and the sex part felt really good sometimes. I was almost thirteen when I stopped going to Bob's. I don't remember why I stopped, but I just did. I was confused and really depressed because Bob and I couldn't be friends anymore. I missed him. I missed all the fun we had. But I kept my promise. I didn't tell . . . for what seemed like a long, long time I didn't tell. But then I did.

SECTION 2. THE FIRST TIME I TOLD

I still don't know why I told Mr. Stone, my ninth grade physical education teacher. It was early November, and my class was outside running track. Mr. Stone was talking to us about something, and all of a sudden it was like I wasn't there anymore. I was remembering riding by Bob's house on Saturday with my dad. It was like there was this video playing in my head. I saw a bunch of little kids, eight and nine-year-old guys, from around the neighborhood at Bob's. They were getting into the back of his van. Then I realized I couldn't hear what Mr. Stone was saying anymore. His mouth was moving, but I didn't hear any sounds. I started to feel sick to my stomach and dizzy. My head ached. I must have looked dazed, or something, because Dave, the guy next to me, elbowed me and asked if I was okay. I didn't answer him, but just turned away, and started walking across the football field. I don't know where I was going. Dave came after me. He kept asking what was wrong. I kept walking.

Then Mr. Stone came running after me. "Joe. Joe." He was calling to me. It sounded like his voice was calling from a tunnel, all hollow and echoey. He finally caught up to me and put his hand on my shoulder. His touch startled me out of my daze.

Mr. Stone was taller than me, and he had to bend down so he could see into my eyes. "Joe," he said, "What is it? Can I help you?"

I couldn't answer at first. I looked from his face to the ground. I shuffled my feet around, and then, I don't know why, but I just kind of blurted it out. "I was molested by Bob." For a minute after I said it, everything seemed so quiet and still I thought for sure the world had ended. But it didn't. I was still there. Mr. Stone was still there.

Then I kind of started to cry. Mr. Stone just kept saying, "It's okay, Joe. It's okay." He put his arm around me, but that felt horrible to me. I don't know why it felt so bad because Mr. Stone was really nice. But I managed to squirm away from his arm without saying how bad it felt. He maybe understood even if I didn't because he didn't touch me again.

We sat on the field for awhile. I was nervously pulling at the grass, twisting it in my hands, and tossing it into the air. Finally Mr. Stone asked, "Joe, who is Bob?"

"He was my neighbor and the youth leader for the Jefferson Avenue Club," I said. "Bob was my best friend . . . the little guys I saw at his house . . . they looked so small and helpless . . . I wonder why Bob isn't my friend anymore . . . Oh no." I covered my face with my hands and started to cry. I didn't want to cry, but I couldn't stop it. The tears seeped through my fingers. He could see me crying, I just knew it.

Mr. Stone talked to me very quietly and calmly. He said it was okay to cry. He said guys my age had all kinds of thoughts and emotions going on all the time, and we needed to cry sometimes. But, I felt ashamed, anyway. I wished I could sink into the ground and disappear from this place. I didn't want anyone to see me. I didn't want the other guys to know I was crying. I mean, how embarrassing. I especially didn't want anyone to know about me and Bob. What would all the kids say about me? Why did I tell Mr. Stone? Oh no, why did I tell when I promised Bob I wouldn't?

Mr. Stone called Dave over and asked him to tell the class to "hit the showers" and wait in the locker room for the bell. After the guys left, Mr. Stone and I walked into the school building and went to the counseling office. I kept staring at the ground and didn't say a word. I was upset about Bob, for sure, and confused about what he did . . . about what I did. Almost like he could read my mind, Mr. Stone said I did the right thing by telling him about Bob. He said I was brave. It was nice of him to be encouraging, but really, I was so ashamed about making such a scene at school, and so angry at myself for breaking my promise to Bob, that I wasn't feeling "brave."

My guidance counselor, Ms. Feldman, was able to see me right away. It was nice of Mr. Stone to stay around; since he was the first person I told, I just sort of needed him to be there with me. Mr. Stone explained that my high school had standard procedures about how to handle a **disclosure** of sexual abuse and that Ms. Feldman would call the principal, who came quickly to the guidance office after he was called. I felt embarrassed about all the attention I was getting from these adults . . . for such a terrible reason, besides. And I sort of felt like I must be in a lot of trouble because the principal was there. They all assured me that I was not in trouble and I didn't do anything wrong. Ms. Feldman said that telling about what happened with Bob was "right," not "wrong" in any sense.

Since Bob was our youth leader, as well as being my neighbor and friend, the principal said he was in the role of "caretaker." And he said that the Commonwealth has a **mandated reporting law** and a report needed to be filed with the **Department of Social Services (DSS).** "But," the principal said, "I think I should notify your parents first, if you feel okay about me doing that." I nodded. And so, he called my parents. He told my mom and dad it was an emergency, and asked them to come to school right away. Dad wasn't able to leave work, but Mom arrived about thirty minutes later. I waited for her in Ms. Feldman's office. I was really nervous. Ms. Feldman and Mr. Stone and the principal were totally super to me. But I was too upset and confused to be consoled by much of anything.

SECTION 3. I'M SORRY

Mom arrived to find me sitting in Ms. Feldman's office, staring at the floor, bending and unbending the paper cup I held in my hands. Mom right away said she was worried and confused about this emergency especially because she didn't know what it was all about. When she saw the principal, she asked me if I was in some kind of trouble.

Ms. Feldman answered her question. "No, Joe's not in any trouble. But today during his P.E. class, Joe told Mr. Stone that he had been sexually molested by Bob, his neighbor and youth leader." I was looking up at Mom from the corner of my eye. I realized how important it was for me that my parents believed me.

I could tell Mom was genuinely shocked when she said, "What? Bob?"

She looked at me, and I nodded. "I'm sorry, Mom," I mumbled.

Mom started to cry. "Oh no, Joe," she said. "I'm so sorry. I never should have let you spend so much time with him. But he seemed like such a nice man, and so dedicated to you boys."

The principal continued the discussion. "Our school has procedures in place for handling the disclosure of sexual abuse. Since Mr. Stone is a **mandated reporter,** we are required by law to file an official report with DSS." Then the principal told Mom it was important for my family to be supportive of me, particularly if we intended to follow through with prosecution.

I don't think I've ever seen my mom react so quickly. She jumped out of her chair, and was almost yelling, "Of course we intend to prosecute!" Then she asked to use the phone to call my father. I felt so relieved and grateful . . . Mom believed me.

Dad managed to get away from work when he heard what the emergency was about. He was so mad that I heard him yell, "What? Bob did what?" through the telephone receiver. Dad arrived at school within the hour.

Dad was really upset, I could tell because his face was red and his forehead was wrinkled. Mom was crying, and I was still staring at the floor. What a scene. But, you know, in spite of all the upset and confusion, I must admit, it was a relief to have let out the secret.

I still felt kind of sad and guilty about telling on Bob, though. I didn't want him to get into any trouble. I loved Bob. He was my friend.

SECTION 4. MAKING A REPORT

While Mr. Stone and the principal were filing the report with DSS over the telephone, my guidance counselor, Ms. Feldman, explained some things to my parents and me about what would happen next. Even though I couldn't look at her, and couldn't really even listen to her, she explained anyway.

Ms. Feldman told us that once a report was received and evaluated a **social worker** would be assigned to my case. Then DSS would have ten days to investigate. Although they legally had ten days to investigate, Ms. Feldman said that a social worker might be in touch with us sooner.

She said that the next several days could be particularly stressful for me. Then she gave me this telephone number for a twenty-four-hour **crisis line,** "just in case" I needed to talk to someone. Like I wanted anyone else to know about this! I was embarrassed enough now that Mr. Stone, Ms. Feldman, the principal, and my parents knew. I mean, what was going to happen when the kids at school found out? They would think I was some weird pervert; I just knew it. And probably none of the other guys from Bob's would want to hang around with me anymore. They would think I was a snitch. And I was sure no one would want to go out on dates with me because I was abused and damaged. This was a terrible mess I'd gotten into.

I wanted to disappear, or run away maybe . . . go someplace new, change my name and start over. But instead, I went home with Mom and Dad, knowing that the DSS social worker would call in a few days to schedule a meeting with me.

When we got home, I went right to my room and turned on a CD—loud! I was trying to drown out Dad's yelling downstairs. He was so mad. I was so ashamed and so scared and so confused. I just sat and stared out the window, tapping my fingers on my desk. After all Bob had done for me, I still couldn't believe I had betrayed him. I didn't know what I was going to do, what was going to happen. I felt like I was being torn in two. Part of me felt so relieved that I had told. Part of me wished I had never said a word.

I was very tense, and when Mom called me for dinner a couple hours later, I almost jumped out of my chair. We ate dinner. No one said anything. Except for the quiet, everything at home seemed just the same as usual. And everything was the same, except inside of me.

I was different inside. I knew that it was important for me to let people know about Bob because I just could not get the picture of all those little guys in his van out of my mind. I was scared about what was going to happen next, but I was sad, too. I remembered how much I loved Bob, and how much I thought he loved me. Bob had a way of making me feel so special.

After dinner that night I met a bunch of guys and played basketball for awhile. At first I tried to watch TV, but I was too nervous to sit still, and I knew I had to move around. Basketball was good, but boxing would've been better. I wanted to punch Bob right in the face. Why did he do this to me? When I got home that night I started to cry again. I thought I should be tougher, but I just couldn't help it.

SECTION 5. THE INVESTIGATION BEGINS

One of the hardest parts of the whole prosecution process was all the waiting. Especially waiting and not knowing what was going to happen to me, to Bob, to the other kids, and to my mom and dad.

Fortunately, at the beginning, I didn't have to wait very long before the **investigation** started happening. It was only three days later, although it seemed like ages, when Patrick O'Neill, my DSS social worker, called me at home. I was very nervous. He was very nice. He said I could call him "Pat."

First thing, Pat asked me how I was doing.

"OK."

Then he asked me if I understood why he was calling me. I knew all right, but it was a hard question to answer. He repeated the question, "Joe, do you know why I'm calling you this afternoon?

"Because of Bob," I whispered into the phone. "Because I told Mr. Stone that Bob had sex with me."

"Yes," Pat said. Then he explained his role as my DSS social worker and the procedures.

In the middle of his explanation, I just blurted out this question that had been haunting my mind . . . for years probably. "Why did Bob do this to me?"

Patrick O'Neill was quiet for a minute, then he said, "I know this isn't a very good answer, Joe, but it's the only true answer I know." He took a very deep breath, kind of like a sigh, and continued. "The truth is, I don't know why Bob did these things to you. But I do know you did the right thing by telling us. So now we can stop Bob and help you. But Bob really needs help, too, so he doesn't hurt you or any other kids ever again."

I nodded in response, but of course Pat could not see my nod over the phone.

"Joe? Joe, are you still there?"

"Yeah, I'm here. I just don't understand."

"I'm really sorry I can't give you a better answer right now, Joe. But maybe as we get to know more about Bob we'll all understand this better."

"Yeah, yeah sure," I said. "It's OK."

Then Pat started to talk about this **team interview,** which he wanted to schedule as soon as possible. To him, soon meant within the next day or two. He said it was an important part of the DSS investigation, and it's done as a "team" so I won't have to be interviewed too many times by too many different people. He said, "We use the team interview here because we think it makes things easier for you and is better for the investigation. But in other places they do the interviewing differently, because they think other ways are easier for kids."

Pat went on to explain that they gather all the people who need to know what happened. This includes my investigative social worker, Patrick O'Neill, the **assistant district attorney,** the **victim witness advocate,** the **child interview specialist,** a police officer, and a **therapist** from a local mental health clinic.

I almost had a heart attack on the spot when I realized I would have to say what Bob did in front of all those people, but Pat calmed me down right away. He said that I would only have to tell one person at the interview, and that would be the child interview specialist. The others would observe the interview from behind a two-way mirror. They would be able to see me and hear me, but I wouldn't be able to see or hear them. Telling one person sounded better, but I still didn't like the idea of more people knowing. It was embarrassing enough already, and the more people who knew, the more embarrassed I felt. I mean really, what was going to happen when the kids at school found out? I was really afraid and ashamed, I felt like I was shrinking. I was glad about that actually. I kept hoping that maybe I would totally disappear.

But Pat said if we were going to stop this type of abuse from happening to other kids, the people from the different agencies needed to know what happened to me. And, that meant that we needed to do the team interview. It was kind of cool that he said, "WE." I didn't feel so alone.

I knew that Pat and I needed to talk this over with Mom and Dad, but I also knew that my parents wanted Bob to be prosecuted. So, I knew the team interview would be happening. It was just a matter of time . . . a short time.

SECTION 6. THE INTERVIEW

About 5:30 that same afternoon, Patrick O'Neill called back. He had called Dad at work and he wanted to let me know about the team interview. It was scheduled for 3:00 the next afternoon at the district attorney's office. They have a special Child Unit set up there to handle all the child abuse cases in the county.

Dad went with me to the **interview.** We arrived about ten minutes early. Pat was there and it was comforting to see him. I felt a little bit better with him around because he had been so nice to me already. But I really couldn't get over how scary this was, and how exciting it was at the same time. I was amazed. All these important people, and my dad, were here because of me.

Everyone on the team was already meeting in a big conference room with a very long table and lots of chairs. At 3:00 p.m. this woman, Lisa, came out to the reception area where Dad and I were waiting. She was my interviewer. When she shook my hand, I did manage to glance up at her face. I was surprised to see that she looked very friendly. She said, "Hi, Joe. I'm Lisa Lance-White."

I mumbled, "Hello."

She smiled at me, and said, "I'll be conducting the interview with you today."

I mumbled again, "OK."

After another few minutes, Lisa and I went into a small, very neat room. In the room were two chairs, a small table, sort of like a coffee table, this huge mirror that covered one whole wall, and a box of tissues. It was weird, you know, sort of uncomfortable, to see myself in the mirror. I felt totally self-conscious. Lisa explained that the people on the team were on the other side of the mirror, and they could see and hear us. She said she thought it might be easier for me to talk with only her in the room. I knew it wasn't going to be easy for me, it didn't matter who was there.

Before the interview started, Lisa explained why certain people needed to observe. Pat would be observing as a part of his investigation for DSS. In his report, Pat needed to indicate whether or not he **supported the allegations** of the sexual abuse. The assistant district attorney would be making **prosecution** decisions, and the victim witness advocate would be concerned about how I'm feeling and reacting to all of this. I wasn't sure what it all meant, but I was sure this interview was important. As hard as it was for me to talk about Bob and the sexual abuse, I had to tell the truth. I had been dreaming about Bob . . . about those little guys in the van. Bob had to stop.

Then Lisa started asking questions. I was nervous. I couldn't focus my thoughts very well. I felt sick. I felt weird. I felt like crying. For awhile I didn't think I could breathe. Lisa asked me if I could speak louder. And then she asked me to tell exactly what Bob did. I didn't say it all. I could never say it all. But I made myself say some of it. Saying the words "penis" and "anus," talking about Bob and me and the other guys in the neighborhood club, made me feel ashamed and guilty. I know I mumbled. I'm very sure I stared at the floor most of the time, and shuffled my feet around a lot. I noticed some smudges on my new sneakers and a piece of string on the floor. Lisa had on black shoes. I remember. And then I didn't even realize it, but I started to cry. I covered my eyes because I didn't want anyone to know. Lisa noticed and she told me it was definitely OK to cry, but I tried not to.

Lisa was very understanding about me being so upset and nervous. She told me I was brave. I looked at her then, really confused, because I didn't feel anything resembling "brave" at that moment. But later I realized that buried somewhere deep underneath my confusion and upset, I felt proud of myself for being strong enough to do something to stop Bob.

After the interview, Lisa explained what would happen next. She said that if Dad and I wanted to talk with the team today, we could wait in the reception area while they reviewed my interview. We could meet with them today or later, separately or together. There was "no pressure," she said. It was totally my choice. I talked it over with Dad, and we decided to stay and meet my team.

SECTION 7. AFTER THE INTERVIEW

I wandered around the reception area for about twenty minutes while Dad tried to look calm and read a magazine he had taken out of his briefcase. I felt best about meeting with the team with Dad in the room, so when Lisa came out to get me, Dad and I went into the big conference room together. It was hard to be with all these people because I felt ashamed that they knew such private things about me. It was a struggle to even look at them, but when I did, I was surprised to see kind faces.

All the people in the room explained their job responsibilities to me, and what they would do next regarding my case. It was hard for me to understand everything they said. But it was mostly hard for me to even listen because I was so distracted by my own upset and embarrassment. But everyone was nice and patient. It was clear they were used to working with kids and that they knew what they were doing. I got the feeling that they were all on my side.

Patrick O'Neill spoke first. He said there was enough evidence to support the allegations of child sexual abuse in his report for DSS. Then the Assistant District Attorney, Nina Santiago, talked about the prosecution process. She explained that with my testimony, there appeared to be enough evidence to proceed with the criminal prosecution of Bob. She said the Commonwealth of Massachusetts would file the charges against him in **superior court.** She was careful to explain that I would not be responsible for taking Bob to court because the commonwealth is responsible for prosecuting people who commit crimes. But in order for the case to go forward, I needed to be willing to be a **witness.** My next interview would be videotaped and presented to the **grand jury.** Nina said my testimony would be taped so I would not have to say what happened live, in person, in front of the members of the grand jury.

I asked her what a grand jury was.

She said it was a jury of citizens who consider evidence brought before the superior court and decide if there is cause to believe a crime has been committed.

I told her I'd never heard of a "grand jury."

And so Nina explained more about it. She said that not all states have grand juries, and in those states, the **probable cause hearing** takes place before a judge. She also said that sometimes the states that do have grand juries don't use them for child abuse cases. "It is one of those legal procedures that really varies from state to state," she said. "And since we do have the grand jury here, we must present the evidence for your case to them. The videotaping of your **testimony** will hopefully make that part of the process easier for you, Joe. But, if the case goes to trial, you need to be able and willing to **testify** in court."

This information and my emotions were overwhelming. Although my team was very nice, they were also very serious about wanting Bob to take responsibility for what he did. I asked what would happen to Bob if the case went forward. My victim witness advocate, Andrew Kane, explained that there were a variety of possible **dispositions** of a criminal case, and that he and Nina would seek my input about what I would like to see happen if Bob were found **guilty.**

While Andrew was talking, I couldn't keep my eyes off of the police officer, Detective Rapucci. I wasn't planning to say anything, but I just blurted out the question anyway. "Are you going to arrest Bob?" I was upset about the possibility of Bob going to jail, and at the same time, that's exactly what I wanted to happen to him.

Detective Rapucci said he would not be arresting Bob at this time. He said he might ask Bob some questions, and would probably seek a warrant to search Bob's house for photographs and additional evidence, but would discuss everything with the assistant district attorney before deciding whether an arrest should be made.

Andrew continued the discussion by saying there would be time to talk about what might happen to Bob, and that my feelings would certainly be considered.

The next person to speak was the therapist from the mental health clinic. She said it was clear that this experience was upsetting for me, and assured me that upset was a normal reaction under the circumstances. I was relieved to be "normal." But then I started to cry when the therapist suggested that it might be helpful for me to talk with a counselor who works with kids my age. I was confused. A second ago I was "normal," and now I felt like there was something wrong with me because they wanted me to go to a **counselor.** I wondered if maybe these people thought I was crazy. I asked, kind of angry about it, and they all said they didn't think I was crazy. Patrick reminded me how important it would be for me to talk about my feelings and fears with someone I trusted.

Then Dad spoke for the first time. He said, "Joe's mother and I have already been looking into therapy for Joe, for all of us actually. We think it's important for Joe to have as much support through this process as we can provide for him."

I just looked at Dad, totally surprised. I didn't think that my parents believed too much in therapy. But everyone said they were pleased to hear there would be additional support in my life during this difficult time.

I wasn't sure how I felt about it, and I asked, "What if I don't want to go to a counselor?"

Dad said that I could think about it, and that I didn't have to do anything I didn't want to do.

"OK." That made me feel better about it. It felt important for me to be able to decide.

Dad asked the team if he and I could have a few minutes alone together to talk things over, so everyone left the room. Although a public trial would for sure be a hard experience for me, Dad and I decided that going forward with prosecution was the right thing to do. I'm telling you, I just could not get the picture of those little guys getting into Bob's van out of my mind. I wanted to make sure that he was stopped from hurting any more boys. Only God knew how many boys Bob had already abused. Dad agreed. We needed to stop Bob. But Dad also wanted me to know that his first priority was to help me. "Whatever you want to do, Joe."

I got a little teary when Dad said that, but I looked away because I didn't want him to know. I said I wanted to stop Bob.

When the team returned, Dad told them that we would cooperate with the district attorney's office in preparing the case against Bob for trial. They were all very businesslike as one by one, they thanked us.

Before we left the office, Andrew scheduled an appointment for me to come back to videotape the interview of my testimony for the grand jury. Then he said, "The police will begin an investigation, and they might be in contact with some of the other guys from the Neighborhood Club."

I just nodded, wondering again what I had done.

Andrew gave me his business card, and told me I could call him if I had any questions about the legal process, or didn't understand something that happened, or even if I just wanted to talk to somebody. I put his card in my backpack along with Pat's. Having their telephone numbers with me all the time helped me feel safe somehow.

As Dad and I were leaving the office, Andrew shook our hands and said he would be in touch very soon. He said it was his job to answer my questions, explain the court process, provide support to me and my family, and keep me notified of the case status. He also said that he had originally hoped to explain the court process to me that afternoon, but it seemed like too much for one day. "Another time, then, OK?" he asked.

That was fine with me.

Andrew looked right at me, and assured me he would be there for me. And I believed him.

SECTION 8. COUNSELING

I went to school the next couple days, and being there was a relief. I wanted to forget all about Bob and abuse and going to court. I wanted to pretend that everything was just fine with me.

I hadn't told any of my friends or teachers what was going on. But I knew I needed to talk to some of the other guys who were at Bob's with me. And I knew I needed to talk to them soon. I just didn't know what to say. I wanted them to agree with my decision to testify against Bob. But what if they didn't? What if they protected Bob and said I lied? After all, we all took an oath never to tell.

I didn't know what to do. I was afraid if I told even one friend that all the other kids would find out and then they would tease me. They might think it was all my fault, or that I wanted Bob to have sex with me. I didn't think I was overreacting, because I know how mean kids can be to each other. They can get ahold of any piece of information and torment a guy to death with it. I've seen it. I know. Every time I started to imagine what they were going to say about me, or what they were going to do to me, I shuddered. I felt afraid and ashamed.

My parents convinced me that seeing a therapist was a good idea. I guess I did need to talk to someone. I went to see Dr. Catherine Clayton. She said I could call her "Cathy." I liked that better than calling her "Doctor."

During that first appointment, I couldn't talk much about anything. I stared out the window, and at the floor. I fidgeted. I didn't want to look at Cathy at all. She didn't say anything about my nervous behavior, and when the time was up I scheduled another appointment for two days later. I didn't know how this was going to help me, especially if I couldn't or didn't talk about anything, but having the appointment made me feel better.

When I was leaving the office, Cathy gave me her business card with her telephone number on it. She told me I could call her any time, day or night, if I wanted to talk to her . . . or if I wanted her to talk to me. I smiled—I actually smiled—when I put Cathy's card into my backpack with Patrick's and Andrew's. I felt like I had a whole team of people in there helping me get through this.

During my next appointment with Cathy, I was calmer. I had made a list of things I wanted to talk about. My questions were written on a piece of paper that was folded about thirty times and stuffed into the inside pocket of my jacket.

First on my list was what to do about feeling so isolated. I still hadn't told anyone. Although I didn't want to feel so alone, I also didn't want anyone else to know. But I knew it wasn't going to be a secret for long. I mean, there were a lot of other guys at Bob's. I saw him abusing them, just like he did to me. I knew I needed to deal with this before the police talked to the other kids. But maybe they already talked to them, and the other guys were feeling the same worries as me about talking to anyone else. This situation seemed liked a volcano getting ready to explode, and I wanted to be braced for it.

Second on my list was my mixed emotions about what I called my "sexual identity." It was confusing to me because I liked being around girls, but lots of times the sexual experiences with Bob felt really good. I didn't know what it meant, but I wondered if it meant that I was gay.

And then I started to worry about "practical" things. Like what if Bob had AIDS, or some other sexually transmitted disease. When I thought about AIDS, I started to panic, so I tried not to think about it.

I was so ashamed about all of this that sometimes I wanted to hide out, or be invisible maybe. I figured people could tell that I'd had all those sexual experiences for all those years just by looking at me. I felt ruined.

I still couldn't figure out why Bob did this to me, and to all the other kids. I asked Cathy "Why?" over and over. It was too hard for me to understand. I kept wishing it didn't happen.

Finally I managed to tell Cathy that I had been feeling so terrible and nervous when I was alone at night that I actually thought I might rather be dead than to feel this way. I thought maybe she would be surprised by this because I had been trying to hide my real feelings, and thought I was being "totally cool" about it all. But I wasn't feeling all that cool. I was having these horrible nightmares. I also wasn't sure if I did the right thing by telling, or if I was doing the right thing by planning to testify. I felt guilty. Bob might go to jail, and maybe it wasn't his fault. I mean he didn't force me. I liked what we did. I liked how it made me feel. It was hard for me to admit, but sometimes I wanted him to do it. Lots of times I even called him to get together.

I told Cathy I wasn't sure if I felt like swearing or crying. She said it was fine to go ahead and do either or both, but I was too embarrassed.

Cathy sat quietly while I went down my list of questions and concerns, which I read pretty fast, stumbling over a lot of my scribbled words. When I finally finished, I looked up at her over the crumpled piece of paper I held in my hands, and she smiled at me. Then she leaned forward a little bit and she said, "Joe, I can see that you are feeling nervous and sad and confused about all of this. And before I say anything else, I want to tell you that it is completely normal under these circumstances to be experiencing all of those feelings."

What a relief! I breathed, I think, for the first time since I came into her office that day. I felt myself relax a little.

Cathy continued. "Your list is terrific, Joe. I can see that you worked very hard putting it together, and I know it took a lot of strength to put your thoughts and feelings onto paper and bring them here."

Then she said that dealing with sexual abuse issues was tough for everyone, and that it was "a real act of courage" for me to tell Mr. Stone about Bob.

Cathy also said she was glad I trusted her enough to bring my list to her. She said we would talk about whatever I wanted whenever I wanted, whether it was on the list or not. "We can talk about the details of the abuse when you feel ready to do that, Joe. That will be an important part of our work together. But it's also important for us to talk about your reactions to what is happening in your life right now regarding the trial, as well as your relationships with your family and your friends, and the experiences you are having at school." It felt good not to be pressured to talk about what Bob did right then.

Unfortunately, Cathy didn't think we'd be able to answer all of my questions in that hour on that day. I was upset about this because I really wanted the answers. But she asked me to say where I wanted to begin, and we would begin. And so we did. It was hard to talk about my feelings. My fear about doing this was huge. But I made myself do it as best as I could. Somewhere deep down inside, I knew it was important to get my feelings out of me and into the world. Cathy helped me to talk by asking me clear and direct questions.

The hour passed quickly, but it was a hard time for me. We decided I would come to see her on Mondays and Thursdays for the next month. That way, Cathy said, I wouldn't feel so isolated and alone.

Because I didn't talk about it, and because Cathy knew that wanting to be dead rather than deal with all of this on my list, she said she wanted to take some extra time before I left to talk a bit about those feelings, if that was OK with me.

"That's OK," I said, but I couldn't look at her. I was too ashamed.

Cathy suggested that I keep the telephone number of the twenty-four-hour crisis line Ms. Feldman gave me handy at all times. She encouraged me to use it, to talk to someone there, especially another teenager, if I wanted. She reminded me that everything I said would be kept absolutely private. Cathy asked me to promise that the next time I felt so bad, I would call her, no matter what time.

"Yeah, OK," I promised, but I knew I wouldn't. I didn't want to bother her.

I couldn't believe what she said then. "Honestly, Joe, anytime will be fine to call. You won't be bothering me at all. If I'm tied up when you call, I'll get back to you just as soon as I can."

I nodded, but inside I thought, "She read my mind."

Cathy suggested that I put the crisis line telephone number and her telephone number on a piece of paper right next to my bed so they would be there for me at night when I was feeling scared and alone.

SECTION 9. PROSECUTION BEGINS

The next week, my victim witness advocate, Andrew Kane—he said everyone called him Drew and that I could, too, if I wanted—called from the district attorney's office. He wanted to follow up on our meeting and to answer any questions I might have. He also wanted to explain the investigation, interview, and court processes to me.

But before doing any of that, Drew asked me how I was feeling. He asked about my therapy, "How's that counseling going?"

"OK."

Drew said that he knew this was really hard for me. He assured me that the case would only be brought to trial if my therapist, my parents and I thought it was advisable for me. Everyone wanted to make sure I would be OK, and that the court process was the right choice for me.

We confirmed a date for making a videotape to present to the grand jury. Then Drew offered me some options for talking about the details of the prosecution process. He said we could talk on the phone, or meet earlier on the day of the interview, or I could come into the office for a separate meeting. I decided I wanted to come in to his office to see him, so we scheduled a meeting for the next day after school.

When we got together the next afternoon, Drew explained more about the grand jury. He said, "The grand jury consists of a group of citizens who are registered to vote in our county. They are called for jury duty and are assigned to review the evidence for superior court cases for about three months. Their job is to hear evidence on serious cases to determine if the case should go forward into the superior court system."

He continued, "Nina will present the case against Bob to the grand jury, and then the jury will watch the videotape of your testimony. Neither Bob nor his lawyer will be here. And because your testimony is on tape, you don't have to be there either. After the grand jury reviews the evidence, they vote on whether or not they think there is sufficient evidence to prosecute. If they think YES, they issue an **indictment.** If they think NO, this case is closed."

All these legal terms sounded like a foreign language to me, and I was pretty confused. So confused actually, that I didn't know what to ask when Drew wanted to know if I had any questions.

He went on to explain about the **criminal justice system.** He said it was designed to protect the rights of the accused, which was Bob. He was accused of sexually abusing me. Drew reminded me of the phrase we learned in junior high civics class, **"presumed innocent** until proven guilty." The assistant district attorney had to convince a trial **jury,** beyond a **reasonable doubt,** that Bob was guilty of abusing me.

Drew told me that the criminal court system is designed for adults and that it sometimes can be especially hard for kids. "Things can be said, things can happen," he said, "that kids don't understand. But I'm always here to help you, Joe. Please, just ask me. Anything. Feel free to ask me anything."

Finally I did manage to ask a few questions, just to see if I could make some sense of all that Drew was saying. Then I realized it would be helpful to write some things down in case I forgot, or so I could think about this and ask more questions later.

Before we ended the conversation, Drew reminded me again that it was OK for me to call him if I wanted to talk about the case or if I had any questions. I'm not really the type to ask a lot of questions or to call people, but it seemed that so far everyone—Pat, Cathy, Drew—kept inviting me, encouraging me to call whenever, and to ask whatever. I began to think that maybe I wouldn't be such a bother after all.

Drew reminded me again of my appointment with Lisa to videotape the grand jury interview. He also reminded me that it would only happen if I felt ready. He assured me I could decide if and when the time was right for the interview. Drew and Nina, the **ADA,** would be there observing the interview from behind the two-way mirror.

Drew said he would call my parents some time during the next few days to tell them what happens next and to answer their questions.

"Good-bye, Joe." Drew said as he walked me to the door of the office. "Take care. And call me. I'm here for you."

I felt some tears in my eyes. "Bye, Drew. And thanks," I said.

I stood outside the building for a long time, staring at the cars whizzing by. Everyone seemed to be going somewhere. That's where I wanted to go. Somewhere. Anywhere away from here. I suddenly felt furious that this was happening to me. Why? Why did I have to deal with this?

SECTION 10. PRETRIAL TESTIMONY

My mom went with me to the district attorney's office on the day we were making the videotape for the grand jury. These past few weeks had been a really hard time for my family. Mom and Dad had also been to see a therapist, and I felt guilty about that. I mean, if I had just kept quiet about Bob, everything would be just like it had been a month ago. Fine. Everything would be just fine. Cathy told me over and over that none of this was my fault, and that Mom and Dad going to a therapist was a good thing. It showed that they were committed to helping me. I was confused. Cathy helped me sort things out when I was confused.

Lisa, Drew, and Nina Santiago were all going to be a part of the interviewing process. Before beginning the taping, they spent some time just talking to me. Although I felt nervous beneath my "totally cool" act, I also felt like a very important person at a business meeting with other important people. I tried to act especially cool because I didn't want anyone to know I was really "totally nervous."

Drew asked me how I was feeling.

I said, "Fine."

He asked how my therapy was going and how I liked Cathy.

"Fine. Fine."

Drew wanted to make sure I would be OK if I gave my testimony that day, and when I told him I was ready, and would be seeing Cathy later, he said that was a "good plan." It was Cathy's idea for me to see her after the interview. That way I would feel "supported," she said.

The interview room was the same room I was in before when I talked to Lisa. Everything was just the same. I sat in a chair facing the mirror and the camera hiding behind it. Lisa spoke to the mirror and asked for the camera to be turned on. Drew and Nina were behind the mirror, so I guess one of them did it.

Lisa spoke to the camera. "Good afternoon. Today is December 8. My name is Lisa Lance-White from the district attorney's office. I'm here today meeting with Joe."

Then Lisa spoke to me. "Joe, do you understand that it is important for you to tell the truth when you answer the questions I'm going to ask you today?"

I answered, "Yes," but my voice was very soft because there was a huge lump in my throat, and Lisa asked me to speak louder. I said it again, "YES."

Then she asked, "Do you promise to tell the truth today, Joe?"

I replied, "Yes, I do." I felt a shiver go through my body. I shut my eyes tight and took a deep breath. I was really doing this!

Lisa began asking me some simple questions like my full name, my birthday, where I went to school, what grade I was in, my address, and Bob's address. While I was answering those questions, Lisa had to remind me a couple of times to speak up.

I was very nervous, and even laughed a couple of times during those first questions. I couldn't believe I laughed because it definitely was not a funny experience, but I was just so nervous and scared. I laughed, I think, to keep from crying. I actually clutched the arms of my chair the whole time, maybe so I wouldn't get up and run away.

And then came the hard questions. Lisa asked, "Joe, did something happen with your neighbor Bob? What happened? When did it begin? How often did it happen? Where did it happen? Who was there? When did it stop? . . ." As I answered these questions for Lisa, I remember reaching up and touching my face. It felt so hot.

It seemed like I was in the interview room answering these questions forever. I was surprised to find out that the whole thing only took about fifteen minutes.

At the end of the interview Lisa thanked me, and we went back out into the reception area to get Mom. Then we all met for a short time in the big conference room. Nina, Drew, and Lisa said that my testimony was "excellent." But all I cared about was that it was over. I just knew I did the right thing, and I felt so relieved.

Drew said he would call in a couple of days to discuss the next step. That's what I liked best about Drew, he kept me informed and he always called me when he said he would. That was so important because I really needed someone to count on.

When we left the office, Mom offered to take me to McDonald's, but I wasn't hungry. Later I went to see Cathy.

SECTION 11. COUNSELING SUPPORT

Have I mentioned how tired I was? During those weeks after I first told Mr. Stone about Bob, I was so tired all the time. Sometimes I felt sick and I didn't eat much. I was also very confused. Yes, for sure. I felt tired and sick and confused that afternoon when I went to see Cathy.

I know it's hard for people to understand, but I loved Bob, and I felt guilty about turning him in. And now my testimony was on videotape. A grand jury was going to hear what Bob did to me. I was embarrassed even thinking about it. I was also sad because I didn't want Bob to get into any trouble, and I didn't want Bob to be mad at me.

When I saw Cathy I told her I wasn't sure that I should be involved in the prosecution process.

Cathy said she understood my confusion. That afternoon she helped me to understand it too, and to accept being confused. I wanted everything in my life to be fine and smooth and simple, and for everyone I knew, including Bob, to be happy. I felt like such a troublemaker.

Cathy said it was OK for me to love Bob and to still want him to take responsibility for his actions. After all, Bob abused me. "Bob has some problems, Joe, and he needs help," Cathy said. "However," she continued, "what he did was also a crime. Legally it was wrong, and morally it was wrong." She explained that the child abuse laws were made to protect me, and that I, and all those other "little guys" I kept mentioning, had a right to be protected. Cathy and everyone at the district attorney's office had a way of making me feel important. Since they believed that I had "rights," I came to believe it, too.

Pat O'Neill told me, and Lisa told me and Drew told me that if testifying felt too hard for me, I could withdraw from the process and stop the prosecution at any time. Although other guys might come forward and be willing to testify, for the time being, I was the primary witness. Without my cooperation, there was really no case.

Cathy reminded me again that feeling reluctant about the court process is normal. Then she said, "Know that you do have a choice about testifying, Joe."

I left Cathy's office feeling less tired, but I was definitely lost in thought about what she told me. I was "important." I had "rights." I could "choose." I felt better because I knew I had some control over my life.

SECTION 12. WAITING

The holiday season came and went. I hardly noticed. However, I did notice that those weeks after my interview seemed endless. I think the time seemed longer than it really was because I didn't know what was happening. And mostly it didn't seem that anything was happening. But, even though I couldn't tell, the justice system was, in fact, operating.

Some of the time I was kind of in a panic, and I think I called either Drew or Nina or both of them at least once a day to see how my case was going. I needed to know. Nina was in court a lot, so sometimes she couldn't call me back right away and I would panic even more, worrying that she forgot me. But Drew always called me, and even though he sometimes didn't have much new information, just talking to him helped me to calm down.

Then finally, one day after school, Drew called. *The Commonwealth of Massachusetts vs. Bob* would be heard by the grand jury the following Tuesday. "And then shortly after that," he said, "we'll know if an indictment will be issued." I felt a surge of excitement rush through my body that shot like an electric current up and down my back and through my legs and arms.

But when I hung up the phone I went numb. I sat in the living room for a long time waiting for my parents to come home from work. As the sun went down I watched the house get dark, and the shadows appear. I never even turned on the lights. I wasn't even sure if I could move. The only sound I noticed was the ticking of the clock.

Waiting . . . waiting . . . it seemed like forever.

SECTION 13. AT SCHOOL

Some days it was great to go to school. The distraction of school was good. But some days I didn't want to go. Sometimes it felt best to put on my earphones, turn up the music—loud—and just walk. It didn't matter where to. I felt lost in the music, and safe wandering around. I was sure that Bob was following me to school. I was afraid of him.

My mom had a meeting with the principal at school, who then talked with all of my teachers. Without being specific, the principal explained that I was experiencing a "personal crisis," and that I might be late or absent, and that sometimes I might have difficulty concentrating, or that maybe I would need some extra help with my work or some extra attention. I was embarrassed about getting any special treatment because I didn't want the other kids to notice it and give me a hard time. But deep down, I appreciated everyone's help and concern. And this truly was a crisis.

Cathy and Mom helped me decide which friends to tell and how to tell them. Cathy also helped prepare me for their possible reactions, especially the other guys who I knew Bob had also abused. It was going to be totally hard if they denied it happened to them, or especially if they denied it happened to me.

My parents really helped with this. They talked to my friends' parents so they could understand what was happening, and to offer them support if their sons had also been involved. It felt weird to me when this secret thing wasn't a secret anymore. I felt ashamed, but I needed people to know so I could feel supported, so they could help me deal with all of this.

I sometimes felt as if the whole world knew my dirty secret. I just knew that everyone was looking at me. I wished that no one could see me. I prayed that one day I would disappear and then it would all be over.

Even on the days I felt like going to school I didn't say much in classes because I didn't want to attract attention. I didn't know what to say to people, even my friends. Should I talk about what was constantly nagging at my thoughts—Bob and the trial? Should I bring it up to the other guys I knew were involved? Or, should I talk about sports and music and classes and dates, and just pretend that everything was cool? It was hard. I didn't know what to do, how to be, where to start.

It helped a lot when my friends would come up to me and start conversations. Like at lunch one day, Dan came over and said, "Hey, Joe. So what do you think about that substitute teacher in history class? Is he a total bore or what?" He broke the ice, and just acted natural around me. I remember smiling that day. I didn't feel so isolated or weird.

I was pretty nervous and jumpy a lot. One day at school the hall was kind of empty and I was getting a notebook from my locker. This girl, Joy, called to me from down the hall. "Hi, Joe!" She startled me and I dropped all of my books from my locker on my foot. I felt so stupid. Joy helped me pick up my stuff. She said she was sorry for startling me. I was embarrassed. But whatever it was she said next started me laughing. It felt good to laugh!

That afternoon after school, Joy and Dan and I went out for some fries and a Coke. I had fun. We didn't talk about my real life. The trial, I mean. We talked about school and movies and concerts. It was so good just to have some fun.

As things about the abuse and the trial became public, more people found out. And not all the kids were as nice to me as Joy and Dan. Some were cruel, and I hated them. Some days I thought I'd never go back to school. Some days I was going to leave town, change my name, and start a whole new life. Cathy helped me through the tears and hate about those kids. It's times of trouble like this that you find out who your true friends are.

I was beginning to learn about trust. I had been pretty mixed up about that.

SECTION 14. THE INDICTMENT

It had been an uneventful day. I was beginning to feel a little calmer, and didn't even jump when the phone rang at home late that afternoon. It was Drew calling to tell me that the grand jury had handed down an indictment against Bob. He said that because Bob still had access to kids, a **warrant** had been issued and Bob would be arrested. The **arraignment** would be in superior court within the next few days. My hand felt frozen to the phone. Bob going to jail. My thoughts were whirling.

I knew that Drew had explained arraignment to me before, but I guess I forgot. I wanted to understand, so I asked him, "What's arraignment, again?"

He explained. "Arraignment is the public reading in court of the formal charges against Bob. At this time, the charges filed against Bob will be read to him, and he will **plead** "guilty" or "not guilty." Just so you know, Joe, it is pretty standard for all defendants charged with serious crimes to plead "not guilty" at the time of arraignment. This has nothing to do with whether or not they plead guilty later in the process. Joe? Joe, are you still there?"

I was there, but I had drifted off into my whirling thoughts. Was this all really happening? I came back, "Yeah, yeah."

"Oh, by the way, Joe," Drew continued, "remember we mentioned that although it's not very common, sometimes indictments handed down by the grand jury might appear in the local newspapers. It's more likely in this case to get news coverage because of the number of potential victims, but your name won't be revealed. The law in the commonwealth says the media cannot use your name. However, Bob's name and address might be in the papers."

"Oh no," I said. "Now everyone will know." I hid my face in my hands and just cried. Drew said that he understood I was upset and frightened about being publicly exposed. He spent a lot of time that afternoon talking with me, listening to me . . . comforting and supporting me.

SECTION 15. THE ARRAIGNMENT

Generally, time was moving very slowly for me. But the day of the arraignment arrived quickly. I didn't have to go to the arraignment. It was a "brief procedure," Nina said, so she was the only one who needed to be there. She said it was important for Bob to understand that the charges were being brought against him by the Commonwealth of Massachusetts, not by me or any of the other boys who might be witnesses. That fact would be clearer to Bob if I wasn't there for the arraignment. But I might as well have been there, though, because I couldn't think of anything else all day. I imagined the scene over and over in my mind. I could see the court officers leading Bob into the room. Would he be handcuffed? That image troubled me. Bob, handcuffed. All because of me.

Late in the day Drew called. I stayed home from school waiting to hear from him. Believe me, it was a very long day! As expected, Bob pled "not guilty." They had a **bail hearing,** and bail was set so Bob wouldn't have to be in jail before the trial. I was nervous about that. I worried that Bob would come after me to get even with me for telling.

Awhile ago, I told Nina I was worried that Bob was following me to school, and she got a **restraining order,** "to keep you safe," she said. But I was really worried now. Bob indicted and out on bail. Drew interrupted my worries by saying that court dates had been set for a **pretrial conference** and **motions hearing.** But I didn't have to go to them. "The actual trial date," he said, "could be scheduled anytime from three months to a year from now."

"A year!" I yelled at him. I know I yelled even though I didn't mean to. "A year!" I was totally shocked.

Drew said calmly, "Joe, it might even be longer. Sometimes there are **continuances** in court that we can't control. Realistically the trial could happen in October or November." This was January. October, November. That seemed like never.

After I calmed down, I called Drew back. "What's a continuance?" I needed to hear the explanation again even though I knew Drew had explained this to me before.

And so he explained it to me again. "A continuance is a change in the date when something is scheduled to happen in court."

Now I had more questions: "Why does that happen? Will it happen to me?"

He answered, "A continuance happens for a lot of different reasons. Sometimes the lawyers need to do more research on the legal issues. Sometimes a witness is not available. Sometimes a previously scheduled trial takes longer than expected, so the judge is busy with that and not ready for us." Drew didn't know if a continuance would happen for us. "But if it does," he said, "we will most likely be notified well in advance about any delays or changes. When it is time for the trial you will receive a **subpoena** telling you when to appear in court. By then, things should be pretty well set and ready to go."

SECTION 16. WAITING AGAIN

I just could not believe that it took so long for a trial to be held in superior court. It's about "scheduling" they told me, and lots of cases for the judges to hear. It was hard for me because there was nothing I could do about it but wait. Sometimes I was very nervous inside because of all the waiting, and mostly there was just nothing anyone could do about it.

Eventually I settled down into a routine, and a routine felt nice for a change. I still called Drew a lot with questions and needing updates. He called me regularly to check in about how I was doing and to keep me informed about the progress of the case. I saw Cathy every week, and I started to feel OK about her, and to trust her, too. Sometimes I wasn't sure why I went to see Cathy because I didn't really want to talk about the abuse. Sometimes I just wanted to forget the whole thing.

Things were quiet at home. My parents said they wanted to help me, and they did by being there for me. We didn't talk about the trial or the abuse or Bob very much because Mom and Dad usually waited for me to bring it up, which wasn't often.

Mom would make attempts to talk about it by saying things like, "How are you feeling about 'things' today?" But since she was never too specific in her questions, I was never too specific in my answers either.

Usually I said something like, "Yeah, it's cool."

It was all so hard for me to talk about. But even though I didn't say much to my parents, I appreciated their love and support. They consistently asked me how I was doing. And even though they didn't say directly "about Bob and the trial," I knew what they meant. I knew they were there to help me. Eventually, with Cathy's help, I was able to tell my parents how I was, and to thank them for their support.

SECTION 17. THE EMPTY COURTROOM

Although I went on with my regular life, I felt as if a gray storm cloud was hovering over me all the time. It followed me everywhere. I wondered if Bob had one, too.

In mid-August, Drew called to tell me that a trial date had been set for October 4. I shivered, and it was ninety degrees outside! He reminded me, right then, that things could come up to cause delays.

In September, Nina, Drew, and I met a few times to go over what would happen in court. First they talked to me about the verdict. Drew said, "We know Bob is **guilty,** Joe. But during the trial, we need to prove his guilt, beyond a reasonable doubt. Remember? We talked about reasonable doubt."

I nodded.

Drew was being very serious. "In cases like this, sometimes the **defendant** is found **not guilty.** If that happens, Joe, it doesn't mean that Bob is innocent, or that he didn't abuse you. It means that the district attorney's office did not provide sufficient evidence to convince the jury of his guilt beyond a reasonable doubt." Drew told me that to prepare me for the possibility that Bob might be **acquitted** rather than **convicted.** I knew it was a possibility, but I told Drew that I didn't even want to think about it. I couldn't think about it.

One morning Drew and Nina took me to an empty courtroom so I wouldn't be going into a totally strange place when the trial started. We went into the courtroom. It looked dark and somber, and felt cold.

In fact, a shiver went up my back as I stood in the doorway and looked around. I knew right away this was a serious place.

Nina coaxed me into sitting in the **witness stand.** She and Drew were going through some papers deciding on what questions to ask me. They were talking together, and I sat in the stand and looked around. I had to remind myself to breathe. I felt hot. Tears started welling up in my eyes. I squeezed my eyes shut really tight, hoping the tears would go away, hoping when I opened my eyes I would be away. In Florida maybe, in Hawaii, or maybe Spain. I've always wanted to go to Spain. My hands clutched the arms of the chair. I was hoping with all my might.

And then I heard Drew's voice. "Joe. Joe. What's happening?"

I opened my eyes and was surprised to see him and Nina and the empty courtroom. It didn't look so scary now because it wasn't the first time I was seeing it. It actually looked familiar.

"I'm OK," I said. So while I continued to sit in the stand, supposedly "getting comfortable," Nina spent some time preparing me for what might come up in the trial. This was going to be hard.

When I stepped down from the stand, I felt a little shaky, but I also felt very mature and grown-up.

SECTION 18. PRETRIAL DETAILS

A lot of paperwork goes into a trial. I learned that first thing. Before the trial actually happens, the ADA and the **defense attorney** meet in court with the **judge** and the other court workers (the **court officers,** the **judge's clerk,** and the **court reporter**), to submit and decide about the **pretrial motions.** That's when the attorneys address certain legal issues with the judge, including special procedures and special conditions. For example, Nina asked for a microphone to use during my testimony. She knew I had a hard time speaking up when it came to the details of the abuse. She wanted to make sure the judge, the jury, and everyone could hear me. The defense attorney didn't want Nina to refer to me as a **victim,** but to use the term **complaining witness** instead. Drew explained that this was because the word victim implied that Bob hurt me and that is what the prosecution has to prove. It was a "technicality," he said.

The judge decided to "wait and see" about the microphone, but I wish he hadn't done that. He instructed Nina to use the phrase "complaining witness" instead of victim.

The court process—the whole thing—was really hard for me. Sometimes I didn't understand what was going on, and sometimes I really started to wonder whose side they were on.

SECTION 19. DELAYS AND PREPARATIONS

There were continuances. I'm glad Nina and Drew warned me about them, but even their warnings didn't help my stress about all the delays. I'd be all ready for the trial to start, and either Drew or Nina would call to say it had to be rescheduled for later.

It happened a few times, and each time I got mad at Drew or Nina, whichever one called to tell me the news. But then I felt bad about being mad at them. They were really nice to me, and on my side, I knew it. After all, the judge was the person who was in charge of the courtroom, and the delays were mostly for "administrative reasons," they said. Nina and Drew assured me it was nothing personal against me. But I could never figure out how those reasons, whatever they were, could be more important than a person's feelings. I was very upset about all this waiting and delaying. I kept wondering if they cared about me at all. I had waited so long already, and I didn't know if I could stand waiting one minute longer. Dad called my upset "apprehension." Fear of future evil! That felt like an accurate description. But, somehow, I made it through all the waiting.

For months before the trial I spent some of my free time preparing myself by watching lawyer shows on television. I almost never missed *Judge Judy* or *Law and Order* or *The Practice*. And sometimes I'd stay up late and watch the old reruns of the original *Perry Mason*. I prayed that Nina was a better prosecutor than poor Mr. Burger!

The television law fascinated me. Even though Drew talked to me a lot about the legal process and the language that would be used in court, I thought I could become some kind of "expert" through my TV research. And then, I'd be less afraid. Drew and Nina both talked to me about television law, warning me that some of it was "realistic" and some of it was "just drama" geared to entertain TV audiences. But I watched the shows anyway.

Unfortunately, those TV shows didn't help me to feel more confident when my real day in court finally came. But they did keep me occupied during the long months of waiting. Watching them helped me feel that I was doing something productive to prepare myself.

SECTION 20. THE TRIAL BEGINS

The trial was finally scheduled to begin on November 11. "A firm date," Nina said. I received a subpoena in the mail requesting my appearance as a witness for the prosecution in the case of *The Commonwealth of Massachusetts vs. Bob.* I was impressed by the official-looking importance of the document, so I hung it up on the wall in my room. It felt like a "Red Badge of Courage."

The trial did start on November 11. It lasted for five days from the jury **empaneling** to the reading of the **verdict.** Those were by far the longest, yet the shortest, five days of my entire life. When the trial was in progress, even the minutes crawled by. The days seemed endless. And the sleepless nights were definitely endless. But when the trial was all over, it seemed to have lasted no longer than the blink of an eye.

SECTION 21. IN COURT

Court was a tense place. It was extremely organized, and the people who worked there seemed to know exactly what was going on. But in spite of their knowing, even they seemed tense.

There were a lot of people in court. There were two lawyers (Nina and Mr. McCarthy, who was the defense attorney for Bob). There were two court officers. They had on uniforms sort of like police officers. There was a court clerk who sat at a desk in front of the judge's bench, and a court reporter who recorded every word of the trial. I was surprised that there were fourteen people on the jury instead of twelve. I kept counting them, thinking I made a mistake. When I asked Drew, he explained that two jurors were alternates in case someone on the jury got sick or something. There were also a few people in the audience. Drew explained that most trials are open to the public. I wanted to know who the people were and why they were there.

I appreciated Drew more as each minute passed. He stayed with me the whole time. I didn't realize it, but I couldn't be in the courtroom through the whole trial. There's this thing called being **sequestered.** It means that one witness can't hear the testimony of other witnesses, so as not to be influenced by what someone else says. So I had to spend a lot of time with Drew in the victim/witness "waiting" room (what a perfect name for it), wondering what in the world was going on inside the courtroom. There was this huge clock on the wall in the waiting room, and I just stared at it, watching the endless seconds tick by. At first I asked Drew a lot of questions because I was so nervous, but then I drifted off into my own thoughts. I was so worried. I was going to have to say all those embarrassing things in the courtroom. But I had to do it. I wanted Bob off the streets, away from helpless kids.

I was at the courthouse on the third, fourth, and fifth days of the trial. Mom and Dad were there with me the whole time. We didn't have to be there for the jury selection or the pretrial motions which happened during the first two days.

When the actual trial part started, Nina and Mr. McCarthy gave their **opening statements.** Then Nina called me to the witness stand to testify. My hands were sweaty. My stomach was upset. And for a minute I thought I might throw up, but I didn't. It was hard to testify, for sure. But I did it. I was OK.

Nina stood across the courtroom and asked me questions. The easy ones were first. My name, address, age, school, where I live . . . and then came the hard ones. Nina began to ask me questions about the sexual experiences I had with Bob. Oh no. She kept asking me to speak up, but I could barely speak at all.

Then, all of a sudden, the judge jumped up from his chair. This unexpected movement, right in the middle of my testimony, startled me. He abruptly said, "We're in **recess.** Counsel, in my chambers." Surrounded by a cloud of swirling black fabric, the judge disappeared from the courtroom, followed by the lawyers.

I started to cry. I couldn't help it. I couldn't figure out what was happening. But then, I was out in the corridor and Drew was right beside me. I got some water, and Drew tried to comfort me. The next thing I knew, the court officers were installing a microphone on the witness stand for me to use. Nina came out into the corridor and explained that the judge couldn't hear my answers and asked that the microphone be set up. I wished that the judge had approved Nina's pretrial motion for a microphone in the first place, because now I was upset and feeling afraid of him.

Fifteen minutes later court was back in session, I was back in the witness stand. The judge spoke to me directly and apologized for the disruption. He asked me to speak clearly into the microphone, "So the jury can hear every word." I think he smiled at me. I didn't smile back. I just nodded.

SECTION 22. CROSS-EXAMINATION

When Nina finished asking me questions, Bob's lawyer, Mr. McCarthy, **cross-examined** me. He was loud and abrupt. At times I felt attacked by him. He tried to confuse me by asking me the same question over in different ways.

Mr. McCarthy's confusing questions were making it hard for me to think. I was getting really tense and I felt hot tears stinging my eyes. My fists were clenched in my lap. I wanted to run out of the courtroom, and not stop running until I got to Spain. But I tried to hold it together, and I answered the questions in the best way I could. Mr. McCarthy kept saying he didn't understand. So he'd ask the same question again, and again. I didn't know what to do. Finally, the judge interrupted. He clearly rephrased Mr. McCarthy's last question, which had been asked several times, and my answer. He then looked directly at me and asked, "Is this what you're saying, Joe?"

"Yes," I said as I nodded.

The judge turned to Bob's lawyer and said, "Well, then. That's quite enough for this question, Mr. McCarthy. I think that both the jury and I understand the witness's answer. Please move on."

I felt such relief, I can't even say. The judge's interruption helped me to calm down, and Mr. McCarthy didn't seem so mean from then on. But still, I was totally glad when it was finally over. I was questioned for almost three hours.

That afternoon and part of the next day there were other witnesses. After that, Bob testified even though his lawyer didn't want him to, and he didn't have to. Drew explained that Bob didn't have to testify because of the **Fifth Amendment,** and because the **burden of proof** is on the prosecution. A couple of people testified for Bob as **character witnesses.** I didn't hear any of the testimony because I was sequestered.

At the end of the examination of all of the witnesses, both lawyers gave their **closing arguments** to the court, first the defense attorney, Mr. McCarthy, and then Nina. I was there for that. It was very scary hearing Mr. McCarthy speak. He seemed so convinced that Bob was not guilty. He said that I was mistaken. "Children misunderstand and misinterpret." He said that I lied. "Children have vivid imaginations, and they sometimes fabricate dramatic tales to get attention." That's what Mr. McCarthy had to say about me. Drew had prepared me for the types of things Mr. McCarthy might say, but it was still hard for me not to get angry and scared.

But Nina's closing argument restored my faith and confidence. She said, "Why would Joe lie? Why would he come before this court and this jury and discuss the most embarrassing, painful details of his life? Being here, talking about sexual abuse is absolutely the last thing a teenaged boy wants to do. Joe has no reason to lie."

I felt like I was on a roller coaster. I wondered how the jury felt.

SECTION 23. INSTRUCTIONS TO THE JURY

After the closing arguments, the judge spoke directly to the jury for what seemed to be a very long time. I wondered how they could remember everything he said.

The judge told the jury to weigh the **credibility** of the witnesses, and to decide whether to believe some, none, or all of what each person said. I thought it must be very hard to be a juror. I mean, I said Bob had sex with me, and he said he didn't. How does the jury decide who's telling the truth and who's telling a lie?

The judge went on to further instruct the jury. He reminded them that Bob was **"presumed innocent."** I shivered when I heard those words. The judge said that the prosecution must prove guilt beyond a "reasonable doubt," but not all doubt.

Then the judge went over the elements of the charges against Bob for the jury to hear, reminding them that Bob was charged with several counts of rape of a child. Then the judge read these things called **statutes.** "Whoever has sexual intercourse or unnatural sexual intercourse . . . abuses a child under the age of sixteen." It all sounded so impersonal, I couldn't believe he was still talking about me. The jury was then told that they had two choices for a verdict: either not guilty, or guilty as charged.

When the judge finished talking to the jury, the court clerk took this wooden box and shook it up. It looked like he was going to draw the winning name for a raffle. I was startled by this familiar, friendly action which seemed so out of place. The clerk chose two names from the box, but instead of winning something, the names identified the alternate jurors. The other twelve jurors left the courtroom and went into the jury room to **deliberate.**

"All rise." The judge swiftly left the courtroom followed by his fluttering black robes. The trial was suddenly over.

I turned to Drew with hope in my eyes and a question in my voice. "It's over?"

"Not yet, Joe," he replied. "It's not over yet."

SECTION 24. THE VERDICT

Nina suggested that my parents and I go to the cafeteria in the courthouse for lunch. She didn't want us to go home or leave the courthouse. She wanted us to "stay close" as we waited for the verdict. We went to the cafeteria and ate lunch, although I wasn't very hungry. Then we spent the rest of the afternoon waiting with Drew in the victim/witness waiting room. I swear, I have every single detail of that room memorized!

At exactly 3:39 p.m. Nina appeared in the doorway of the waiting room. The jury had reached a verdict.

And then we were back in the courtroom. I have never in my life been so scared. Drew stayed right beside me the whole time. This was a totally terrible situation. I was feeling panicky because I wasn't sure what I would do if Bob was found "guilty." I wanted him to go to jail. But I worried about that. I couldn't help it. I still loved Bob. But what if he was found "not guilty?" Then everyone would think I was a liar. I had a splitting headache. My teeth were clenched. So were my fists.

Drew kept trying to get me to be more relaxed, but there was absolutely no possibility of relaxed!

The jury filed in. The judge appeared. "All rise." I was becoming accustomed to the routine. "This court is now in session." What followed seemed like a dream . . . or a movie. Something unreal, anyway. In fact, if I think about it, I can still play back the entire scene in my mind just as if I were seeing it happen all over again.

The judge spoke. "Women and men of the jury, have you reached a verdict?"

The foreman of the jury stood and replied. "We have."

The clerk asked Bob to stand, and he did. So did his lawyer. And then the verdict. **"Guilty as charged."** Guilty as charged . . . guilty as charged . . . guilty as charged. An echo. I'm sure I heard an echo in the cold, hollow courtroom.

Movement and sound happened slowly and distinctly. I couldn't see Bob's face, but when the guilty verdict was announced, his whole body slumped forward. My face and hands finally relaxed. Bob sat down and held his head in his hands. Was he crying? I was.

The judge spoke. His voice startled me as it filled the hushed courtroom. "The jury is dismissed. The court thanks you for your service. The defendant will be held over for sentencing, which will be in two weeks. This court is adjourned." In that now familiar flurry of swirling black, the judge was gone.

SECTION 25. AFTER THE TRIAL

In slow motion, I turned to Drew. I looked up at him and whispered, "Is it over?"

"Well, not quite, Joe," he answered. "The trial is over, but the court process is not. In two weeks, at the sentencing hearing, the judge will listen to sentence recommendations from both Nina and Mr. McCarthy. And if you want to say something, there will also be time for you, and your parents, as well, to make a **victim impact statement.** Or, you can write a letter to the judge telling him how you feel about Bob's sentence. In fact, sometimes before the sentencing, people write to the judge on behalf of the defendant, and you need to be prepared for that. Bob may have character witnesses who suggest that he receive **probation** and not be sentenced to jail at all, or that he receive a short sentence."

I just nodded in response, and Drew continued. "I know that you've thought a lot about what kind of sentence you want Bob to receive, Joe. And now is the time for you to decide if you want to make a victim impact statement. You can either say your statement in court the day of the sentencing, or you can write it to the judge. We encourage you and your parents to communicate your feelings to the court in some way, so your voices will be heard. But you don't have to. You don't have to say anything. You don't have to write anything. You don't even have to go to the sentencing hearing. However, I encourage you to let the judge know how important this case is to you."

Drew and I had similar talks before, but hearing it all again put me in a kind of a daze. Maybe I was dazed because I thought it was over. I hoped it was over. I wanted it over. Two more weeks seemed like another eternity, but I knew I'd get through it somehow. I mean, really! Look at what I'd been through already!

During the next days, I spent my time after school alone, going for long walks, mostly. Thinking. I walked and walked, trying very hard to get to the bottom of my feelings about Bob. Talking with Cathy helped, but I knew that getting down to my deep feelings was a solitary activity. And so I walked some more. Finally, after ten days I sat down very late at night and wrote the victim impact statement I wanted to read in the courtroom.

My statement was short. I thought that was best. I honestly didn't know how much I would be able to say.

SECTION 26. VICTIM IMPACT STATEMENT

Since I'm only sixteen years old, I can't know for sure, but I think that being here in this courtroom under these circumstances may be the hardest thing I will ever do in my whole life.

But it's important for me to be here because I want to do everything I can to make sure that Bob can't do to other kids what he did to me. Bob hurt me. He scared me and threatened me. He confused me and used me. He stole things from me that I can never, ever recover. My body was violated and I am so ashamed.

Bob did something wrong, something very wrong. It seems only fair that he should be punished. I don't want him to hurt me or threaten me anymore, or to hurt other kids. I want to feel safe. If Bob is in jail, and can't see me or call me, then maybe I can actually feel safe.

SECTION 27. SENTENCING

The day of the sentencing hearing finally arrived. My parents and Drew and I were sitting in the courtroom at exactly 2:00 p.m., the time the hearing was scheduled. Except for Nina and the court officers, the room was empty. I was nervous and confused. At five minutes past 2:00, more people started coming, but I didn't know who they were. In and out. People kept coming in and going out of the courtroom.

I whispered to Drew a question I had asked him several times before, "What kind of sentence will Bob get?"

"Well," he whispered in reply, "there are guidelines regarding appropriate sentencing for every crime, but the decision in each case is really up to the judge."

At ten minutes past 2:00, more people came in. "Who are these people?" I asked Drew. He told me that other activities were scheduled in court that afternoon. The people were lawyers and victim witness advocates and witnesses and friends and reporters. Some of the people were Bob's friends. I noticed that the lawyers seemed friendly to each other, even if they were on opposite sides. When Mr. McCarthy arrived, Nina shook his hand and spoke to him. I didn't want them to be friendly.

At 2:15, I started going in and out of the courtroom. Getting a drink, going to the bathroom, generally moving around because I was too nervous to sit still. This waiting was so hard. Drew told me that sometimes the waiting is the worst part because it leaves lots of room for apprehension and worry. At that moment, I thought that he was right.

At 2:20, the court officer started talking on his phone and this one lawyer over in the corner was throwing his pen up in the air catching it each time it came down again. Was he nervous, too? Or just passing the time? It seemed to me that nothing at court ever started on time. I wondered if whoever was in charge had any idea how nerve-racking all this waiting was. My heart was pounding so hard, that I worried I might be having a heart attack. But I wasn't.

Finally, people slowly began taking their places. They sat down one by one and became quiet. Bob was brought in, and he sat on the other side of the courtroom. He didn't look at me.

"All rise." The judge appeared. "Be seated. This court is now in session." A solemn quiet. The clerk announced the other cases, stated who was present and who the lawyers were. Now things seemed to happen very quickly, and soon the courtroom was nearly empty.

The clerk announced our case and acknowledged Nina and Mr. McCarthy as the lawyers. Bob went forward and sat next to Mr. McCarthy.

Then Nina stood. I stopped breathing. Nina spoke directly to the judge. Her voice was clear and loud. It echoed in the solemn space. "Thank you, Your Honor. On behalf of the commonwealth, the district attorney's office recommends a state prison sentence. The planned and manipulated sexual abuse of children is the most disgusting and heinous crime. Bob is a pro at this type of abuse. And as it has been proved in this court of law, he is a sophisticated, deliberate, and aggressive abuser of children. He has made Joe's life into a living nightmare. Joe was a helpless, defenseless, appreciative child, and he suffered the ultimate betrayal of a trusted, adult friend and caretaker. Nothing we do here today can totally heal Joe's wounds. However, what we can do is hold Bob responsible for his crimes. We cannot even guess at the number of children Bob has victimized, but we do know he has been actively abusing boys in the neighborhoods of our county for years. Bob was found guilty of the sexual abuse of this victim by a jury of his peers. Although we cannot take away Joe's suffering, we can send a message to all child molesters, through this molester, that our society will not tolerate the mistreatment of our children. Therefore, the commonwealth recommends a state prison sentence, to be followed by a **suspended sentence** from and after the committed sentence, during which time sex offender counseling will be mandatory."

When Nina was finished there was a hush over the courtroom. It was my turn to speak. I walked up to the witness stand and sat down. I unfolded my paper and looked at Nina and then at the judge. I looked at my parents. I looked at Drew. Then I looked at Bob. Whew, that was hard. I thought he might look at me, but instead he stared at some papers on the table in front of him. I read my statement, grateful that it was short, because I almost started to cry. This whole situation was a terrible nightmare. I still couldn't believe it was all happening.

I finished my statement, folded up my paper and went back to my place next to Drew. Then my dad took the stand. He had prepared an impact statement to read to the court. Dad's statement was a lot longer than mine. He told the court about my fear, about how I wondered how old I would be when Bob got out of jail. How I wondered if I would be able to protect myself from him. How I wondered if I'd always be afraid. Dad talked about how ashamed I was because of being sexual with Bob. Then my dad got choked up as he asked the court to "respect the bravery of my son." As Dad continued, his voice was kind of shaky. "Joe is just a kid, a kid acting and speaking in the face of fear for his own safety, and in the fear of public shame, to protect other kids. He has come forward at great cost to himself, a cost that I don't think we as adults can imagine. How dare this man harm this boy, my son!"

I thought Dad was going to cry. I couldn't help myself. I did cry.

Dad continued. "How dare he! I have watched and supported my son as he dealt with the legal system, knowing how hard it was for him, knowing the pain it was causing him, knowing that it was the only rational way to deal with this. And the legal system has worked. Bob has been convicted. And now I ask the court to ensure that what my son has tried to do, does, in fact, come to pass. Protect other kids from Bob by removing him from access to kids for as long as possible."

When Dad stopped talking no one moved for a minute or so. It seemed that no one was even breathing. Then Dad looked at the judge and said, "Thank you. Thank you for this opportunity to speak." Dad had tears in his eyes.

Dad returned to his seat next to me, and the sentencing hearing continued. Mr. McCarthy spoke on Bob's behalf. "He is not a one-dimensional person. We cannot deny him his humanity. He has been a responsible citizen. The judge has received a number of letters from friends and relatives who have known him for more than twenty years. He has a friendly, generous spirit . . . " Mr. McCarthy went on and on saying what a great guy Bob was. It was hard for me to believe that Nina and Mr. McCarthy were talking about the same person.

And then the judge talked, for what seemed like a really long time before he got to the sentencing. Finally, he asked Bob to stand. Then the clerk announced the sentence. "You have been found guilty . . . you are sentenced to a prison term in the state prison . . . to be followed by a suspended sentence . . . will include mandatory counseling . . . sentence to begin immediately." The court officers came up to Bob and led him away through a mysterious door in the back of the courtroom. Drew said that door led to the jail.

As I watched Bob walk away, time stopped for me. Shocked, stunned. I don't know. A shiver went through my whole body. People were talking to me, but I couldn't hear them. I was stunned, I guess. Drew steered my parents and me out of the courtroom and into the victim/witness waiting room. I sat down, relieved, exhausted, grateful that Bob couldn't hurt me or those little guys I saw getting into his van. He couldn't hurt any kids anymore.

Well, the trial was finally over. Now the part about putting my life back together was about to begin.

SECTION 28. TOWARD RECOVERY

It hasn't even been two years since I first told Mr. Stone about the sexual abuse, but it seems like it all happened centuries ago. The investigation and trial sort of happened in addition to my regular life, and now that the trial is over, I want to pick up my life where I left off.

In some ways I feel lucky. Not lucky that Bob abused me. He asked me to do things I was not ready to do, and then I had to deal with the court process, which I really was not equipped to deal with. Bob was a fright in my life. He was destructive. But I do feel lucky because there are people who care about kids. And I'm grateful that those people helped me. In fact, they still help me. I see Cathy every week, and probably will keep seeing her for awhile. She has helped me to understand the experience of sexual abuse and to work on my feelings about it. Sorting out my feelings can be very, very hard work, and will "take some time" Cathy said. I mostly hate doing this "work," but then the upset and the work seem worth it when I finally come to understand more about my experience and to accept it.

I feel sad and angry every time I think about Bob. He was a great friend. We had such good times. But still, what he did—I don't think I can ever forgive him for that. I don't think I want to forgive him. You know, he never ever said he was sorry. I sure hope Bob learns something while he is in jail. I hope he understands how much he hurt me and all the other kids he abused over the years. I hope he understands that what he did was wrong and that he can never sexually abuse a child, ever again.

Given what I've been through in my life so far, things are going as well as can be expected. I'm doing okay in school, I guess. My grades aren't bad, and in the spring I'm planning to try out for the track team. Mr. Stone is the coach. I've even dated a little, very little, but enough to realize that I have a lot to learn about relationships and sex.

"But doesn't everyone!" Cathy said.

Sometimes it's tempting to think about burying my past and my pain with drugs and alcohol, like some kids at school do, but I resist. I know that keeping things buried won't help me much in the long run. Sometimes I have the worst nightmares that just won't end. Sometimes I'm tired, real tired. Sometimes I'm sick. I still have a lot of headaches. Sometimes life isn't exactly fun for me. But now, at least, I know I'm in control of my own body and my own life. It was so important to come forward and stop Bob. My dad told me that by coming forward like I did took as much courage as he has ever seen in his life. And my dad has been with a lot of courageous people, like when he was in Vietnam. My parents' support meant so much to me. They didn't blame me for what happened. They were proud of me for coming forward and stopping Bob.

In a way, I'm sorry I can't end this story by telling you that I "lived happily ever after." But I'm only sixteen years old, so this isn't anywhere near the end. Anyway, that happily ever after stuff is for kids and fairy tales. This is real life, my life. And in a way, it's the beginning of the best part of my life. Oh, I'll never forget what Bob did, and I'll never forget the pain. But I'm going to keep working at understanding myself and what happened, because I firmly believe that with work and persistence, life will be better. I have lots of hope for the future thanks to Mr. Stone and Patrick O'Neill and Drew and Nina and Cathy and my parents . . . well, you know, thanks to everyone who helped me and everyone who cared.

SUPPORT PEOPLE I CAN DEPEND ON

	Name	Telephone #
Therapist/Counselor	_____	_____
24-Hour Crisis Line	_____	_____
Victim Witness Advocate	_____	_____
Child Interview Specialist	_____	_____
Assistant District Attorney	_____	_____
Police Officer	_____	_____
Doctor	_____	_____
Friend	_____	_____
Friend	_____	_____

HOW IT HAPPENED FOR ME: A DIAGRAM

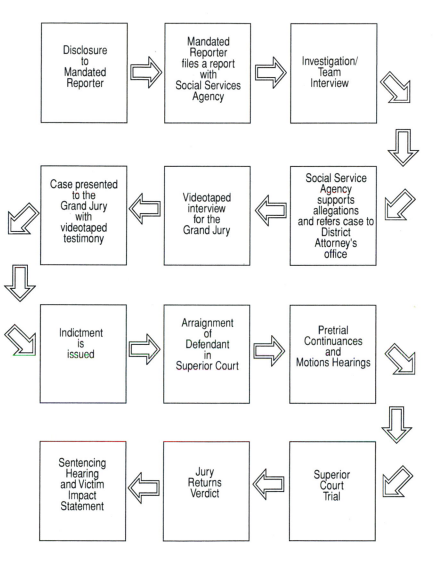

PART IV:
GUIDING ADOLESCENT VICTIMS THROUGH THE ADJUDICATION PROCESS

INTRODUCTION

The **Workbook Guide** for the *We Are Not Alone* workbooks found in Chapter 7 is designed to help multidisciplinary professionals, parents, and other concerned adults use the workbooks as a tool to enhance the effectiveness of their interactions with adolescent victims of child sexual abuse throughout the adjudication process. To make particular issues or pertinent material easy to access, the chapter titles appearing in the personal accounts of the victims in Chapters 5 and 6 and in the workbooks are grouped into the following parts:

A. Disclosure
B. Investigation
C. Prosecution: Pretrial
D. Prosecution: Trial
E. Counseling and Personal Issues

Each of these parts addresses a specific aspect of the adjudication process. Since the typical court process is linear in nature, the chapter titles appear chronologically. However, since the chapters dealing with counseling and personal issues are interspersed throughout the process, these chapters appear twice: chronologically, with a brief mention, and grouped together in their own section, with more detail about key points. The workbook for boys and the workbook for girls have minor differences in chapter chronology and titles; these differences are noted in the appropriate part. The chapter titles are simple, clear, and descriptive so professionals and parents can easily refer to and guide victims to a specific issue.

Each part includes **Key Points** and **Additional Resources**. The Key Points are intended to assist helping professionals and parents who are unfamiliar with and/or continuing to learn about the adjudication process, and/or unfamiliar with or learning about the issues and reactions experienced by adolescent victims, more readily identify areas for concern and focused attention. Additional resources, which will provide professionals and parents with more in-depth material about the topic, are identified for each section.

The **Guiding Questions** in Chapter 8 are organized to coincide with the chapters in the workbooks. These questions are intended to provide a springboard for beginning a dialogue with victims.

The **Glossary of Terms** will help to clarify the vocabulary used throughout the adjudication process. The Questions and the Glossary also appear at the end of each workbook as a support for adolescent readers.

Chapter 7

Workbook Guide: Key Points and Additional Resources

A. DISCLOSURE

The handling of the initial disclosure of child sexual abuse may affect the decision to prosecute a case as well as the outcome of the case; and it may ultimately contribute to the impact of the prosecution process on the victim. Most jurisdictions have specific procedures in place if a victim discloses to a school professional as Joe and Jane do. These procedures provide security during a painful and difficult time for both the victim and the individual receiving the disclosure and making the report. However, not all individuals who are privileged to receive a disclosure from a sexually abused child or teenager are informed about procedures or know what is necessary in such a situation to protect the victim and the legal case. The Key Points in this section help to identify the legal and personal issues which most need attention during the disclosure of child sexual abuse.

Section 1. (Girls) I'm Jane / (Boys) I'm Joe
Section 2. The First Time I Told
Section 3. (Girls) Making a Report
        (Boys) I'm Sorry
Section 4. (Boys) Making a Report

Key Points

1. *Victims may experience fear.*
a. At the time of disclosure, victims may experience distress and confusion, but the underlying and most powerful feeling they experience may be fear. They may fear being blamed for the abuse or being

153

disbelieved. They may fear retaliation from the abuser for revealing the secret, or they may fear the destruction of their families.

b. It is important for an individual who receives a disclosure to reassure the victim that he or she did the right thing by telling someone and that he or she is not to blame for the abuse.

c. Making a disclosure of child sexual abuse puts a victim in an extreme and vulnerable position. It is critical that the disclosure be received with compassion and belief. Often a disclosure generates disbelief, particularly when the individual receiving the disclosure knows and respects the accused. However, it is not the responsibility of the individual receiving the disclosure to judge the victim or even to express opinions about what the victim has revealed. It is the responsibility of the person receiving the disclosure to support the victim and report the disclosure to the proper authorities.

d. Most victims of child sexual abuse have been sworn to secrecy by the abuser, or threatened into silence. Determine if the abuse is ongoing, and if the child remains at risk for further abuse or retaliation for disclosing. If so, take steps either with Child Protective Services or the police to be certain that the victim will be physically safe following the disclosure—particularly if the abuser is a family member.

2. *Most victims of child sexual abuse are abused by people they know and trust and love. Therefore, the sense of loyalty victims feel toward their abusers is powerful, and disclosing often leaves the victims vulnerable to feeling guilt and regret.*

a. Both Jane and Joe loved their abusers in spite of what they did to them. Jane and Joe had ambivalence about doing or saying anything that might cause trouble for the abusers, or that might result in the abusers going to jail.

b. The feelings of guilt and regret may be intense enough for the victim to recant following the disclosure, particularly if any disbelief is expressed or any family pressure to recant is evident.

c. After disclosing, a victim may come to regret the consequences, particularly if he or she is removed from the home and sent into a foster care situation, or if the disclosure disrupts his or her family by leaving a nonoffending parent alone and financially vulnerable due to separation by incarceration or divorce. Unpleasant consequences may also incite a victim to recant.

3. *Disclosing is the right action.*

Appreciating and encouraging child or adolescent victims at the time of disclosure may help them find the strength to continue through the investigation phase. Convey that what the abusers did to them was wrong, and that telling someone who could help was the right action to take. It is also important to acknowledge and appreciate the victims' strength and courage.

4. *Every state has a child abuse reporting law and identifies mandated reporters.*

a. All who have regular contact with children will benefit from being knowledgeable about this law in their state. State senators' or representatives' offices can provide a copy of the law.

b. Know who the mandated reporters are in your state. Some states identify "any person" as a mandated reporter. Most mandated reporters are protected from liability and prosecution if a report of child abuse is made in good faith. Since teachers and school administrators are mandated reporters, public schools require training for all school personnel in the Child Abuse Reporting Law and reporting protocols. However, many other professionals who are in regular contact with children do not have this specialized training, for example, physicians, dentists, clergy, religious educators, and Sunday school teachers. Educating these professionals about reporting laws and protocols is essential.

c. Know whom to call to file a report.

5. *Do not question the victim.*

Individuals who receive disclosures of child sexual abuse can jeopardize the legal case if they inappropriately question the victim. Therefore, it is recommended that no questioning take place, except to identify if the victim is in imminent danger. Although it may appear dispassionate and harsh to remain detached from the details of the abuse and not engage in discussion with the victim about the abuse, it is critical to do so.

6. *Provide information and support and encourage the victim to seek these as well.*

a. It is unlikely that an adolescent who has just disclosed sexual abuse will be able to retain many details about the reporting and investigation procedures, but it is important to explain anyway. Professionals at every stage of the adjudication process will explain what is happening and what happens next. These explanations are important so that victims feel a sense of security and learn to trust the system. Encourage the victim to take notes and ask questions.

b. It is likely that an adolescent who has just disclosed sexual abuse is in distress. Let the victim know of available supports, particularly if the victim is not involved in a therapeutic relationship. Teen and crisis "hotlines," especially those with twenty-four-hour access will be most beneficial. Encourage the victim to reach out and to ask for help.

Additional Resources

1. The Child Abuse Reporting Law from your state. Call your state legislator's office to request a copy of the law.

2. *The APSAC Handbook on Child Maltreatment.*

   "Reporting of Child Maltreatment" by Gail L. Zellman and Kathleen Coulborn Faller. *The APSAC Handbook* can be ordered from Sage Publications. Telephone: (805) 499-0721; e-mail <order@sagepub.com>.

3. *The Future of Children,* Volume 4, Number 2: Summer/Fall 1994.

   "Reporting and Investigating Child Sexual Abuse" by Donna M. Pence and Charles A. Wilson. *The Future of Children Journal* can be ordered from the David and Lucile Packard Foundation, Center for the Future of Children. Telephone: (650) 948-3696.

4. *The User Manual Series:*

   "A Coordinated Response to Child Abuse and Neglect: A Basic Manual" by Diane DePanfilis and Marsha K. Salus.

   "The Role of Educators in the Prevention and Treatment of Child Abuse and Neglect" by Cynthia Crosson Tower. *The User Manual Series* is available from the National Clearinghouse on Child Abuse and Neglect (NCCAN). Telephone: (800) FYI-3366 or (703) 385-7565.

5. *Preventing Sexual Abuse,* Volume 2, 1987.

   "Pervasive Fears in Victims of Sexual Abuse" by Linda T. Sanford.

B. THE INVESTIGATION

In most jurisdictions, a disclosure, particularly one made to a mandated reporter who is familiar with the reporting procedures, will automatically set off an investigation. Whether the report is made to Child Protective Services, the police, or the district attorney, an investigation will commence within a relatively short period of time. If the victim is currently being abused, or if the safety of the victim is in question, the investigation is likely to begin within hours. In the case of adolescent victims, such as Joe, who report abuse that took place years earlier and who are no longer in contact with the perpetrator, the investigation may not begin for up to ten days following the disclosure. It is a simple case of triage in the social service or police departments. The disclosure of a victim who is at greater risk than Joe—for example, one who is currently being abused and/or living in the same house with the abuser, such as Jane—is likely to be responded to within two to twenty-four hours. Whether the investigation begins in ten hours or ten days, that time of waiting will seem like eternity to an adolescent victim. Therefore, it is advisable to factor in some kind of support, protection, and consolation into your interactions with a disclosing adolescent while waiting for the next step to begin.

Section 4. (Girls) The Investigation Begins
Section 5. (Girls) I'm Sorry, Mom
Section 5. (Boys) The Investigation Begins
Section 6. The Interview
Section 7. After the Interview
Section 8. Counseling

Key Points

1. *Waiting is stressful.*
a. Under the best of circumstances, waiting is aggravating. When a victim is dependent on others for information and protection, waiting can be an excruciating experience. Victims do not understand the adjudication process and waiting in the unknown creates enormous apprehension. It will be helpful to give the victims—as accurately as possible—an idea about how long they will wait at each stage. Particularly after the disclosure, it will be difficult for the victim to wait for

the investigation to begin. Depending on the jurisdiction and the victim's situation, the investigation may begin immediately. Some jurisdictions and situations may allow several days before a contact is made with the victim by the authorities. It would be helpful to know when the victim can expect to be contacted by authorities and to clearly communicate this information to him or her.

b. Encourage the victim to reach out for support while he or she is waiting. Be available to answer questions and to provide understanding and encouragement. Let the victim know specifically when you will and will not be available so as not to set up expectations that will not be met. The business cards in their backpacks were symbolic to Jane and Joe of the support which was available to them. There is a page at the end of the *We Are Not Alone* workbook for victims to write in the names and telephone numbers of people they can contact.

2. *The prospect of foster care is threatening.*

a. If a child or adolescent is being abused or has been abused by a family member—particularly a custodial parent—the most common practice is to remove the victim from the home into a foster care placement. To a child, this act of protection is often experienced as punishment, and can reinforce the feeling that the victim is at fault. Abusers have been known to coerce the victims into silence by threatening them with foster care if they reveal the abuse.

b. Foster care is not necessarily a refuge for abused children. Many child victims of physical and/or sexual abuse have been reabused in foster care situations.

c. No matter how abusive the home situation, the majority of child victims prefer to stay with their families. This is a phenomenon of attachment, dependence, and security. Many children do not know the extent of the dysfunction in their homes because they have never known anything different.

d. The best interest of the child must be kept in the forefront. If a nonabusive parent is supportive of the child, it is recommended that the abuser be removed from the home, and the child be given the safe haven of people and places that are familiar.

3. *Therapy is recommended.*

a. Therapy is recommended for victims and will unquestionably be useful. However, many victims, particularly adolescents, will be reluctant to participate in therapy. Well-meaning adults or friends may be encouraging them to "put it behind you and move on with your life." Reopening the wound by talking about what happened does not feel like moving on—and yet, it is the most effective way to truly move on.

b. Many victims cannot afford private therapy, so it is important that community resources and/or programs providing financial assistance for healing be made known to them. (Victims of Violent Crimes Programs in many states offer financial assistance for certain victims.)

c. Family therapy is a helpful option if nonoffending parents and siblings are open to participating. In this situation family members can learn about the dysfunctional dynamics in their home and take steps toward change. They can also learn and understand more about the experience of the victim.

d. Therapy for the abuser is crucial. Most states make sex offender therapy a mandatory part of any sentence for child sex abusers, and failure to attend will result in a stiffer sentence or revocation of parole. This is one reason why prosecution of sex offenders is so strongly recommended. As a group, they are not likely to seek counseling support without the external mandate of the court. Although sex offender therapy does not guarantee that abusers will not reoffend, short of incarcerating them for life, it is currently the best intervention available for protecting children from them.

4. *Victims may feel out of control once the adjudication process begins.*

a. Generally, they *are* out of control. The standard procedures and policies tend to take over the process once a disclosure is made. The most important intervention concerning this point is to inform victims and their families of this reality and invite them to ask questions and to openly express their concerns. Communicating about the process will help victims to feel that the process is more manageable.

b. Victims need to know that although they cannot control the process, they do have choices about their participation in the prosecution. After all, they are the eyewitnesses to the crime, and without their cooperation, in most instances, there is no case.

5. *The primary purpose of legal intervention is to protect the victim.*

a. The social service agencies, and juvenile or family court, are usually focused on protecting the victim and/or preserving the family unit. However, once a case is referred to the police or the district attorney, the focus becomes one of punishing the perpetrator. Adult victims often complain about feeling revictimized by the justice system. In many instances their complaints are justified. It is important to keep in mind the extra vulnerability of child and adolescent victims, and to take deliberate steps to protect them from further harm throughout a process intended to help them.

b. One way of protecting victims is to believe them. The abusers—usually adults—are much more capable of manipulating the system than are the victims. The first action abusers are likely to take is to deny the abuse, or to suggest that the victims misunderstood or initiated the sexual encounter. Attempts to discredit the victims will materialize in creative and unexpected ways. Jane and Joe repeatedly express the need to be believed, and this need will carry over to the majority of victims of child sexual abuse.

c. It is important to stress—over and over—to the victims that their disclosures are the first step toward protection. After all, their disclosures launch the social service and legal initiatives to protect the disclosing victims from further sexual abuse, and will ultimately protect additional children from being victimized while the perpetrators are incarcerated.

6. *Forensic interviews intensify victim vulnerability.*

a. Helping and legal professionals need to remain sensitive throughout the adjudication process to the vulnerablity of the victims, especially when they are required to communicate (possibly repeatedly to intimidating strangers) the details of the sexual abuse. Shame is a primary experience during this process. Adults would not welcome the necessity for revealing personal sexual encounters to social service workers, police officers, legal professionals, or juries. Sexual encounters are not common topics for discussion in our culture, and asking children and, especially adolescents who crave privacy, to reveal these details is a stress-provoking and shame-provoking request. Since the majority of victims are not in therapeutic relationships, most do not have experience in talking about the abuse, and most do not have support for the emotions that will surface once they begin talking about it.

b. Victims will be required to reveal specific details about the abuse. The forensic interviews in the *We Are Not Alone* workbooks are intentionally vague. However, the use of the words "vagina" and "penis" are an attempt to communicate the reality that victims will be required to be explicit. It will be helpful if victims are informed, in advance of the interviews, that they will be asked to describe exactly what happened using accurate names for body parts.

c. In many cases, the results of the forensic interviews determine whether the allegations are supported and the case is referred for further investigation and prosecution, and/or whether the prosecutor feels the allegations can be proven in court.

d. The forensic interviews are highly stressful for the victims. Professionals and supportive adults may want to consider and plan for a support system to be in place for the victims before and after the interviews.

7. *Victims feel isolated.*

a. Most victims feel confusion about what to tell to whom, and some guidance in this area is essential. Help victims to identify individuals who will be appropriate and safe to receive this vulnerable information.

b. Victims need a safe person/place to talk with about the feelings they are having in the present as a result of the prosecution process, as well as the opportunity to talk about the abuse. Group therapy is recommended for adolescents and these programs are often available through community mental health centers. Be aware of the resources that are available in your community.

Additional Resources

1. The National Criminal Justice Clearinghouse has multiple resources available. Call (800) 851-3420 for a list of their services and publications.

2. *Portable Guides to Investigating Child Abuse.*

   "Criminal Investigation of Child Sexual Abuse."
   "Interviewing Child Witnesses and Victims of Sexual Abuse."
   "Law Enforcement Response to Child Abuse."
   "Understanding and Investigating Child Sexual Exploitation."

   The Portable Guide series of pamphlets is a publication of the U.S. Department of Justice, Office of Juvenile Justice, and can be ordered by calling (800) 638-8736; e-mail: <askncjrs@ncjrs.org>.

3. *The Future of Children,* Volume 4, Number 2: Summer/Fall, 1994.

"Responding to Child Sexual Abuse: The Need for a Balanced Approach" by Douglas J. Besharov. *The Future of Children Journal* can be ordered from the David and Lucile Packard Foundation, Center for the Future of Children. Telephone: (650) 948-3696.

4. *The APSAC Handbook on Child Maltreatment.*

"Criminal Investigation of Sexual Victimization of Children" by Kenneth V. Lanning. "Interviewing Children In and Out of Court: Current Research and Practice" by Karen J. Saywitz and Gail S. Goodman. *The APSAC Handbook* can be ordered from Sage Publications. Telephone: (805) 499-0721; e-mail: <order@ sagepub.com>.

C. PROSECUTION: PRETRIAL

The pretrial phase of the prosecution process is actually where the organization of the case begins to take shape. The victim officially offers testimony in a pretrial hearing or for the grand jury; the charges are filed against the defendant; the defendant enters a plea; motions for courtroom accommodations and/or modifications take place; and a trial date is set. During this phase, the prosecutor will attempt to negotiate a plea bargain with the defense, in an effort to avoid the expense and emotional distress of a jury trial. A majority of crimes, including child sexual abuse, are disposed in this manner. Because most cases of child sexual abuse do not culminate in a jury trial, it is important to not just focus our supportive attention on those victims. The victims whose cases are settled in the Pretrial phase also need support. They have participated fully in the investigation and discovery phases and these are highly stressful and frightening experiences in themselves. Do not abandon victims just because their cases do not go to trial.

Section 9. Prosecution Begins
Section 10. Pretrial Testimony
Section 11. Counseling Support
Section 12. Waiting

Key Points

1. *Prosecution will only go forward if it is advisable for the victim.*

This point cannot be stressed enough. Victims, especially adolescents, need to know that they have choices. Now that they have disclosed the abuse, they will not be forced to testify in court. Even if a victim is not involved in a therapeutic situation, he or she will not be left alone in the decision to testify. Victim Witness Advocates and Child Interview Specialists are trained to observe victims for signs of distress which may indicate that they are not emotionally prepared to participate in a trial. In such cases, the prosecutor may be inclined to shelter this information and push the defense for a plea bargain.

2. *Explain, explain, explain the process.*

a. Victims and their parents cannot receive too much information about the investigation and prosecution processes.

b. Each professional who meets with the victim is likely to explain the process from his or her perspective as a means of informing the victim, but also as a means of making a meaningful contact during an initial meeting.

c. Encourage victims and their parents to take notes, to ask questions, to consult the glossary at the end of the *We Are Not Alone* workbook whenever a word comes up that they do not completely understand, and to contact a professional affiliated with the case if they need support at any time during the process.

3. *Address critical aspects of the criminal justice system.*

a. The foundational aspects of the criminal justice system may be illusive, confusing, and exasperating for victims of crimes and their families. Do not excuse the inadequacies of the system or to try to cover up its limitations. Explain the system factually and support the victims who will inevitably feel frustrated by laws designed to protect the rights of the defendant.

b. Be prepared to explain the concepts of "presumed innocent until proven guilty" and "reasonable doubt" in a way a child can comprehend. These concepts are generally misinterpreted in ways which can impose undue pressure on young victims. When misinformed, children and adolescents can believe that they must prove their innocence in court. They can also assume that a "not guilty" verdict is an indictment of them as liars, when the true meaning of the verdict is a judgment of the presentation of the prosecution's case.

c. Enormous guilt and grief are likely to surface for victims when defendants are found not guilty. Although this outcome does not happen often, it does happen, and it is crucial to provide attention and support for these victims.

d. The criminal justice system was designed for adult defendants and adult victims, and the influx of child victims has stretched the limits of the system and challenged its effectiveness. Some state statutes make courtroom accommodations available for child victims and witnesses, but in many instances prosecutors hesitate to use accommodations, fearing grounds for appeal of a conviction. Know what accommodations are available and consider what accommodations will be helpful to or necessary for a particular victim.

5. *Pretrial testimony is a significant stress for the victim.*

a. The victim may be required to provide pretrial testimony at a preliminary hearing in court, before a grand jury, or for a videotape to be used in lieu of live testimony. Any of these options will be a stress-provoking situation for a victim even though the testimony will not directly affect the guilty or not guilty verdict. It will, however, affect the decision whether or not to prosecute the case further. The victim will be asked to provide testimony similar to that which will eventually be offered in a trial court, which will involve clearly speaking explicit details of the abuse he or she experienced.

b. Some victims will be interviewed multiple times for pretrial discovery and testimony and will experience more shame and guilt each time they have to repeat the details of the abuse. The goal is to limit the number of interviews and times the victims must make themselves vulnerable and reveal the details of the abuse. Parents and other helping professionals can intervene on behalf of the child and discuss the number of interviews required with the prosecutor. This is an opportunity to ask questions and to be certain that the purpose for each interview is completely understood before subjecting the victim to perhaps unnecessary exposure.

6. *Establishing trusting relationships with helping and legal professionals will be healing for victims.*

a. Whether abused by a parent, a relative, an older sibling, a teacher, a priest, or a Scout leader, the victim's sense of trusting others has been shaken. In the situation of abuse by a parent, the victim's trust has probably been shaken to the very core. Adults who are working with victims of child sexual abuse have the opportunity to make a significant impact on the lives of these victims, an opportunity to begin healing the wound of trust. This opportunity should not be taken lightly. It is a heightened emotional time for the victims and some are likely to forget many of the details, however, they may, in fact, remember words and gestures which touch them. Other victims may remember the entire experience in exact detail for years.

b. Reliability is a quality that may help to heal shattered trust. To plant this seed of healing, helping and legal professionals need to keep their word. They need to call when they say they will; they need to do what they have informed the victim they will do; and they need to communicate all pertinent information as soon as possible. Failing to uphold these simple, respectful, interpersonal agreements will add more pain to the already wounded trust.

c. Return phone calls. Every victim and family I interviewed mentioned the importance of having access to the professionals handling the case. They are anxious and do not want to fear that they have been forgotten. Return the call even when there is nothing new to report, even when you do not yet have the answer to their questions. Professionals involved in legal cases are often overwhelmed with work, and some victims and/or their families have difficulty understanding this reality. They may be compulsive talkers, or inclined to talk more when they are nervous. It is a fine art for helping and legal professionals to learn how to be available to people who need their attention, and still to keep on track with their other responsibilities. Seeking training and guidance on achieving this balance will be far better for the victim than just choosing not to return the phone call until time is available or until there is something new to report.

8. *Child sexual abuse is a crime.*

a. This is the blunt truth. Until recently, child abuse, particularly within the family was considered a "family matter" to be worked out among the members of the family, and it was not taken too seriously by legal authorities. Times and laws have changed, but some attitudes have not. Because of these antiquated attitudes, victims may have difficulty grasping the criminal nature of the act. Particularly if overt coercion or violence were not part of the abuse they experienced. Sexual abuse can often feel good to the victim, and since it is most often perpetrated by a person the victim knows, it is hard to categorize this act as a crime.

b. Let victims know that laws exist to protect children. Show them copies of the laws if they are old enough to read them and understand.

c. Explain children's "rights." Since their rights were violated, often before they were able to comprehend the concept, they do not understand that they have a right to privacy and to protect their own bodies by saying "No."

d. Explain the "age of consent" and know what the legal age is in your state. This concept is important because many victims will believe that they were willing participants in the abuse. In many instances the perpetrators have coached them to believe this. In many instances victims believe this because they did not forcibly resist.

9. *Waiting is a fact of life throughout the adjudication process.*

a. The court process involves standard procedures, but because each case is unique, the process is not necessarily predictable. The schedule is one highly variable aspect of the process. Since the case load in most courts is quite heavy, trials can be scheduled six to nine months in advance. During that time many situations, from the defense requesting additional discovery to the judge's vacation plans, can interfere with a projected schedule. Waiting is a fact of life in the court system, and waiting longer than is expected should be anticipated. Preparing victims for this fact in advance will help to soften the blow when they are informed that the trial has been delayed.

b. It is important to receive the victim's feelings about delays and waiting, but since it is a fact of life, making the best of it is advisable. Asking the victim how he or she is doing is important so as not to appear avoidant. However, talking about the case or the abuse needs to be balanced with some other conversations and activities for the victim. School and socializing with safe friends and relatives are ideal distractions and give the victim a renewed sense of normalcy.

c. Joe and Jane watched legal shows on TV, trying to become "experts" about courtroom procedures. Although this is not the most reliable method of gathering accurate information about the court system (particularly when most cases get resolved within forty-five minutes), Joe and Jane felt a sense of meaning from these efforts. They felt they were doing something "productive" to prepare themselves. It may help victims to have productive activities while they are waiting. Reading the *We Are Not Alone* workbooks or other more realistic resources may help to better prepare victims than TV programs designed to entertain.

Additional Resources

1. *The Future of Children,* Volume 4, Number 2: Summer/Fall, 1994.

   "Adjudication of Child Sexual Abuse Cases" by John E. B. Myers. *The Future of Children Journal* can be ordered from the David and Lucile Packard Foundation, Center for the Future of Children. Telephone: (650) 948-3696.

2. *The User Manual Series:*

   "Working with the Courts in Child Protection" by Janet Nusbaum Feller. *The User Manual Series* is available from the National Clearinghouse on Child Abuse and Neglect (NCCAN). Telephone: (800) FYI-3366 or (703) 385-7565.

D. PROSECUTION: TRIAL

As mentioned in Chapter 1, 9 percent of child sexual abuse cases are referred for trial. This number seems low, but it is actually three times greater than other felony cases overall. Therefore, the lives of a relatively large number of sexually abused children and adolescents will intersect with the criminal justice system. In considering this intersection, it is important to acknowledge and understand that the criminal justice system was not/is not designed with the needs of children at the forefront, and accommodating their needs is still controversial. Keeping child and adolescent victims and their families adequately and clearly informed about the system and how it works is currently the best means available to prepare them for the experience of a criminal trial.

Key Points

1. *Prepare the victim for the courtroom experience.*

The criminal courtroom is a familiar place to legal, law enforcement, and social service professionals who work with sexually abused children. These professionals frequent these courtrooms, perhaps, daily. The personnel, the schedules, the procedures, and the activities are all familiar. However, it is significant to remember that this familiar place is totally foreign to victims and their families. It is, therefore, important to inform victims about all the details of the courtroom.

a. Victims, particularly adolescents seeking control and privacy in their lives, will be sensitive to the number of people in the courtroom. Take time to explain who all the court personnel are and what their responsibilities will be during the trial. Since the number of jurors will vary according to the type of crime (misdemeanor vs. felony) and type of court hearing the case (superior court, district court), as well as the policies of the jurisdiction, it is important to inform the victim about the number of jurors assigned to his or her case.

b. Because witnesses are not always sequestered during the practice of TV law, this practice may take victims and their families totally by surprise and may feel threatening both to victims and parents. It may be difficult for parents to even consider leaving their child during such a stressful time, therefore, helping them to understand this law and giving them time to process and prepare for this reality will be helpful. In certain circumstances where the well-being of the victim and/or his or her ability to testify will be negatively impacted by being separated from a significant support person who is also a witness, accommodations may be considered.

c. It is advisable for everyone—victims and their families and sea-soned professionals as well—to be prepared for the unexpected. In general, a legal proceeding has predictable parts and is usually a se-date and serious experience. However, in this emotionally charged microcosm of life, things happen that just cannot be anticipated. Vic-tims, witnesses, and family members of both the victim and the de-fendant are experiencing heightened stress and anxiety. Many are still in disbelief by the time they reach the courtroom. Many sob before, during, and after testifying, and experience despair as they watch their lives, as they knew them, shatter. The judge, who is considered the "boss of the courtroom" could be abrupt, and/or may exhibit be-havior that cannot be anticipated. In Jane's and Joe's cases, the judge could not hear the victim's testimony and he disrupted the proceedings in a brusque manner, which confused and frightened Jane and Joe.

d. The defendant is not required to testify. This may be a difficult reality for a victim to consider and experience. After all, the victim must endure the pressure of publicly testifying and answering ques-tions about humiliating experiences, and the defendant is not required to even speak on his or her own behalf. The decision whether the de-fendant testifies is a judgment call made by the defense. If the defense believes testimony from the defendant will help the case, he or she might testify; otherwise, the defendant might not testify. Some defen-dants insist on testifying, believing they can convince the jury of their innocence. In some jurisdictions, this decision will not be made until the trial is underway, so it is important to prepare the victim for either possibility.

2. *The court process is adversarial.*

a. The court process is adversarial by nature and cross-examina-tion of witnesses is the pinnacle of adversary. During cross-examina-tion, the defense attorney will attempt to discredit or blame the vic-tim. This will not be a pleasant or affirming experience, and it may fall to both the prosecutor and the judge to intervene and protect the victim from inappropriate or unfair questioning or badgering.

b. The closing arguments will accentuate the opposing positions of the prosecution and the defense. The prosecution will seek to hold the defense accountable for the crime of child sexual abuse, and the de-fense will again attempt to blame the victim by offering the argu-ments that the victim misunderstood, was mistaken, misinterpreted, imagined, fabricated the abuse to get attention or revenge, or simply lied.

c. The sentencing hearing will again emphasize the adverse positions of defense and prosecution. The defense will argue that the defendant, although a convicted child molester, is a good person in all other aspects of his or her life, and is well respected and responsible; or the defense may offer the explanation that the defendant was himself or herself abused and this behavior is in reaction to that abuse. Character witnesses may come forward to speak on the defendant's behalf, telling the court of his or her good character. The prosecution will present the picture of the defendant as one of society's most despicable criminals.

3. *The jury's assignment.*

a. In the adversarial system of criminal court in which two convincing arguments are professionally presented, one of the most difficult assignments of the jury is to determine who is telling the truth and who is lying. Motives for truth-telling or for lying must be weighed considerably and carefully. But determining who has the most compelling motive for lying, particularly in child sexual abuse cases when the defendants are often upstanding, law-abiding citizens, may not be all that easy. Imagine a case in which the defendant is a fifty-year-old, well dressed, educated, employed man, who is a deacon at his church and is well liked and respected by everyone in the community. He volunteers his time as a Boy Scout leader, and the prosecution contends that over the past ten years he has sexually molested more boys than can be counted. The man before the court does not resemble society's definition of a despicable criminal in any way imaginable, and the defense will feature this inconsistency in the case. The man will take the witness stand and deny that the abuse occurred, using reasonable and convincing language, insisting that he would never harm a defenseless child. He may ultimately express horror at the accusation. The jury may not be familiar with the realities of child sexual abuse and it may appear inconceivable that this defendant could have perpetrated such heinous crimes. Therefore, the victim's integrity may come into question. Is it possible that the victim is lying? What motive does the victim have for lying, for going through the grueling court process if the abuse did not happen? What possible motive? The defense will attempt to convince the jury that the victim is lying, or at least to plant the golden nugget of "reasonable doubt" in the jury's thoughts.

b. The next dilemma for the jury is to determine if the prosecution met the burden of proof. Was evidence presented to the court that proved the defendant's guilt beyond a reasonable doubt according to the laws and definitions of their jurisdiction? The jury may believe that the defendant is guilty, but if the evidence is not conclusive then they must reach a verdict of not guilty. The concept of reasonable doubt is worth exploring with victims and their families prior to going to court, so they understand what is actually being considered by the jury. Refer to the glossary for a very basic definition of reasonable doubt.

c. The jury must reach a verdict. In superior court criminal trials, the verdict must be unanimous, which means all jurors must be in agreement about the verdict. If after deliberating for a reasonable amount of time, the jurors cannot reach a unanimous decision, a mistrial is declared and the trial may be repeated with a new jury. In other types of courts and other levels of crimes, the number of jurors needing to be in agreement in order to reach a verdict may vary. It is important to communicate this information to victims and their families during courtroom preparation.

4. *Sentencing.*

a. As with the pretrial motions and hearings, the victim is not required to attend the sentencing hearing. However, many states and many judges invite victims and witnesses to prepare a statement for the court expressing how they have been affected by the crime and what they think the defendant's sentence should be. The judge will consider these statements, which may be written and sent to the judge or stated in court, when imposing the sentence. These statements may also be received from the defendant and/or witnesses, relatives, friends, colleagues, etc., on behalf of the defendant. The victim is not mandated to prepare an impact statement; however, it is an opportunity for the victim to be heard by the court and to have his or her wishes about sentencing known and considered by the judge.

b. Many states have sentencing guidelines for specific crimes and/or mandatory sentencing. Within these guidelines and mandates, the judge exercises his or her discretion when imposing sentences on convicted defendants. It will be helpful to know these guidelines and mandates in your state to help the victim better understand what the possible outcomes of the sentencing could be.

c. The prosecutor and the defense attorney will also make sentencing recommendations. Before the judge passes sentence, each attorney will make a statement before the court offering suggestions for sentencing, which the judge may consider. The defense will undoubtedly request a lenient sentence. The prosecutor, being aware of the sentencing guidelines and mandates, will request a sentence within the guidelines in the best interest of the state.

d. The sentence imposed on the defendant may not reflect reality. The formulas for calculating how much actual time (versus sentence received) will be served in prison by the defendant are complex and vary by jurisdiction. Parole options also differ based on type of crime and jurisdiction. The victims need to know how many years the abuser will be incarcerated, how many on parole, how many in mandatory counseling. It is a safety issue for victims, and knowing how long the abusers will *actually* be in jail respective to the sentence received is a critical piece of information. Some states offer a service to victims and will notify them when their abusers are about to be released from prison.

Additional Resources

1. *The APSAC Handbook on Child Maltreatment.*

   "Child Abuse and Neglect Laws and Legal Proceedings" by Josephine Bulkley, Jane Nusbaum Feller, Paul Stern, and Rebecca Roe. *The APSAC Handbook* can be ordered from Sage Publications. Telephone: (805) 499-0721; e-mail: <order@ sagepub.com>.

E. COUNSELING AND PERSONAL ISSUES

The psychological and physical vulnerabilities of sexually abused children and adolescents cannot be underestimated. Acknowledging, assessing, and addressing these vulnerabilities throughout the adjudication process will be helpful to both the victim and the legal case. Depending on the type and length of abuse, as well as the age when the abuse began, and/or if the victim has received any support or counseling prior to the disclosure, the impact of the abuse on the victim will vary. However, given the current understanding that no victim of child sexual abuse will emerge from the experience unaffected, some type of counseling support is recommended. If the victim becomes involved in the adjudication process, counseling is doubly recommended because on top of the abuse experience has been piled a confusing, stressful, and emotionally intense legal process.

The teen characters in the workbooks are insightful and reflective. It is unrealistic to expect any adolescent victim of child sexual abuse to have this level of self-awareness during such a stressful time. Victims *need* understanding, guidance, and support. Parents, although well-intentioned, probably cannot provide the type of support needed because they are also involved and may be distressed and in need of their own support. Since parents and other well-meaning relatives are generally not informed about issues teens may experience as a result of child sexual abuse, expecting them to provide the type of help a teen victim needs while going through the adjudication process is impractical and may even be dangerous for the victim.

The legal and helping professionals involved in the case will be knowledgeable about community and private counseling resources, and they will be prepared to make appropriate referrals. It is recommended, however, that other professionals who may receive disclosures (i.e., school personnel) or who may be sought out by victims or their families for help (i.e., pastors or physicians), educate themselves regarding counseling resources for sexual abuse issues both for victims and perpetrators, and to be prepared to make referrals.

Section 3. (Boys) I'm Sorry
Section 5. (Girls) I'm Sorry, Mom
Section 5. (Boys) The Investigation Begins

Key Points

1. *The reactions of people hearing a disclosure of child sexual abuse, and/or learning about the abuse for the first time, are important to the victim.*
   a. The most common reactions include empathy and compassion from people (i.e., mandated reporters) who are knowledgeable about the issues and know what to do when receiving a disclosure. Com-

mon reactions from people who are not prepared to receive the information include shock, disbelief, and denial. These reactions are most notable when the abuser is someone known and respected. Guilt and anger are also common reactions. Nonoffending parents commonly feel responsible for the sexual abuse of their child because they believe they should have/could have done something to prevent the abuse—*if only* they had been more protective, spent more time with their child, etc. The *if only* list could be endless. Nonoffending parents may be infuriated to learn their child has been violated. This reaction, if not taken to an extreme or directed at the victim, may be the most healing reaction for the victim to experience. It could help the victim to feel his or her own justified anger at the violation.

b. "I realized how important it was for me that my parents believed me" (Joe); "I just knew I needed my mom to believe me" (Jane). Victims have taken a huge risk by revealing the sexual abuse. Some may have been threatened by the perpetrator to keep silent or else expect a horrible disaster, such as another child being abused or a parent dying as a result of knowing the truth. Receiving disbelief in response to a disclosure of child sexual abuse is devastating and emotionally destructive for the victim. It may, indeed, be difficult to believe that a known and respected person, such as a teacher, neighbor, relative, friend, priest, church member, could have sexually abused any child. In such circumstances it is preferable not to express disbelief, but to allow the authorities to conduct an investigation. False accusations of sexual abuse do happen, but not very often. Therefore, it is best when receiving a disclosure to err on the side of believing the victim, to offer comfort and support, and to seek professional assistance as soon as possible. Receiving disbelief and denial in response to a disclosure of child sexual abuse may be damaging for the victim's already wounded psyche.

2. *The victim will be likely to have emotional reactions to people knowing about the sexual abuse.*

As more people learn about the sexual abuse—either through the investigation process or by the victim's voluntary revelations—the victim is likely to feel shame and remorse for telling. The shame is a natural result of feeling exposed and the remorse is almost inevitable in child sexual abuse cases because of the relationship between perpetrator and victim. The power of these emotions may facilitate a recantation. Legal and helping professionals familiar with the issues surrounding child sexual abuse cases are likely to be prepared to deal effectively with victims who recant.

3. *Talking about the details of the abuse is difficult for victims.*

a. This point seems so obvious, why even mention it here? It is a reminder for professionals who routinely talk about anal rape over lunch that not everyone shares their sensibilities. A child or adolescent victim of child sexual abuse, who must actually say "penis" or "vagina" out loud in public, may experience embarrassment and/or anxiety. This may be a wild speculation, but it is assumed that most adults who find themselves saying "penis" or "vagina" out loud in public—for much more benign reasons—do so with at least a tinge of embarrassment. Professionals working with this information every day may be desensitized, but it is important to remember that throughout the adjudication process, sexually abused children are asked to ignore their own boundaries of privacy and to reveal explicit, humiliating details about how their bodies were molested. In addition, victims must reveal precise details about the bodies of their abusers. These are never easy or effortless revelations.

b. Victims know that the more people who know about the abuse, the more likely it is that the abuse they experienced will soon be common knowledge among their relatives and friends, and throughout their neighborhoods and schools. Worrying about what people will think of them once the sexual abuse is known is of grave concern for adolescent victims. It is important to receive this worry with respect and not to dismiss it. Adolescents, in particular, can be cruel to their peers and can take pleasure in teasing and taunting the vulnerable among them. Be prepared to provide victims with support and strategies for protecting themselves from peer, family, and community pressures and/or judgments.

Section 7: After the Interview

Key Points:

1. *The victim is not responsible for taking the defendant to court or for putting the defendant in jail.*

a. Thinking that they are responsible for putting their abusers into jail may give some victims a rush of power and it may cause some to feel enormous pressure and distress. Others may feel a combination of power and pressure. Depending on the relationship to the abuser, the intensity of the reactions may vary. It is important to explain to victims that the state is filing the criminal charges to protect the victim and the residents of their state. The victim is a witness for the prosecution, but is not responsible for the legal actions being taken against the defendant.

b. Child and adolescent victims are likely to have mixed emotions about their abuser receiving a jail sentence. Although the victims want the abuse to stop, they may not want their fathers or uncles or pastors, etc., to be in jail. It is important to explain to victims that child molesters will usually not stop sexually abusing children unless they are forced to by an external intervention.

2. *It is "normal" for victims to be upset during the adjudication process.*

a. Our culture does not encourage people to openly express emotions. However, at times people may experience overwhelming feelings—for example, during a child sexual abuse investigation—and it may be impossible and ill-advised to withhold their emotions. Although acknowledging and expressing their intense feelings may cause some people to feel unstable, it will help victims and their families to hear that these overwhelming emotions are normal reactions to a difficult experience.

3. *Attitudes about and experiences with therapy vary.*

a. Recommending therapy for sexually abused children and adolescents is a common practice. Knowing these victims have been seriously violated and may have lifelong emotional scars, therapy is the treatment of choice. However, some individuals or families may have negative attitudes about therapy, and, therefore, do not support the victims in this treatment. Without family support, it is unlikely that adolescent victims will pursue or persist in a therapeutic relationship.

b. Misunderstandings about what therapy is and what it is for may cause adolescent victims to react in anger when treatment is recommended for them. They may feel that they are being judged as crazy or at fault. They may confuse therapy with punishment. Generally, their reference point for therapy is the knowledge that their peers who are in trouble are "sent" to therapy. These attitudes will be difficult to overcome.

Section 8. Counseling

Key Points

1. *Victims feel isolated.*
a. Victims of child sexual abuse live under a shroud of secrecy which causes them to feel isolated because they cannot show their true selves to the world. After disclosing the abuse, the isolation may increase because the victims feel different from their peers.

b. Helping the victims determine who to confide in regarding the abuse is an important step toward relieving the isolation. Confiding in close friends and/or the parents of close friends who will be kind and supportive can be a helpful intervention. However, confiding in un-trustworthy companions or relatives who are not understanding or supportive, or who greet the disclosure with denial may be harmful to a victim.

c. Relieving isolation by talking with a counselor who is trained in sex abuse therapy is the best approach. This provides an opportunity for the victim to be seen in a place of safety and to develop a trusting relationship with an adult. When choosing a therapist for a sexually abused adolescent, be particularly mindful of the victim's comfort level with adults who are the same gender as the abuser.

2. *Parental support for therapy is critical.*
Adolescent victims will not be eager to begin therapy. Parents are encouraged to take the lead by making the appointment and accompanying the victim to the first session and/or subsequent sessions as needed. The adolescent's desire for independence may not coincide with his or her need to be taken care of during a stressful time. Careful negotiation of these needs is recommended until the victim feels safe enough and committed enough to the process to go to therapy alone.

3. *Jane and Joe project keen awareness about issues and feelings.*
a. Actual victims are not likely to have the same level of awareness as the teen characters in the workbooks. Actual victims are likely to be confused to the extreme. The purpose of the characters' awareness is to help victims identify their own feelings or project their own feelings onto the characters as a jumping-off point for discussion.

b. Reassure the victims that their feelings—even if they differ from Jane's and Joe's—are normal feelings in reaction to the abnormal experience of abuse.

Section 11. Counseling Support

Key Points

1. *Victims may experience physical symptoms.*

As a result of the emotional strain from the abuse and the adjudication process, victims of child sexual abuse may experience a number of idiosyncratic physical symptoms that cannot be explained by medical diagnosis. These symptoms may include fatigue, headaches, insomnia, or nausea. Do not discount these symptoms because a physical cause cannot be determined. Stress puts enormous pressure on the body, and this stress will often be manifested in physical symptoms.

2. *Victims may regret disclosing.*

a. It is common for victims to regret disclosing the abuse. Most do want the abuse to end, but feelings of confusion spark the regret anyway. Victims may be overcome with feelings of guilt and shame. They know that disclosing means people will know what they have done. Victims, not understanding the dynamic of child sexual abuse may, indeed, believe the abuse was their fault.

b. The victims may feel that they have caused trouble for themselves, their families, and/or the abuser and his or her family. It may be very difficult for children and adolescents to understand that the abuser—not the victim—has caused the trouble for all those involved.

c. Victims may feel such extreme distress after disclosing that they will choose to recant.

d. Victims may experience confusion about the prosecution process, particularly if their cases are headed for court. They may fret about this, wondering if it is a good idea to be involved or if they want to do this at all.

3. *Children have rights.*

a. Communicate to child and adolescent victims about "Human Rights," and help them understand that their human rights of privacy and control over their own bodies have been violated. Jane and Joe came to believe in their rights because the helping and legal professionals involved in their cases were strong proponents and protectors of these rights, *and* they transmitted their beliefs to the victims.

4. *Victims have choices.*

Victims need to know that they have some control over what happens during the adjudication process. They are not, once again, victims in a situation that is completely outside of their control. The most important choice to stress is the choice about testifying against the defendant in pretrial testimonies and/or courtroom testimony.

Section 12. Waiting

Key Points

1. *Waiting sparks a range of emotions.*

Anger and fear top the list of the emotions sparked by waiting. Victims and their families can feel ignored or neglected by the waiting which is an integral part of the adjudication process, and anger—which is already at the surface because of the abuse—begins to intensify. Normal fear about the process, mixed with apprehension, can expand to panic when left unchecked during times of waiting. Unfortunately, not much can be done to hurry the process. Therefore, waiting must be acknowledged, endured, and effectively managed.

2. *Victims may feel excitement and fear.*

In this highly charged emotional situation, the adolescent victim is the center of attention. He or she may feel excited and powerful. Do not deny, diminish, or judge any of the victim's feelings. Many victims of child sexual abuse are emotionally neglected, which is why they are more easily subjected to sexual abuse. When the spotlight of attention from the investigation and prosecution is focused on these neglected children, they may actually enjoy it and flourish within in it. They may be excited by being a part of the court process and by the critical role they play. Adolescents, in particular, may feel very grown-up and respected. It may be the first time in their lives that they feel they have been taken seriously. It may be difficult for victims to understand and accept their excitement and to keep it in a proper perspective. It also may be difficult to separate their excitement from the fear they will inevitably experience.

Section 13. At School

Key Points

1. *Victims may experience difficulties at school.*

a. Adolescent victims of child sexual abuse—even those who previously have not had problems at school—may experience difficulties at school following a disclosure and throughout the adjudication process. This is a time of emotional and physical upheaval and expecting the life of the victims to go forward according to the status quo is unrealistic. The stress of the trial may cause insomnia and fatigue, and as a result, victims may experience difficulty in concentrating. They may be unusually anxious, easily startled or provoked to tears, and distracted during class. Their grades and performance in extracurricular activities may falter. Jane's and Joe's parents notified school administrators about this stressful time in the lives of their children, seeking as much support as possible for Jane and Joe. Each situation should be considered individually and the helping adults and parents should determine with the victim what kind of support would be helpful.

b. Victims may become withdrawn at school. In an effort to avoid drawing attention to themselves, victims may become extremely quiet, not participating in class discussions or social activities. These behaviors are a form of protection from exposure and vulnerability. Once victims disclose sexual abuse they may experience unreasonable fear and shame that everyone now knows and that people can tell just by looking at them what has been done to their bodies. Withdrawal is a coping technique to avoid the fear and shame.

2. *Social aspects of school.*

In the lives of adolescents, school represents much more than a place for intellectual learning. School is the primary source of social interaction and peer relationships. Adolescents are peer conscious to an extreme, and how peers react to the sexual abuse will be important to a victim. The question about which friends to tell and/or how to tell them will be a concern. Parents and therapists can help with this dilemma. Talking with friends' parents, coaching friends to help to "break the ice" by starting conversations about typical teenage interests and extending invitations to usual activities, and helping the victim develop coping techniques to deal with cruel reactions are some ways to be supportive. Ready or not, peer interactions following a disclosure of child sexual abuse will provide the victim with ample opportunities to learn about friendship and trust.

Section 26. Victim Impact Statement

Key Points

1. *A paradox of feelings.*

In her victim impact statement, Jane projects deep insight into her paradoxical feelings about her father. She is able to communicate clearly about her conflicted feelings. Although she still feels love for her father, she is able to acknowledge that he did something wrong, and to feel and believe that he must be held accountable.

2. *The safety of other children is at stake.*

Victims of child sexual abuse need to understand the pivotal role their participation in the prosecution process has on their own safety as well as the safety of other children. In his victim impact statement, Joe mentions twice that he wants to make sure Bob cannot hurt any other boys. Joe's father stresses how much Joe has sacrificed to protect other boys. Since most child molesters are repetitive and compulsive, prosecuting them is the most effective way to interrupt their abusive behaviors with either the outcome of incarceration or mandatory counseling.

3. *Victims want and need to feel safe.*

The disclosure and subsequent prosecution may set off a series of threats directed at the victim by the abuser. Practical steps, such as a restraining order, can help to ensure the victim's safety during the adjudication process, however, more protection is needed. The perpetrator in jail represents the ultimate protection for the victim. Although the purpose of a prison sentence is accountability—to punish the perpetrator for his or her crimes—it is also the one sure way a victim will feel protected from further abuse by this person. Other means of protection, both physical and emotional, can be explored on a case-by-case basis. What does the individual victim need to feel safe? Therapy can help victims and families to determine how to establish and maintain safety for the victim.

Section 28. Toward Recovery

Key Points

1. *A sense of control.*

The end of the abuse, particularly abuse which ends due to a victim's disclosure, may help to give the victim a sense of control over his or her body—perhaps for the first time. This feeling of control may be empowering, and may even spill over into other areas of the victim's life.

2. *We are not alone.*

The awareness that there are adults in the world who want to protect and respect children may have a healing impact on a victim. Many victims have lived much of their young lives burdened by isolation and fear, and it can be a relief to discover that there are people who care about children, and who will help them. Just experiencing adults who are not exploitative will have a healing effect.

3. *Forgiveness.*

a. Some victims may be pressured to forgive. In situations of intra-familial abuse this pressure may be extreme. Other victims may come from religious traditions that stress forgiveness as a prerequisite for salvation. Forgiveness is a complex topic from both a moral and a practical perspective. Victims and their families are encouraged to explore this topic with therapists and religious leaders to reach a comfortable and healing conclusion.

b. Jane raises two points that are crucial to consider in the forgiveness discussion: (1) Has the abuser apologized to the victim? Does the abuser feel true remorse and regret for his or her actions? Or, is the abuser truly sorry that he or she got caught and is facing punishment? (2) Has the abuser repented—taken sincere and serious steps to change his or her behavior?

c. Do not use the concept of forgiveness as a method to manipulate a resolution to a conflicted relationship and "get on with life." The sexual abuse of a child is an extreme violation of the child's body and soul, and of the child's trust. Do not advise or urge the child to forgive the abuser for any purpose outside of the child's best interest.

4. *Courage.*

The courage of a child or adolescent who discloses child sexual abuse and participates in the prosecution process cannot be underestimated. It is a risky and painful path for a child to walk, and encouragement and support for his or her courageous decision are critical.

5. *A conviction does not make it "all better."*

a. Sexually abused children and adolescents may experience physical and emotional posttraumatic symptoms related to the abuse for years, and some for life. Although a trial resulting in a conviction draws closure to one phase in the victim's life, parents and other supportive adults should not assume that this is the end of the issue for the victim. Helping the victim to understand that the end of the trial will not necessarily be a cure-all will give the victim a more realistic view of what to expect.

b. At the end of the trial, the victim may feel depressed. After months of intensity, the absence of this intensity may cause the victim to feel alone and let down. Although this reaction may be interpreted as depression, it is a usual and anticipated reaction at the end of an emotional and stressful time. Professional support will be helpful and is recommend for any victim experiencing symptoms of depression at any time during or after the adjudication process.

6. *Hope for the future.*

Young lives are not ruined forever by sexual abuse. Although the lives of the victims may be more painful and more challenging than the lives of their peers, they can succeed at living healthy and fulfilling lives. Without denying the reality and the effects of the abuse and the trial, encourage the young survivors to learn to truly live.

Additional Resources

1. *The APSAC Handbook on Child Maltreatment.*

   "Treating Abused Adolescents" by Mark Chaffin, Barbara L. Bonner, Karen Boyd Worley, and Louanne Lawson. *The APSAC Handbook* can be ordered from Sage Publications. Telephone: (805) 499-0721; e-mail: <order@sagepub.com>.

2. *The Future of Children,* Volume 4, Number 2: Summer/Fall, 1994.

   "Immediate and Long-Term Impacts of Child Sexual Abuse" by John N. Briere and Diana M. Elliott. *The Future of Children Journal* can be ordered from the David and Lucile Packard Foundation, Center for the Future of Children. Telephone: (650) 948-3696.

3. *Lasting Effects of Child Sexual Abuse,* edited by G.E. Wyatt and G.J. Powell. "Treating the Effects of Sexual Abuse on Children" by J.R. Wheeler and L. Berliner. *Lasting Effects of Child Sexual Abuse* can be ordered from Sage Publications. Telephone: (805) 499-0721; e-mail: <order@sagepub.com>.

4. *Psychotherapy with Sexually Abused Boys: An Integrated Approach* by William N. Friedrich. *Psychotherapy With Sexually Abused Boys* is part of *Interpersonal Violence: The Practice Series,* edited by Jon R. Conte, and can be ordered from Sage Publications. Telephone: (805) 499-0721; e-mail: <order@sagepub.com>.

5. *Portable Guides to Investigating Child Abuse.*

   "Sexually Transmitted Diseases in Child Sexual Abuse."

   The Portable Guide series of pamphlets is a publication of the U.S. Department of Justice, Office of Juvenile Justice, and can be ordered by calling (800) 638-8736; or e-mail: <askncjrs@ ncjrs.org>.

6. *The Survivor's Guide: For Teenage Girls Surviving Abuse* by Sharice A. Lee, can be ordered from Sage Publications. Telephone: (805) 499-0721; e-mail: <order@sagepub.com>.

7. *Treating Abused Adolescents* by Eliana Gil can be ordered from Guilford Publications. Telephone: (800) 365-7006.

8. *The User Manual Series:*

   "The Role of Mental Health Professionals in the Prevention and Treatment of Child Abuse and Neglect" by Marilyn Strachan Peterson and Anthony J. Urquiza.

   "Treatment for Abused and Neglected Children: Infancy to Age 18" by Anthony J. Urquiza and Cynthia Winn. *The User Manual Series* is available from the National Clearinghouse on Child Abuse and Neglect (NCCAN). Telephone: (800) FYI-3366 or (703) 385-7565.

Chapter 8

Guiding Questions

Section 1. (Girls) I'm Jane / (Boys) I'm Joe

1. Do you remember how old you were when the abuse you experienced started?
2. When and how did you realize that what was happening to you was abuse?
3. What feelings and reactions did you experience while the abuse was happening?
4. (Girls) As a result of her abuse, Jane felt confusion, fear, anxiety, upset, and physical illness. But she pretended that everything was fine. Were your reactions similar to Jane's? Did you experience other feelings and reactions as well?
4. (Boys) Joe had confusing feelings about Bob, his abuser. Did/do you have confusing feelings your abuser? What are some of your feelings?

Section 2. The First Time I Told

1. How did you decide to tell someone about the abuse?
2. Whom did you first tell about the abuse? What was helpful about his or her reaction?
3. (Girls) After she told Mrs. Winston about the abuse, Jane felt a mixture of feelings: relief, gratitude, guilt, fear, shame. These are *some* of the feelings teens experience after disclosing abuse. What feelings did you experience after you told?
3. (Boys) After he told Mr. Stone about the abuse, Joe felt a mixture of feelings: shame, guilt, confusion, sadness. These are *some* of the feelings teens experience after disclosing abuse. What feelings did you experience after you told?

4. Did the person you told notify anyone else? If so, how did/do you feel about other people knowing?
5. (Girls) Did you know that your state had a Mandated Reporter Law regarding child abuse?
5. (Boys) How did you feel about yourself after disclosing the abuse?

Section 3. (Girls) Making A Report

1. How did/do you feel about your abuse being reported to the social service and legal authorities?
2. Jane's guidance counselor gave her a telephone number for a twenty-four-hour crisis line. How do you think that calling the crisis line would have helped Jane? How do you think it would help you to call a crisis line?
3. After Jane's disclosure, her feelings became very intense. She tried to manage her feelings by retreating to her room, listening to music, watching TV, pacing, and hurting herself by twisting her fingers. What do you do to help manage intense feelings?

Section 3. (Boys) I'm Sorry

1. Sometimes parents are supportive and helpful to an abused teen, as Joe's parents were. Sometimes their initial reactions, such as Joe's dad's anger, can be scary. Sometimes parents and other family members are too upset about the abuse and worried about what will happen to be supportive of the teen. What was it like for you when your parents first learned about the abuse?
2. Did you know that your state had a Mandated Reporter Law regarding child abuse? How did/do you feel about your abuse being reported to the social service and legal authorities?

Section 4. (Girls) The Investigation Begins

1. When the legal investigation began, it was difficult for Jane to wait for the various steps in the process to happen. How do you react to having to wait? How do you react to not knowing what the outcome of your situation will be? How do you calm and comfort yourself during the necessary times of waiting and not knowing?

2. If you felt afraid during the disclosure and investigation, were you also able to feel brave for doing the right thing and telling someone about the abuse?

3. Why do you think that the person who abused you did it?

Section 4. (Boys) Making a Report

1. Joe's guidance counselor gave him a telephone number for a twenty-four-hour crisis line. How do you think that calling the crisis line would have helped Joe? How do you think it would help you to call a crisis line?

2. Joe worried that if the kids at school found out about the abuse and that he told about Bob, they would think he was "weird" or "a snitch" or "damaged." Did you/do you have similar worries? Are you worried about additional things kids might think about you if they knew?

3. After his disclosure and the abuse was reported, Joe's feelings became very intense. He tried to manage his feelings by retreating to his room, listening to music, watching TV, playing basketball, and not talking about the situation. What do you do to help manage intense feelings?

4. Crying was difficult and embarrassing for Joe. How do you feel about boys crying?

Section 5. (Girls) I'm Sorry, Mom

1. Sometimes a parent can be supportive and helpful to an abused teen, as Jane's mom was. Sometimes parents and other family members are too upset about the abuse and too worried about what will happen to be supportive of the teen. What was it like for you when your family first learned about the abuse?

2. How do you feel about the idea of going to counseling? How do you think it will help you to talk with someone about the abuse that happened to you?

3. How did/do you feel about telling more people about the abuse?

4. How did/do you think that your friends and relatives and teachers and other people you know will feel about you after they find out about the abuse?

5. Jane did not want to have to tell more people about the abuse, but her mom said "Yes" to the interview in order to protect Jane. How do you feel about taking steps to stop your abuser?

Section 5. (Boys) The Investigation Begins

1. Why do you think that the person who abused you did it?
2. How did/do you feel about telling more people about the abuse?
3. How did/do you think that your friends and relatives and teachers and other people you know will feel about you after they find out about the abuse?
4. Joe didn't want to have to tell more people about the abuse, but he knew it was important to tell in order to stop Bob from abusing more boys. How do you feel about taking steps to stop your abuser from abusing other kids?

Section 6. The Interview

1. What were some of the feelings you experienced before, during, and after your interview?
2. How did/do you feel about saying exactly what happened to you?
3. (Girls) Jane felt ashamed and guilty saying words such as penis and vagina. What words are hard for you to say?
3. (Boys) Joe felt ashamed saying words such as penis and anus. What words are hard for you to say?
4. (Girls) Jane felt proud of herself for being strong enough to do something that was so scary. How do you feel about yourself when you do something that is very hard for you to do?
4. (Boys) Joe felt proud of himself for being strong enough to do something to stop Bob even though he was scared to do it. How do you feel about yourself when you do something that is very hard for you to do?

Section 7. After the Interview

1. (Girls) The investigation and prosecution processes were confusing to Jane because they were all new and different. If the processes seem confusing to you or your family, what can you do to help yourself better understand what is happening?

1. (Boys) The investigation and prosecution processes were confusing to Joe because they were all new and different. If the processes seem confusing to you or your family, what can you do to help yourself better understand what is happening?
2. What do you want to happen to your abuser if he or she is found guilty?
3. How will you feel if your abuser is found not guilty?
4. How do you feel about not knowing what the outcome of the case will be?
5. How do you feel about the possibility of your abuser being arrested?
6. What opinions do you and members of your family have about counseling?

Section 8. Counseling

1. How did you feel (physically and emotionally) before you told people about the abuse? How did you feel after you told?
2. Do you think you would call a therapist or a crisis line if you wanted or needed to talk with someone? Why? Why not?
3. (Girls) Jane made a list of items to talk about with her therapist, Cathy. How do you feel about the items on Jane's list? How is your list the same and different? Write a list of items you want to talk about or know more about.
3. (Boys) Joe made a list of items to talk about with his therapist, Cathy. How do you feel about the items on Joe's list? How is your list the same and different? Write a list of items you want to talk about or know more about.

Section 9. Prosecution Begins

1. Sometimes it is not a good idea for a victim of child sexual abuse to go forward with prosecution. How will you know if it is a good idea for you to go forward?
2. What do you think about the concept that someone accused of a crime is considered innocent until proven guilty?
3. What are some of the words or practices in the criminal justice system that you find confusing?

Section 10. Pretrial Testimony

1. How has the fact of your abuse affected other members of your family?
2. How was the interview handled in your case? How did/do you feel about this process?
3. What was/is the hardest thing for you to talk about regarding the abuse?
4. What helps you trust that you can count on people to be there for you?

Section 11. Counseling Support

1. How were/are you feeling about your abuser after your disclosure and during the investigation process?
2. Who can you talk with about any feelings you have that are difficult for you or that you do not understand?
3. How do you feel about having the power to stop the prosecution at any time?

Section 12. Waiting

1. What information do you need to help you better understand why the court process takes so long?
2. Waiting is difficult for most people. How do you cope with waiting?

Section 13. At School

1. What kind of support do you need at school? How can you ask for what you need?
2. How did people in your life (friends, family, teachers) react when they learned that you had been sexually abused? Which reactions were helpful? Which ones hurt you? Why?
3. How do you know whom to trust?

Section 14. The Indictment

1. How do you feel about the possibility that your abuser's name will appear in the newspaper and on television?

2. What do the laws in your state say about keeping the victim's name private? (*Note:* You can check with your state legislator's office for this information or ask your victim witness advocate.)

Section 15. The Arraignment

1. How do you feel about the amount of time your case is taking?
2. Do you understand the reasons for any delays? What are they?
3. What kind of support do you need to help you through this long process?
4. Are there any words in this chapter that you don't understand? (*Note:* The vocabulary used in court and about the court process is unique. Consult the glossary and ask questions anytime you do not understand a word.)

Section 16. Waiting Again

1. How do you feel about the possibility of your abuser contacting you or trying to see you?
2. If you feel afraid of your abuser, what steps have been taken to keep you safe?
3. If you think it's a good idea to put your troubles aside sometimes, how do you do that?

Section 17. The Empty Courtroom

1. What do you think it means to prove the defendant's guilt beyond a reasonable doubt?
2. How will you feel if your abuser is acquitted (found not guilty) by the jury? How will you feel if your abuser is convicted (found guilty)?
3. Do you think it is a good idea to visit the empty courtroom before the trial? Would you like to do this? Why? Why not?

Section 18. Pretrial Details

1. Sometimes judges will make minor accommodations for young victims and witnesses. Sometimes they will not make accommodations. But, it is important to ask for whatever you need to

help make the process less stressful for you. What kind of accommodations do you think will be helpful to you in court?
Why? Have you discussed accommodations with your victim
witness advocate? Have you asked what accommodations in the
courtroom have been allowed on other cases and helpful to other
kids?

2. (Girls) When Jane got upset about the court process, she wondered, "Whose side are they on?" Sometimes abuse victims feel
revictimized by the court process. How do you feel about how
your case is being handled?

2. (Boys) When Joe got upset about the court process, he wondered, "Whose side are they on?" Sometimes abuse victims feel
revictimized by the court process. How do you feel about how
your case is being handled?

Section 19. Delays and Preparations

1. How do you feel when you are informed about delays in the trial
date?
2. There will be months of waiting before the trial begins. What
can you do while you are waiting for the trial to start to help
yourself feel prepared?

Section 20. The Trial Begins

1. How did/do you feel about the trial finally starting?
2. The experience of being in court will be different for each victim and witness. What was/is the trial like for you? What part of
the experience surprised you the most? What part did/do you
dislike the most?

Section 21. In Court

1. The courtroom is a tense place, and the beginning of a trial
sparks intense emotions. What feelings do/did you have as you
anticipate(d) the trial?
2. Were there parts of the trial that you did not understand or that
you found particularly upsetting? (For example, the number of
jurors, or the sequestering of witnesses, or the court being open
to the public.) Who can you ask to help you better understand

the process and/or to support you through upsetting experiences?

3. Testifying before open court is stressful for everyone—even adults. How can you be prepared for this stress, and how can you take good care of yourself after testifying?
4. Did any unusual circumstances or events take place during your trial? How did you cope with these?

Section 22. Cross-Examination

1. The purpose of cross-examination is to cast doubt on the witness's testimony. This can be confusing and upsetting. What do you think will be the hardest part about being cross-examined? What can you do to be prepared?
2. How will you feel if the defense attorney says that you imagined the abuse or lied about the abuse? What kind of support do you need to deal with this possibility? Would it be better for you to not hear the closing arguments? Why?

Section 23. Instructions to the Jury

1. How do you determine if someone is telling the truth or lying?
2. How do you think members of a jury go about determining who is telling the truth and who is lying?

Section 24. The Verdict

1. (Girls) Even after going through the investigation and the trial, Jane was not sure about what she wanted the verdict to be. How do you feel about the verdict your abuser received?
1. (Boys) Even after going through the investigation and the trial, Joe was not sure about what he wanted the verdict to be. How do you feel about the verdict your abuser received?
2. Are you surprised at all by your feelings? Why? Why not?

Section 25. After the Trial

1. How do you feel about being able to tell the judge what sentence you think your abuser should receive?

2. How do you think you can best figure out what you want to happen to your abuser?

Section 26. Victim Impact Statement

1. How do you feel about the abuse that happened to you? How do you feel about your abuser?
2. What have been the effects of the abuse on your life so far?
3. What do you want your abuser's sentence to be?
4. How will writing (or not writing) a victim impact statement be helpful to you?

Section 27. Sentencing

1. What was the day of the sentencing like for you?
2. How do you think you will feel when you hear the prosecutor say negative things about your abuser and the defense attorney say positive things about your abuser?
3. How do you feel about helping to make sure that your abuser is held responsible for his or her abusive behavior?
4. How do you feel about helping to protect other kids?

Section 28. Toward Recovery

1. How do you feel about forgiving your abuser?
2. What do you want people to know about the experience you have been through? About the abuse? About the trial?
3. What do you want people to know about how these experiences have changed you—for better? for worse?
4. Who are the people you want to thank for helping you through this process? What do you want to say to them?

Glossary

acquitted: The charges against the defendant have been dismissed. Most often, if a defendant is acquitted, it is as a result of the jury finding the defendant "not guilty."

ADA: Assistant District Attorney.

allegation: A stated or written accusation by a victim of what happened.

arraignment: The beginning step of the trial proceedings. The defendant comes to court and is formally read the charges.

assistant district attorney (ADA): Lawyer or prosecutor who works for the state (or commonwealth) and represents the state (or commonwealth) on behalf of a crime victim. (*Note:* Check in the following list to see what the prosecuting attorney is called in your state.) *Alabama,* District Attorney; *Alaska,* District Attorney; *Arizona,* County Attorney; *Arkansas,* Prosecuting Attorney; *California,* District Attorney; *Colorado,* District Attorney; *Connecticut,* State's Attorney; *Delaware,* Attorney General; *District of Columbia (Washington, D.C.),* U.S. Attorney; *Florida,* State Attorney; *Georgia,* District Attorney; *Hawaii,* Prosecuting Attorney; *Idaho,* Prosecuting Attorney; *Illinois,* State's Attorney; *Indiana,* Prosecuting Attorney; *Iowa,* County Attorney; *Kansas,* District Attorney or County Attorney; *Kentucky,* Commonwealth's Attorney or County Attorney; *Louisiana,* District Attorney; *Maine,* District Attorney; *Maryland,* State's Attorney; *Massachusetts,* District Attorney; *Michigan,* Prosecuting Attorney; *Minnesota,* County Attorney; *Mississippi,* District Attorney or County Attorney; *Missouri,* Prosecuting Attorney; *Montana,* County Attorney; *Nebraska,* County Attorney; *Nevada,* District Attorney; *New Hampshire,* County Attorney; *New Jersey,* County Prosecutor; *New Mexico,* District Attorney; *New York,* District Attorney; *North Carolina,* District Attorney; *North Dakota,* State's Attorney; *Ohio,* Prosecuting Attorney; *Oklahoma,* District Attorney; *Oregon,*

District Attorney; *Pennsylvania,* District Attorney; *Rhode Island,* Attorney General; *South Carolina,* Circuit Solicitor; *South Dakota,* State's Attorney; *Tennessee,* District Attorney General; *Texas,* Criminal District Attorney or County/District Attorney or District Attorney or County Attorney; *Utah,* County Attorney; *Vermont,* State's Attorney; *Virginia,* Commonwealth's Attorney; *Washington,* County Prosecuting Attorney; *West Virginia,* County Prosecuting Attorney; *Wisconsin,* County District Attorney; *Wyoming,* District Attorney or County Attorney or Prosecuting Attorney. (*National Directory of Prosecuting Attorneys,* 2001. Arlington, VA: National District Attorneys Association, pp. 89-97).

bail: The amount of money posted as a guarantee that the defendant will appear in court on all of the specified court dates.

bail hearing: Hearing in court before a judge to decide whether bail should be posted or whether a defendant can be released on his or her own personal recognizance.

burden of proof: By law, the prosecution is completely responsible for proving a defendant guilty in court "beyond a reasonable doubt." The defendant does not have to prove that he or she is innocent, does not have to testify, and does not even have to have any witnesses testify.

character witness: A person (such as a relative, friend, or employer) who knows the defendant well enough to testify about his or her character; that is about what a good person he or she is and what positive traits he or she has (such as honesty, loyalty, compassion, etc.).

child interview specialist: A person trained to ask children and teenagers questions about what happened in a skillful and sensitive way.

closing arguments: The arguments presented by the prosecutor and the defense attorney at the end of the trial. Each lawyer attempts to convince the jury how to decide based on the evidence presented.

complaining witness: The victim.

continuance: A decision by the court to review the case at a later date.

convicted: The defendant has been found guilty as charged by a jury or a judge.

counselor: A helping professional who listens to you and provides support and information about your feelings.

court officers: Officers of the court who make sure the court operates in an orderly way. Like police officers, the court officers wear uniforms and make sure that all the people in court remain safe.

court reporter: The person who makes a record of everything said in the courtroom. The record can be made by speaking into a machine or by typing into a machine, or both.

credibility: The issue of whether or not an individual's statements are believable.

criminal justice system: A system of government consisting of different types of professionals (judges, district attorneys, police officers, parole and probation officers, victim witness advocates, child interview specialists) that is designed to protect the public, and to work with both victims and perpetrators of crimes.

crisis line: A twenty-four-hour emergency telephone service providing support, counseling and information.

cross-examine: An opportunity for the opposing lawyer to ask a witness questions about evidence which has already been presented to the court.

defendant: The person charged with committing a crime.

defense attorney: A lawyer who represents the defendant.

deliberate: When the jury goes into a private room after a trial is over and discusses all of the evidence from the trial, and decides the verdict. A superior court jury needs to be unanimous in their decision, which means that all twelve jurors must agree on the same verdict.

disclosure: A statement made by a person relating the details of an incident or incidents of abuse.

disposition: The final outcome of a court case. This word often refers to the sentence a defendant receives.

DSS (Department of Social Services): Agency mandated by the Commonwealth of Massachusetts to receive and respond to reports of child abuse and neglect, to provide protection to children, and to provide services to children and their families. (*Note:* Check in the following list to see what the child protective agency is called in your state.) *Alabama,* Office of Protective Services; Adult, Child and Family Services Division; Department of Human Resources; *Alaska,* Division of Family and Youth Services; Department of Health and Social Services; *Arizona,* Administration for Children, Youth and Families; Department of Economic Security; *Arkansas,* Division of Children and Family Services; Department of Human Services; *California,* Department of Social Services; *Colorado,* Department of Human Services; *Connecticut,* Division of Children and Protective Services; Department of Children and Families; *Delaware,* Division of Family Services; Department of Services to Children, Youth, and Their Families; *District of Columbia,* Child and Family Services; Department of Human Services; *Florida,* Department of Children and Family; *Georgia,* Division of Children and Family Services; Department of Human Resources; *Guam,* Child Protective Services, Child Welfare Services; Department of Public Health and Social Services; *Hawaii,* Family and Adult Services; Department of Human Services; *Idaho,* Division of Family and Community Services; Department of Health and Welfare; *Illinois,* Department of Children and Family Services; *Indiana,* Family and Social Services Administration; *Iowa,* Adult, Children and Family Services; Department of Human Services; *Kansas,* Children and Family Services; Department of Social and Rehabilitative Services; *Kentucky,* Department for Protection and Family Support; Cabinet for Families and Children; *Louisiana,* Department of Social Services; *Maine,* Child Protective Services; Department of Human Services; *Maryland,* Child Protective Services; Department of Human Resources; *Massachusetts,* Department of Social Services; *Michigan,* Child Protective Services Division; Department of Social Services; *Minnesota,* Department of Human Services; *Mississippi,* Child Protective Services Unit; Division of Family and Children's Services; Department of Human Services; *Missouri,* Division of Family Services; Department of Social Services; *Montana,* Child and Family Services Division; Department of Public Health and Human Services; *Nebraska,* Department of Health and Human Services; *Nevada,* Division of Child and Family Services; Department of Human Resources; *New Hampshire,* Division for Children, Youth, and Families; Department of Health and Human Services; *New Jersey,* Division of Youth and Family Services; *New*

Mexico, Children, Youth, and Families Department; *New York,* Division of Family and Children Services; Department of Social Services; *North Carolina,* Child Protective Services; Division of Social Services, Department of Human Resources; *North Dakota,* Child Protection Services; Department of Human Services; *Ohio,* Office of Child Care and Family Services; Department of Human Services; *Oklahoma,* Division of Children, Youth, and Family; Department of Human Services; *Oregon,* Child Protective Services; State Office for Services to Children and Families, Department of Human Resources; *Pennsylvania,* Office of Children, Youth, and Families; Department of Public Welfare; *Puerto Rico,* Families with Children Program; Department of Social Services; *Rhode Island,* Division of Child Protective Services; Department of Children, Youth, and Families; *South Carolina,* Child Protective Services; Department of Social Services; *South Dakota,* Child Protection Services; Department of Social Services; *Tennessee,* Child Protective Services; Department of Children's Services, Department of Human Services; *Texas,* Department of Protective and Regulatory Services; Department of Human Services; *Utah,* Division of Family Services; Department of Human Services; *Vermont,* Department of Social and Rehabilitative Services; *Virgin Islands,* Division of Children, Youth, and Families; Department of Human Services; *Virginia,* Child Protective Services; Department of Social Services; *Washington,* Child Protective Services; Children's Administration; Department of Social and Health Services; *West Virginia,* Office of Social Services; Department of Health and Human Resources; *Wisconsin,* Child Protective Services; Division of Children and Family Services; Department of Health and Social Services; *Wyoming,* Department of Family Services (U.S. Department of Health and Human Services, 1992; U.S. Department of Health and Human Services, 1998).

empaneling: To select a jury.

Fifth Amendment: The United States Constitution provides rights to people accused of crimes. One of those rights, which is contained in the Fifth Amendment, states that persons accused of crimes do not have to say anything that could be used against them in court.

grand jury: A group of up to twenty-three people who hear evidence and decide whether or not there is reasonable cause to believe a crime happened. Twelve members of the grand jury (a majority) must agree that there is reasonable cause.

guilty: A determination which indicates that the state prosecutor has successfully presented the facts in a way that met the burden of proof beyond a reasonable doubt.

guilty as charged: The decision of the jury that the defendant is guilty of the particular charge specified by the indictment.

indictment: The name used for the formal criminal charge against the defendant.

interview: A meeting with a child interview specialist to talk about what happened.

investigation: The process during which professionals from different disciplines (therapists, child interview specialists, social workers, lawyers, police officers) gather the facts about what happened.

judge: The person who is authorized to hear cases in court and make sure the court is run in an orderly manner.

judge's clerk: The judge's assistant. The clerk sits at a desk in front of the judge and helps the judge run the court by swearing people in as witnesses, keeping track of case documents, and reading verdicts.

jury: A group of up to sixteen people who listen to the facts of the case. Twelve selected jurors will then decide if the defendant is guilty of the charges beyond a reasonable doubt.

mandated reporter: A number of professionals including doctors, therapists, teachers, police officers, foster parents, guidance counselors, or any other person who cares for or works with children in any public or private facility.

mandated reporting law: Requires certain professionals (known as mandated reporters) to file a report when, in his or her professional capacity, he or she has reasonable cause to suspect that a child under the age of eighteen (age varies by state) has been or is being physically or sexually abused or neglected. (*Note:* Investigate the mandated reporting law in your state to see who the mandated reporters are and other points of interest in the law. Every state has a mandated reporting law regarding child abuse.)

motions hearings: *See* PRETRIAL CONFERENCES.

not guilty: A determination which indicates that the state prosecutor has not met the burden of proof beyond a reasonable doubt. This determination does not mean the defendant is innocent.

opening statement: The opportunity for both the prosecutor and the defense attorney to present an outline of what they will accomplish during the trial.

plead: To state on the record whether one is guilty or not guilty of the charges.

presumed innocent: Even after a person has been arrested or charged with a crime, the law says that the accused person must be considered innocent until the prosecution proves him or her guilty.

pretrial conferences: Meetings in court to decide what will happen next on the case. The judge, prosecuting attorney, defendant, and defense attorney take part in the conferences. Victims and witnesses do not have to be present in court. There may be several pretrial conference dates scheduled in court before a trial date is finally scheduled.

pretrial motions: Court appearances by both the prosecuting attorney and the defense attorney before the trial begins in order to discuss the preparation of the case with the judge.

probable cause hearing: In states where the grand jury system is not used, this hearing takes place before a judge for the purpose of determining if the prosecuting attorney has enough evidence of the defendant's guilt to move forward to a jury trial.

probation: A kind of sentence in which the defendant is required to follow rules outlined and monitored by a probation officer. For example: having to go to counseling, meeting with a probation officer regularly, staying away from children. Sometimes a defendant is given probation instead of a prison sentence and sometimes probation is given in addition to a prison sentence. If a defendant does not follow the rules of probation, a judge can then order the defendant to go to jail.

prosecution: A process by which the state (commonwealth) brings criminal charges against someone, and then brings a case to trial.

reasonable doubt: Any doubt that a reasonable, responsible person would have a hard time dismissing.

recess: A break in the trial proceedings.

restraining order: An order issued by a judge specifying that one individual be prevented from abusing another individual, and be kept away from and/or removed from the premises of the person who applied for the restraining order.

sequestered: To be separated, so as not to be influenced by the testimony of one another. A jury can also be sequestered so as not to be influenced by the media.

social worker: A professional trained to provide a range of services to families including support and counseling.

statutes: Laws that are created by the state or federal government.

subpoena: A court order sent to a witness, requiring the witness to be present in court. A subpoena can be sent by mail or delivered by hand by a constable, sheriff, or agent of the court.

summons: A written notification issued by the court that orders the defendant to appear in court on a certain day to be arraigned. A summons can be sent by mail or delivered by hand.

superior court: The level of the court system that handles more serious crimes known as felonies. (*Note:* Some child abuse cases are tried in the district court system. This could be because the crime is considered a misdemeanor [which is a less serious crime—like indecent exposure] instead of a felony. District court procedures will differ from those in superior court. If your case is going through the district court system, be sure to ask your victim witness advocate to explain the different procedures.)

supported the allegations: To support an allegation of abuse means that the state social service agency has reasonable cause to believe that an incident of abuse or neglect of a child or teenager did occur.

suspended sentence: A prison sentence that a defendant is not required to serve right away. Instead the defendant is placed on probation with certain rules that must be followed. Usually these rules include sex-offender treatment and no contact with the victim. If the defendant does not follow the rules of probation, he or she could be made to serve the suspended sentence in prison.

team interview: A team of professionals consisting of a social worker, assistant district attorney, victim witness advocate, child interview specialist, police officer, and a therapist who come together to cooperatively conduct an investigation, including observing an interview and discussing what should happen next in the case.

testify: To answer questions in court under the oath to tell the truth.

testimony: A statement made by a witness under oath in response to questions asked by a lawyer.

therapist: A person trained to assist others in dealing with problems or concerns.

verdict: The decision of the jury. In a superior court criminal trial the decision must be unanimous.

victim: The person who is wronged by the crime.

victim impact statement: At the time of sentencing victims and their families can make a written or a verbal statement to the judge about how they feel about what happened, what the effects of the crime are, and what they think the sentence should be. In deciding what sentence a defendant will receive, the judge considers what the prosecuting attorney, the defense attorney, and the victims recommend.

victim witness advocate: A support person who guides victims and witnesses through the court system.

warrant: A document authorizing the arrest of the defendant.

witness: A person who testifies (tells), under oath, what he or she saw or heard happen.

witness stand: The place in court where the witness sits or stands to testify. At this place, usually next to the judge, the witness will be sworn in and will answer questions.

Resources

The following is a list of agencies and organizations that can provide additional resources and/or training and educational materials on child abuse and neglect issues and/or the criminal justice system:

American Bar Association Center on Children and the Law
  740 15th Street, NW
  Washington, DC 20005
  Phone: (800) 285-2221 or (202) 662-1720
  E-mail: ctrchildlaw@abanet.org
  <www.abanet.org>

American Professional Society on the Abuse of Children (APSAC)
  407 South Dearborn Street, Suite 1300
  Chicago, IL 60605
  Phone: (312) 554-0166
  E-mail: apsacmems@aol.com
  <www.apsac.org>

Childhelp USA (National Hotline for crisis counseling for adult survivors and child victims of abuse, offenders, and parents)
  Phone: (800) 4-A-CHILD or (800) 2-A-CHILD (TDD line) or
  E-mail: help@childhelpusa.org
  <www.childhelp.org>

Child Welfare League of America (CWLA)
  440 First Street, NW, Third Floor
  Washington, DC 20001
  Phone: (202) 638-2952
  <www.CWLA.org>

National Center for the Prosecution of Child Abuse:
  National District Attorney's Association
  American Prosecutors Research Institute
  99 Canal Center Plaza, Suite 510
  Alexandria, VA 22314
  Phone: (703) 739-0321
  <www.NDAA-APRI.org>

National Clearinghouse on Child Abuse and Neglect (NCCAN)
  330 C Street, SW
  Washington, DC 20447
  Phone: (800) FYI-3366 or 703-385-7565
  E-mail: nccanch@calib.com
  <www.calib.com/nccanch>

National Criminal Justice Reference Service
  PO Box 6000
  Rockville, MD 20849-6000
  <www.ncjrs.org>

      Juvenile Justice Clearinghouse
      Phone: (800) 638-8736
      E-mail: askncjrs@ncjrs.org

      National Institute of Justice Clearinghouse
      Phone: (800) 851-3420
      E-mail: puborder@ncjrs.org

      Office for Victims of Crime - National Victim Resource Center
      Phone: (800) 627-NVRC
      E-mail: askncjrs@ncjrs.org

National Organization for Victim Assistance
  1757 Park Road, NW
  Washington, DC 20010
  Phone: (800) TRY-NOVA or (202) 232-6682
  E-mail: nova@try-nova.org
  <www.try-nova.org>

Prevent Child Abuse America
   200 South Michigan Avenue, 17th Floor
   Chicago, IL 60604
   Phone: (800) 835-2671 or (312) 663-3520
   E-mail: mailbox@preventchildabuse.com
   www.preventchildabuse.org

References

American Psychiatric Association (1994). *Diagnostic and Statistical Manual of Mental Disorders,* Fourth Edition. Washington, DC: Author.

Angelica, J.C. (1993). *A Moral Emergency: Breaking the Cycle of Child Sexual Abuse.* Kansas City, MO: Sheed and Ward.

Bass, A. (1992). Study ties teenage pregnancy, childhood sex abuse. *The Boston Globe,* February 25, p. A1, A4. (Used by permission of *The Boston Globe.*)

Besharov, D.J. (1994). Responding to Child Sexual Abuse: The Need for a Balanced Approach. *The Future of Children, 4*(2) Summer/Fall 135-155.

Blume, S.E. (1990). *Secret Survivors: Uncovering Incest and Its Aftereffects in Women.* New York: John Wiley.

Brant, R. (1998). Interview by author. Newton, MA, January, 1998.

Briere, J.N. and Elliott, D.M. (1994). Immediate and Long-Term Impacts of Child Sexual Abuse. *The Future of Children, 4*(2) Summer/Fall 54-69.

Bulkley, J., Feller, J.N., Stern. P., and Roe, R. (1996). Child Abuse and Neglect Laws and Legal Proceedings. In J. Biere, L. Berliner, J.A. Bulkley, C. Jenny, and T. Reid (Eds.), *The APSAC Handbook on Child Maltreatment* (pp. 271-296). Thousand Oaks, CA: Sage.

Chaffin, M., Bonner, B.L., Worley, K.B., and Lawson, L. (1996). Treating Abused Adolescents. In J. Briere, L. Berliner, J.A. Bulkley, C. Jenny, and T. Reid (Eds.), *The APSAC Handbook on Child Maltreatment* (pp. 119-139). Thousand Oaks, CA: Sage.

Cross, T.P., De Vos, E., and Whitcomb, D. (1994). Prosecution of Child Sexual Abuse: Which Cases Are Accepted? *Child Abuse and Neglect, 18*(8) 663-677.

Cross, T.P., Whitcomb, D., and De Vos, E. (1995). Criminal Justice Outcomes of Prosecution of Child Sexual Abuse: A Case Flow Analysis. *Child Abuse and Neglect, 19*(12) 1431-1442.

de Mause, L. (Ed.) (1988). *The History of Childhood: The Untold Story of Child Abuse.* New York: Peter Bedrick Books.

Deaton, W.S. and Hertica, M. (1993). Developmental Considerations in Forensic Interviews with Adolescents. *The APSAC Advisor, 6*(1) 5-8.

Deblinger, E. and Heflin, A.H. (1996). *Treating Sexually Abused Children and Their Nonoffending Parents: A Cognitive Behavioral Approach.* Thousand Oaks, CA: Sage.

DePanifilis, D. and Salus M.K. (1992). *A Coordinated Response to Child Abuse and Neglect: A Basic Manual.* The User Manual Series. (NCCAN/DHHS Publication No. ACF-92-30362). McLean, VA: The Circle.

Elliott, D.M. and Briere, J. (1992). The Sexually Abused Boy: Problems in Manhood. *Medical Aspects of Human Sexuality, 26*(2) 68-71.

Feller, J.N., Davidson, H.A., Hardin, M., and Horowitz, R.M. (1992). *Working With the Courts in Child Protection.* The User Manual Series. (NCCAN Publication No. HHS-105-88-1702). Washington, DC: U.S. Government Printing Office.

Finkelhor, D. (1984). *Child Sexual Abuse: New Theory and Research.* New York: Free Press.

Finkelhor, D. (1994). Current Information on the Scope of Child Sexual Abuse. *The Future of Children, 4*(2) Summer/Fall 31-53.

Finkelhor, D. (1996). Introduction. In J. Briere, L. Berliner, J.A. Bulkley, C. Jenny, and T. Reid (Eds.), *The APSAC Handbook on Child Maltreatment* (pp. ix-xiii). Thousand Oaks, CA: Sage.

Finkelhor, D. and Baron, L. (1986). High-Risk Children. In D. Finkelhor (Ed.), *A Sourcebook on Child Sexual Abuse* (pp. 60-88). Beverly Hills, CA: Sage.

Finkelhor, D. and Ormrod, R. (1999) Reporting Crimes Against Juveniles. *Juvenile Justice Bulletin,* November <www.cjrs.org/pdffiles/ojjdp/178887.pdf>

Fogarty, D. (1997). Interview by author. Dedham, MA, December, 1997.

Friedrich, W.N. (1995). *Psychotherapy with Sexually Abused Boys: An Integrated Approach.* Thousand Oaks, CA: Sage.

Gil, E. (1996). *Treating Abused Adolescents.* New York: Guilford.

Gray, E. (1993). *Unequal Justice: The Prosecution of Child Sexual Abuse.* New York: Free Press.

Grayson, J. (1989). Sexually Victimized Boys. *Virginia Child Protective Newsletter, 29*(fall) 3-16.

Grubman-Black, S. D. (1990). *Broken Boys/Mending Men: Recovery from Childhood Sexual Abuse.* New York: Ballantine.

Jackson, H. and Nuttal, R. (1993). Clinician Responses to Sexual Abuse Allegations. *Child Abuse and Neglect, 17*(1) January/February 127-143.

Lanning, K. (1996). Criminal Investigation of Suspected Child Abuse, Section I: Criminal Investigation of Sexual Victimization of Children. In J. Briere, L. Berliner, J.A. Bulkley, C. Jenny, and T. Reid (Eds.), *The APSAC Handbook on Child Maltreatment* (pp. 247-264). Thousand Oaks, CA: Sage.

Larson, C.S., Terman, D.L., Gomby, D.S., Quinn, L.S., and Behrman, R. (1994). Sexual Abuse of Children: Recommendations and Analysis. *The Future of Children, 4*(2) summer/fall 4-30.

Lee, S. A., (1995). *The Survivor's Guide.* Thousand Oaks, CA: Sage.

Lynch, J. (1998). Interview by author. Boston, MA, January, 1998.

Myers, J.E.B. (1994) Adjudication of Child Sexual Abuse Cases. *The Future of Children, 4*(2) summer/fall 84-101.

Myers, J.E.B. (1997). *A Mother's Nightmare—Incest: A Practical Legal Guide for Parents and Professionals.* Thousand Oaks, CA: Sage.

National Directory of Prosecuting Attorneys (2001). Alexandria, VA: National Attorneys Association, pp. 89-97.

O'Brien, R.C. and Flannery, M.T. (1991). The Pending Gauntlet to Free Exercise: Mandating that Clergy Report Child Abuse. *Loyola of Los Angeles Law Review, 25*(1) 1-56.

Pence, D. M. and Wilson, C. A. (1994). Reporting and Investigating Child Sexual Abuse. *The Future of Children, 4*(2) summer/fall 70-83.

Peters, J., Dinsmore, J., Toth, P. (1989). Why Prosecute Child Abuse? *South Dakota Law Review, 34*(3) 649-59

Pini, K. (1998). *Case Analysis.* Somerville, MA: Middlesex County District Attorney's Office.

Porter, E. (1986). *Treating the Young Male Victim of Sexual Assault: Issues and Intervention Strategies.* New York: Safer Society Press.

Reilly, T.F. (1990). Interview by author. Cambridge, MA.

Rooney, L. (1999). Interview by author. Somerville, MA, December, 1998.

Rush, F. (1980). *The Best Kept Secret: Sexual Abuse of Children.* New York: McGraw-Hill.

Ryle, K. (1999). Interview by author. Somerville, MA, December, 1998.

Sanford, L.T. (1987). Pervasive Fears in Victims of Sexual Abuse: A clinician's Observations. *Preventing Sexual Abuse, 2*(2) 1-3.

Savely, L. (1998). Interview by author. Cambridge, MA. January, 1998.

Saywitz, K.J. and Goodman, G.S. (1996). Interviewing Children in and out of Court: Current Research and Practice Implications. In J. Briere, L. Berliner, J.A. Bulkley, C. Jenny, and T. Reid (Eds.), *The APSAC Handbook on Child Maltreatment* (pp. 297-318). Thousand Oaks, CA: Sage.

Sullivan, T. (1998). Interview by author. Medford, MA, January, 1998.

Summit, R. C. (1983). The Child Sexual Abuse Accommodation Syndrome. *Child Abuse and Neglect, 7,* 177-193.

Summit, R.C. (1988). Hidden Victims, Hidden Pain: Societal Avoidance of Child Sexual Abuse. In G.E. Wyatt and G.J. Powell (Eds.), *Lasting Effects of Child Sexual Abuse* (pp. 39-59). Beverly Hills, CA: Sage.

Urquiza, A.J. and Winn, C. (n.d.). *Treatment for Abused and Neglected Children: Infancy to Age 18.* The User Manual Series. (NCCAN Publication No. HHS-105-89-1730). McLean, VA: Circle Solutions.

U.S. Department of Health and Human Services. (1992). *Child Abuse and Neglect: A Shared Community Concern* (DHHS Publication No. ACF-92-30531). Washington, DC: U.S. Government Printing Office.

U.S. Department of Health and Human Services. (1998). *Child Maltreatment 1996: Reports From the States to the National Child Abuse and Neglect Data System* (DHHS Publication No. ACF-105-97-1857). Washington, DC: U.S. Government Printing Office.

U.S. Department of Justice. (1994). *The Child Victim As a Witness: Research Report.* (OJJDP Publication No. 87-MC-CX-0026). Washington, DC: D. Whitcomb.

Whitcomb, D. (1992). *When the Victim Is a Child* (Second Edition). (NIJ Publication No. OJP-86-C-009). Washington, DC: U.S. Government Printing Office.

Whitcomb, D. (1993). *Child Witnesses: What the Research Says.* (NCCAN Publication No. 90-CA-1451). Newton, MA: Education Development Center.

Whitcomb, D., Goodman, G.S., Runyan, D.K., and Hoak, S. (1994). The Emotional Effects of Testifying on Sexually Abused Children. *The National Institute of Justice: Research in Brief, April 1994.* Washington, DC: U.S. Government Printing Office.

Index

THE HAWORTH MALTREATMENT AND TRAUMA PRESS®
Robert A. Geffner, PhD
Senior Editor

THE INSIDERS: A MAN'S RECOVERY FROM TRAUMATIC CHILDHOOD ABUSE by Robert Blackburn Knight. (2002). "An important book. . . . Fills a gap in the literature about healing from childhood sexual abuse by allowing us to hear, in undiluted terms, about one man's history and journey of recovery." *Amy Pine, MA, LMFT, psychotherapist and co-founder, Survivors Healing Center, Santa Cruz, California*

WE ARE NOT ALONE: A GUIDEBOOK FOR HELPING PROFESSIONALS AND PARENTS SUPPORTING ADOLESCENT VICTIMS OF SEXUAL ABUSE by Jade Christine Angelica. (2002). "Encourages victims and their families to participate in the system in an effort to heal from their victimization, seek justice, and hold offenders accountable for their crimes. An exceedingly vital training tool." *Janet Fine, MS, Director, Victim Witness Assistance Program and Children's Advocacy Center, Suffolk County District Attorney's Office, Boston*

WE ARE NOT ALONE: A TEENAGE GIRL'S PERSONAL ACCOUNT OF INCEST FROM DISCLOSURE THROUGH PROSECUTION AND TREATMENT by Jade Christine Angelica. (2002). "A valuable resource for teens who have been sexually abused and their parents. With compassion and eloquent prose, Angelica walks people through the criminal justice system—from disclosure to final outcome." *Kathleen Kendall-Tackett, PhD, Research Associate, Family Research Laboratory, University of New Hampshire, Durham*

WE ARE NOT ALONE: A TEENAGE BOY'S PERSONAL ACCOUNT OF CHILD SEXUAL ABUSE FROM DISCLOSURE THROUGH PROSECUTION AND TREATMENT by Jade Christine Angelica. (2002). "Inspires us to work harder to meet kids' needs, answer their questions, calm their fears, and protect them from their abusers and the system, which is often not designed to respond to them in a language they understand." *Kevin L. Ryle, JD, Assistant District Attorney, Middlesex, Massachusetts*

GROWING FREE: A MANUAL FOR SURVIVORS OF DOMESTIC VIOLENCE by Wendy Susan Deaton and Michael Hertica. (2001). "This is a necessary book for anyone who is scared and starting to think about what it would take to 'grow free.' . . . Very helpful for friends and relatives of a person in a domestic violence situation. I recommend it highly." *Colleen Friend, LCSW, Field Work Consultant, UCLA Department of Social Welfare, School of Public Policy & Social Research*

A THERAPIST'S GUIDE TO **GROWING FREE: A MANUAL FOR SURVIVOR'S OF DOMESTIC VIOLENCE** by Wendy Susan Deaton and Michael Hertica. (2001). "An excellent synopsis of the theories and research behind the manual." *Beatrice Crofts Yorker, RN, JD, Professor of Nursing, Georgia State University, Decatur*

PATTERNS OF CHILD ABUSE: HOW DYSFUNCTIONAL TRANSACTIONS ARE REPLICATED IN INDIVIDUALS, FAMILIES, AND THE CHILD WELFARE SYSTEM by Michael Karson. (2001). "No one interested in what may well be the major public health epidemic of our time in terms of its long-term consequences for our society can afford to pass up the opportunity to read this enlightening work." *Howard Wolowitz, PhD, Professor Emeritus, Psychology Department, University of Michigan, Ann Arbor*

IDENTIFYING CHILD MOLESTERS: PREVENTING CHILD SEXUAL ABUSE BY RECOGNIZING THE PATTERNS OF THE OFFENDERS by Carla van Dam. (2000). "The definitive work on the subject. . . . Provides parents and others with the tools to recognize when and how to intervene." *Roger W. Wolfe, MA, Co-Director, N. W. Treatment Associates, Seattle, Washington*

POLITICAL VIOLENCE AND THE PALESTINIAN FAMILY: IMPLICATIONS FOR MENTAL HEALTH AND WELL-BEING by Vivian Khamis. (2000). "A valuable book . . . a pioneering work that fills a glaring gap in the study of Palestinian society." *Elia Zureik, Professor of Sociology, Queens University, Kingston, Ontario, Canada*

STOPPING THE VIOLENCE: A GROUP MODEL TO CHANGE MEN'S ABUSIVE ATTITUDES AND BEHAVIORS by David J. Decker. (1999). "A concise and thorough manual to assist clinicians in learning the causes and dynamics of domestic violence." *Joanne Kittel, MSW, LICSW, Yachats, Oregon*

STOPPING THE VIOLENCE: A GROUP MODEL TO CHANGE MEN'S ABUSIVE ATTITUDES AND BEHAVIORS, THE CLIENT WORKBOOK by David J. Decker. (1999).

BREAKING THE SILENCE: GROUP THERAPY FOR CHILDHOOD SEXUAL ABUSE, A PRACTITIONER'S MANUAL by Judith A. Margolin. (1999). "This book is an extremely valuable and well-written resource for all therapists working with adult survivors of child sexual abuse." *Esther Deblinger, PhD, Associate Professor of Clinical Psychiatry, University of Medicine and Dentistry of New Jersey School of Osteopathic Medicine*

"I NEVER TOLD ANYONE THIS BEFORE": MANAGING THE INITIAL DISCLOSURE OF SEXUAL ABUSE RE-COLLECTIONS by Janice A. Gasker. (1999). "Discusses the elements needed to create a safe, therapeutic environment and offers the practitioner a number of useful strategies for responding appropriately to client disclosure." *Roberta G. Sands, PhD, Associate Professor, University of Pennsylvania School of Social Work*

FROM SURVIVING TO THRIVING: A THERAPIST'S GUIDE TO STAGE II RECOVERY FOR SURVIVORS OF CHILDHOOD ABUSE by Mary Bratton. (1999). "A must read for all, including survivors. Bratton takes a lifelong debilitating disorder and unravels its intricacies in concise, succinct, and understandable language." *Phillip A. Whitner, PhD, Sr. Staff Counselor, University Counseling Center, The University of Toledo, Ohio*

SIBLING ABUSE TRAUMA: ASSESSMENT AND INTERVENTION STRAT-EGIES FOR CHILDREN, FAMILIES, AND ADULTS by John V. Caffaro and Allison Conn-Caffaro. (1998). "One area that has almost consistently been ignored in the research and writing on child maltreatment is the area of sibling abuse. This book is a welcome and required addition to the developing literature on abuse." *Judith L. Alpert, PhD, Professor of Applied Psychology, New York University*

BEARING WITNESS: VIOLENCE AND COLLECTIVE RESPONSIBILITY by Sandra L. Bloom and Michael Reichert. (1998). "A totally convincing argument. . . . Demands careful study by all elected representatives, the clergy, the mental health and medical professions, representatives of the media, and all those unwittingly involved in this repressive perpetuation and catastrophic global problem." *Harold I. Eist, MD, Past President, American Psychiatric Association*

TREATING CHILDREN WITH SEXUALLY ABUSIVE BEHAVIOR PROB-LEMS: GUIDELINES FOR CHILD AND PARENT INTERVENTION by Jan Ellen Burton, Lucinda A. Rasmussen, Julie Bradshaw, Barbara J. Christopherson, and Steven C. Huke. (1998). "An extremely readable book that is well-documented and a mine of valuable 'hands on' information. . . . This is a book that all those who work with sexually abusive children or want to work with them must read." *Sharon K. Araji, PhD, Professor of Sociology, University of Alaska, Anchorage*

THE LEARNING ABOUT MYSELF (LAMS) PROGRAM FOR AT-RISK PARENTS: LEARNING FROM THE PAST—CHANGING THE FUTURE by Verna Rickard. (1998). "This program should be a part of the resource materials of every mental health professional trusted with the responsibility of working with 'at-risk' parents." *Terry King, PhD, Clinical Psychologist, Federal Bureau of Prisons, Catlettsburg, Kentucky*

THE LEARNING ABOUT MYSELF (LAMS) PROGRAM FOR AT-RISK PARENTS: HANDBOOK FOR GROUP PARTICIPANTS by Verna Rickard. (1998). "Not only is the LAMS program designed to be educational and build skills for future use, it is also fun!" *Martha Morrison Dore, PhD, Associate Professor of Social Work, Columbia University, New York, New York*

BRIDGING WORLDS: UNDERSTANDING AND FACILITATING ADOL-ESCENT RECOVERY FROM THE TRAUMA OF ABUSE by Joycee Kennedy and Carol McCarthy. (1998). "An extraordinary survey of the history of child neglect and abuse in America. . . . A wonderful teaching tool at the university level, but should be required reading in high schools as well." *Florabel Kinsler, PhD, BCD, LCSW, Licensed Clinical Social Worker, Los Angeles, California*

CEDAR HOUSE: A MODEL CHILD ABUSE TREATMENT PROGRAM by Bobbi Kendig with Clara Lowry. (1998). "Kendig and Lowry truly . . . realize the saying that we are our brothers' keepers. Their spirit permeates this volume, and that spirit of caring is what always makes the difference for people in painful situations." *Hershel K. Swinger, PhD, Clinical Director, Children's Institute International, Los Angeles, California*

SEXUAL, PHYSICAL, AND EMOTIONAL ABUSE IN OUT-OF-HOME CARE: PREVENTION SKILLS FOR AT-RISK CHILDREN by Toni Cavanagh Johnson and Associates. (1997). "Professionals who make dispositional decisions or who are related to out-of-home care for children could benefit from reading and following the curriculum of this book with children in placements." *Issues in Child Abuse Accusations*

Order Your Own Copy of
This Important Book for Your Personal Library!

WE ARE NOT ALONE
A Guidebook for Helping Professionals and Parents
Supporting Adolescent Victims of Sexual Abuse

_____in hardbound at $39.95 (ISBN: 0-7890-0924-2)

_____in softbound at $24.95 (ISBN: 0-7890-0925-0)

COST OF BOOKS_____

OUTSIDE USA/CANADA/
MEXICO: ADD 20%____

POSTAGE & HANDLING_____
*(US: $4.00 for first book & $1.50
for each additional book)*
*Outside US: $5.00 for first book
& $2.00 for each additional book)*

SUBTOTAL_____

in Canada: add 7% GST____

STATE TAX____
*(NY, OH & MIN residents, please
add appropriate local sales tax)*

FINAL TOTAL____
*(If paying in Canadian funds,
convert using the current
exchange rate, UNESCO
coupons welcome.)*

Prices in US dollars and subject to change without notice.

❏　**BILL ME LATER:** ($5 service charge will be added)
(Bill-me option is good on US/Canada/Mexico orders only;
not good to jobbers, wholesalers, or subscription agencies.)

❏ Check here if billing address is different from
shipping address and attach purchase order and
billing address information.

Signature_____

❏　**PAYMENT ENCLOSED: $_____**

❏　**PLEASE CHARGE TO MY CREDIT CARD.**

❏ Visa ❏ MasterCard ❏ AmEx ❏ Discover
❏ Diner's Club ❏ Eurocard ❏ JCB

Account # _____

Exp. Date_____

Signature_____

NAME_____

INSTITUTION_____

ADDRESS_____

CITY_____

STATE/ZIP_____

COUNTRY_____ COUNTY (NY residents only)_____

TEL_____ FAX_____

E-MAIL_____

May we use your e-mail address for confirmations and other types of information? ❏ Yes ❏ No
We appreciate receiving your e-mail address and fax number. Haworth would like to e-mail or fax special
discount offers to you, as a preferred customer. **We will never share, rent, or exchange your e-mail address
or fax number.** We regard such actions as an invasion of your privacy.

Order From Your Local Bookstore or Directly From
The Haworth Press, Inc.
10 Alice Street, Binghamton, New York 13904-1580 • USA
TELEPHONE: 1-800-HAWORTH (1-800-429-6784) / Outside US/Canada: (607) 722-5857
FAX: 1-800-895-0582 / Outside US/Canada: (607) 722-6362
E-mail: getinfo@haworthpressinc.com
PLEASE PHOTOCOPY THIS FORM FOR YOUR PERSONAL USE.
www.HaworthPress.com

BOF00